The China Business Casebook

Edited by

John Storm and John Wilson

The China Business Casebook
Edited by John Storm and John Wilson

This book first published 2023

Ethics International Press Ltd, UK

British Library Cataloguing in Publication Data

A catalogue record for this book is available from the British Library

Print Book ISBN: 978-1-80441-000-4

eBook ISBN: 978-1-80441-001-1

Table of Contents

*Some organisations and authors have been anonymised at the authors' request

Introduction

John Storm & John Wilson

However much we know, or think we know, about China, it is in all our interests to try to know a little more, to devote time to understand developments there. It is an economic, political, and military superpower and, directly or indirectly, affects all of our lives. It is the second largest economy in the world after the United States but projected by some economists and thinktanks to become the largest economy by 2030 if not sooner (CEBR, 2022) (it actually became the largest economy in the world in 2013 on purchasing power parity basis).

China's economic rise represents a remarkable transformation, particularly in the period since the policy of opening up and reform began in 1978-79 (Brown, 2018), a period that has been described as 'spectacular' (CRS, 2019, p1) and 'the fastest sustained expansion by a major economy in history' (World Bank quoted in CRS, 2019, p1). The achievements are as varied as they are impressive (World Bank, 2022). It has experienced rates of growth averaging almost 10%, 800m people have been lifted out of extreme poverty, globally-leading companies such as Alibaba, Tencent and Huawei have been established, Millennium Development Goals have been achieved and the hugely ambitious Belt and Road Initiative, first announced in 2013, continues to expand and, as at March 2022, involved almost 150 countries (Nedopil, 2022).

These achievements are to be taken forward by means of its most recent Five Year Plan (FYP) covering the years 2021-2025 inclusive. On 11 March 2021, the 13th National People's Congress of the People's Republic of China (PRC) approved the 14th FYP for National Economic and Social Development and Vision 2035. The Plan lists key targets across five main themes: economic development; innovation; people's wellbeing; green ecology; security/safety. Achievement of its key objectives will build upon one of its two centennial goals announced at the 18th National Congress of the Communist Party of China (CPC) in 2012 i.e. the goal, said to be achieved in 2021, to build a moderately prosperous society in all respects, in celebration of the centenary of the founding of the CPC in 1921, and will help underpin the goal to be achieved by 2049, in celebration of the centenary of the PRC, to build China into a modern socialist country that is prosperous, strong, democratic, culturally advanced and harmonious (State Council, 2019).

Its unprecedented achievements, however, have been accompanied by major ongoing challenges, including those related to the environment, ageing population, job security, workforce skill upgrading, social inclusion, inequality and how to make further sustainable progress from a low-income to a high-income country (World Economic Forum, 2018). In responding to these challenges, China will continue to adjust to the 'new normal' as introduced by President Xi in May 2014 (Green & Stern, 2015) involving, *inter alia,* reduced economic growth, upgrade of the economy and growth driven by innovation and technology rather than input and investment. The new normal, alongside related policy priorities including, for example, the continued anti-corruption drive and China's commitment to the United Nations Sustainable Development Goals, provided the backcloth to the 14th FYP, agreed in the context of the domestic and global economic impact of the pandemic which potentially will give China even greater global influence depending, in part, on relative rates of economic recovery.

In achieving the strategic goals established by central government, the role of business is critical, and it is important to understand how organisations and individual managers respond to these goals, not least when under the type of extreme and unprecedented pressures arising from the Covid-19 pandemic. To this end, and to seek to contribute to some level of greater appreciation and understanding of developments in China, this book presents case studies written by practising managers for their peers, students and those who simply have an interest in China, to highlight a wide range of issues and management challenges faced in a variety of sectors.

The case studies cover: lessons from business history at a successful joint venture (Tao); how a new enterprise may emerge during market turmoil (Fei); how a business may respond to an externally-driven crisis by changing the business model (Underwood); how lessons may be learnt from the evolution of a start-up (Vermeulen); how to respond to macro trends in a specific sector (Huang & Storm); the gradual demise in China of a well-known European brand (Gunaratna); issues to consider in dealing with unsuccessful promotion applications (Henderson); how to enhance position in the market place through increasing customers' perceived value of products (Jiang, Storm & Underwood); strategies to attract customers through a key video-hosting platform (Zhang & Storm); how to use Design Thinking to improve employee retention (Yang & Storm) and to facilitate organisational development (Metz); how to source talent in an ever-increasing competitive market (Zhang, Kuang & Mackrell); the response of a domestic airline to motivation of its pilots during and post-pandemic (Deng); the analysis of culture through use of the cultural web (Jiang); managerial attitudes to corporate social responsibility, and how financial management influences overseas expansion at a State Owned Enterprise (Seufert & Ding).

Given the variety of the cases and the sectors from which they are drawn, it is not possible to generalise beyond saying that they illustrate specific challenges at a particular point in China's development and, as such, provide insights into the management of business organisations in China and questions for discussion. In the context of major global events and trends, the cases are presented as important micro-level opportunities for learning and reflection and provide a foundation for future studies. It is hoped that the cases, anonymised where necessary, are of use for teaching purposes at undergraduate or postgraduate level, may stimulate ideas for research, are of practical interest and benefit to managers or simply be of general interest to the reader as we all collectively help each other understand a little more of a country the significance of which, for all of us and irrespective of where we are located, can hardly be overstated.

For the most part, the language and expressions used by the case study authors have been preserved by the editors.

References

Brown, K. (2018). 'Reform and opening up, 40 years on' *China Daily* 31 May www.chinadaily.com.cn/a/201805/31/WS5b0fa276a31001b82571d73e.html

Centre for Economics and Business Research (CEBR) (2022). 'China's Economy Could Overtake US Economy by 2030' 5 January https://cebr.com/reports/chosun-ilbo-chinas-economy-could-overtake-u-s-economy-by-2030/

Congressional Research Service (CRS) (2019). *China's Economic Rise: History, Trends, Challenges, and Implications for the United States* https://crsreports.congress.gov/product/pdf/RL/RL33534

Green, F. & Stern, N. (2015). *China's "new normal": structural change, better growth, and peak emissions* London School of Economics: Grantham Research Institute on Climate Change and the Environment https://www.lse.ac.uk/granthaminstitute/wp-content/uploads/2015/06/China_new_normal_web1.pdf

Nedopil, C. (2022). 'Countries of the Belt and Road Initiative' Shanghai, Green Finance & Development Center, FISF Fudan University www.greenfdc.org

State Council (2019). 'The Two Centennial Goals' 11 July https://.english.scio.gov.cn/featured/chinakeywords/2019-07/11/content_74977591.htm

World Bank (2022). 'Overview' 12 April www.worldbank.org/en/country/china/overview

World Economic Forum (2018). *Future of Consumption in Fast-Growth Consumer Markets: China.* https://www.weforum.org/reports/future-of-consumption-in-fast-growth-consumer-markets-china

Building on Local Understanding, Core Competencies and Global Connections: An HR Consulting Company Adapting to an Evolving Market

Huaiyuan Zhang
Teaching Lecturer: International Business School Suzhou at Xi'an Jiaotong-Liverpool University

Fu Kuang
Director: Cornerstone International Group

Alex Mackrell
Director: Manakai Consulting Ltd.

Abstract

International companies frequently enter foreign countries using business models and products inherited from their home territories. However, opaque and rapidly changing markets do not always conform to theoretical frameworks. The success of a global company may be influenced by how it perceives and analyses the changes within its local market, in addition to how its own core competencies relate to that market. This case study concerns Cornerstone China, the Chinese subsidiary of a global HR consulting group, and its successful expansion to a new market in the face of changing macro- and micro-level headwinds in a rapidly developing market. Rather than apply theory and business models to achieve this, the company took a more intuitive and organic approach to develop their new business, with this based on their understanding of both local and international markets, the competencies and vision of their own company, and benefits gained through membership of global professional networks.

Introduction

Cornerstone is a global organisation in the talent recruitment and development consulting field. Established in the United States (US) in 1989, by 2022 Cornerstone possessed 57 offices across 40 countries worldwide. The majority of Cornerstone's operations fall into two categories: retained executive searches; executive development in the form of coaching and leadership training. Cornerstone's clients span a wide variety of industries, including healthcare, manufacturing, and infrastructure. The group sources talent for a diverse range of executive and specialised roles in functions such as human resources, finance, sales, and supply chain management. Cornerstone entered the Chinese market in 1995 with the establishment of a local subsidiary, Cornerstone China. This has expanded to operate in 6 major cities in China, namely Beijing, Shanghai, Guangzhou, Hong Kong, Taipei and Suzhou, and employs a total of 21 consultants (Cornerstone International Group, 2022).

"Executive Search", one of Cornerstone's core offerings, is often referred to as headhunting (Allan, 2019), though this description has been disputed within the industry as too simplistic. Cornerstone follows a "retained" executive search business model, which features a high-impact, high-quality and time-consuming process, where recruiters are paid at beginning of a search. This is in contrast to the "contingency" executive search model, which places emphasis on speed rather than quality and fit, and where payment is only made upon hiring of a candidate (Allan, 2019). Figure 1 features a description of these two approaches based on the work of Dingman (1993) and AESC (2020). Prior to entering China, Cornerstone had extensively tested the retained executive search model, having come to the conclusion that this more rigorous approach was more effective at maximising client value than the contingency search model.

	Retained search	**Contingency search**
Pay to recruiter	Recruiter is paid when the search begins. Payment is guaranteed no matter the results.	Recruiter is paid only after a candidate is hired and has worked in the position for an agreed period.
Price for service	Fees for both models start at a similar level, usually a percentage of the position's annual salary. However, contingency search fees can sometimes be negotiated down far lower than retained search fees.	
Target position	Usually senior management positions.	Can include middle management or junior-level positions.
Style of service	- Values the "chemistry" or fit between candidate and the client organisation beyond just hiring. - Clients generally engage just one executive search company per position.	- Values the speed and result of hiring over long-term fit. - Clients can assign multiple executive search companies to search for the same position.
Speed/ quality of work	- Usually takes longer to locate and screen candidates, but each assignment is given more attention. - The recruiter typically conducts extensive research on the organisation and industry, and talks to candidates in person to achieve best fit.	- Can locate candidates quickly relying on existing candidate databases, but with limited time spent screening for best fit. - The recruiter typically avoids in-depth research, preferring to persuade both their client and the candidate to complete the hiring process in the shortest time possible.

Figure 1: *Differences between retained executive search and contingency executive search*

Problem statement

Following in Cornerstone's footsteps, Cornerstone China went on to use the retained executive search model exclusively, developing a strong client base among the waves of international companies entering the Chinese market in the 1990s and early 2000s. From 1992 to 2008 in China, foreign direct investment (FDI) increased by over 700% from $11.01 billion in 1992 to $92.4 billion in 2008. At the same time, the number of foreign-invested enterprises rose by more than 400% from less than 85,000 to almost 434,000 (China National Bureau of Statistics, 2022). This expansion drove strong demand for senior management personnel and resulted in equally strong growth for Cornerstone China over this period.

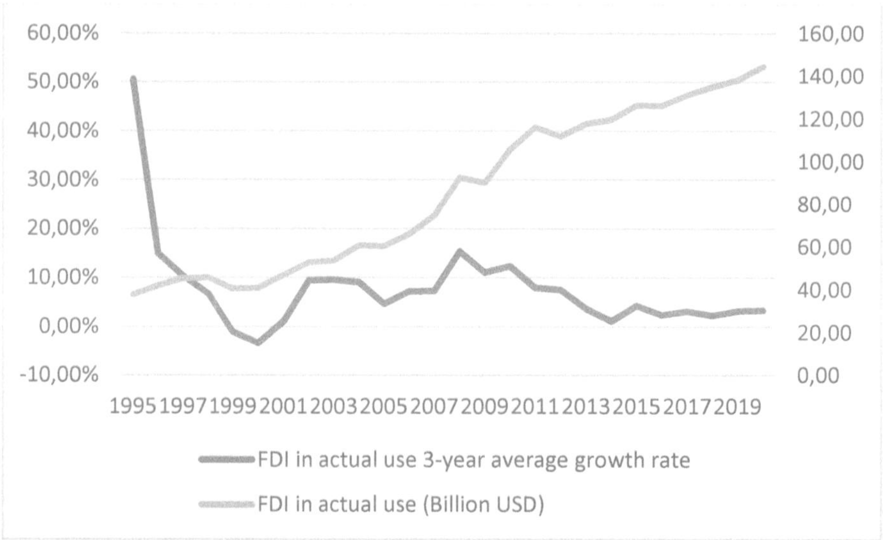

Figure 2: *Change of FDI in actual use in China from 1995 to 2020, calculated according to data from the China National Bureau of Statistics (2022)*

Post-2008, however, several macro and micro level trends began to impact Cornerstone China's market:

1. **Macro-level: Slowdown in foreign-invested enterprises**

   As shown in Figure 2, China experienced a general slowdown of FDI growth beginning in 2008. While FDI grew over this period, the 3-year average growth rate dropped significantly from over 15% in 2008 to approximately 1% in 2014, going on to achieve a 3% average until 2020 (China National Bureau of Statistics, 2022). This macro-level trend indicated that foreign-invested business expansion in China was slowing down, the very expansion that had driven the need for Cornerstone China's international executive search services over the previous decade. With this threat to the company's future revenue growth in this sector came a need to rethink its strategy.

2. **Micro-level: Local preferences differed from Cornerstone's other markets**

   Chinese customers have placed different emphasis on executive search. During Cornerstone China's initial development, differences in local preference were offset by the fact that many of its clients were both international and hiring for scarce and valuable senior level positions – often expatriates. The lucrative era of new business and fast-paced expansion effectively ended after 2010, with the initial wave of foreign businesses in China starting to stabilise. With this came a decrease in demand for senior-level position recruitment services, as well as the localisation of management and operations teams. Cornerstone China found that the lower-priced, faster-paced, and results-oriented "contingency" search model was increasing in popularity with their clients, while Cornerstone's rigorous, process-oriented "retained" search model was becoming less attractive. With this change, the company's focus on the executive search model was increasingly looking like a strategic weakness.

3. **Micro-level: More competitors joined the game**

   In addition to lower demand in general and a change in preference from clients, threat of local competition exploded during 2002 to 2012 as the number of competing executive search firms grew from 51 to 2,367 companies (Chenli, 2013). A great increase in alternative choices resulted in the strengthening of client negotiation power and served as a significant barrier to further growth (Luo et al., 2020). While Cornerstone China could adopt the "contingency" search model as its competitors to survive, this clashed with the company's (and Cornerstone's) global identity as a high-end, quality-service provider. Cornerstone's core competencies and reputation were founded in providing rigorous and quality-oriented talent allocation, and it was unlikely that Cornerstone China could face off against entrenched industry leaders with extensive contingency search experience. In this case, the wisdom of the proverb "if you can't beat them, then join them" (Titleman, 1996) does not apply to Cornerstone China's scenario.

Given the above, decision-makers at Cornerstone China concluded that the executive search market was no longer viable for long-term growth, particularly the sector pertaining to the "retained" search model. Despite this negative outlook, it was understood that Cornerstone China had not lost any of the core competencies that had brought it success in China, and the company embarked on a journey to develop new business opportunities and differentiate themselves from their current competitors.

Strategic or entrepreneurial: Re-positioning with a new vision

To develop new opportunities in the China market, Cornerstone China did not turn to frameworks for strategic analysis, such as Porter's Five Forces Model. Many of these models are built on the assumption that information about the market and competitors is transparent and available, and this definitely was not the reality around the time Cornerstone launched in China (Grundy, 2006). Instead, Cornerstone China chose to leverage the most important assets a knowledge-driven company possessed: the reputation, knowledge, and experience of their expert team of consultants.

Although not restricted by complex supply chains or similar factors of production, intangible assets such as reputation, expertise, diversified offers and connection through partners are crucial factors for executive search companies like Cornerstone China (Harvey et al., 2019). Rather than turning to organisational or management theory to identify a strategically valuable niche, Cornerstone China decided to apply its existing experience, expertise, connections, and market insights to an iterative approach. It was decided that this more organic or entrepreneurial approach, based on trial, error and adjustment, was more suited to the complex, opaque and rapidly evolving Chinese market, as well as the strong emphasis on relationships in a business community.

When establishing a reputation in a new field, it is beneficial to shape perceptions of the company as a well-established "first mover", allowing a company more effectively to "get into the mind" of potential clients (Demaris et al., 1992). This relates to the importance of "being known for something", which brings with it higher returns, increased resilience and interest from customers (Lange et al., 2011). For this reason, instead of answering the question "what is wrong with the current business and how should it be improved?", Cornerstone China implemented the transformation by looking at their business in a different way (Ready & Mulally, 2017) by asking: "what new business will best show our identity as a high-quality global human resources service company in the Chinese market?" It then split this into two main areas concerning the company and its market.

1. **External/Market focus for new value proposition:**
   a. What will be the "next big thing" in our field?
   b. What will be our role to play within this new trend in the market?

2. **Internal/Company focus for capacity building:**
   a. How can we develop internal expertise for this "next round of the game"?
   b. How should we develop a client base in this new field?

Implementation: nurturing a business plan B

These above questions align with Hoffman and Casnocha's (2012) three questions to answer when starting a new enterprise, namely 1) "what the company's assets allow it to do"; 2) "what the company is aspiring to do"; and 3) "what the market needs the company to do". They argue that while it is important to keep a business' most competent resources as its core focus (Plan A), a company should also create a Plan B by aligning its assets, vision and market needs to prepare for a time when Plan A could fail or when the time is ripe for Plan B to offer bigger benefits. In line with this, Cornerstone China did not drastically change its main business focus or invest heavily in exploring a new business, and continued to pursue their Plan A (retained executive search). However, they simultaneously developed their Plan B by answering the two sets of questions above with reference to the following analysis.

Mature markets offer key insights into the future of developing markets

To "predict" China's future, Cornerstone China looked to the past. The US, a mature market in HR management field where Cornerstone had originated, proved to be an excellent guide for pinpointing the direction in which the company's industry in China was headed. Cornerstone China determined that China in the 2010s was following a similar growth pattern to the US in the 1990s. This was characterised by fast economic growth brought by new technologies like the internet, with businesses investing heavily in expansion but largely ignoring the high possibility of the economic contractions endogenous to capitalism (Sherman, 2014). The US experienced severe downturns in the IT and internet industries in the late 1990s, and the China economy was showing a similar trend in the face of years of rapid expansion. Therefore, Cornerstone China concluded that, similar to the US, the upcoming stagnation and contraction in China would result in increases in labour costs, competition, corporate bankruptcies and layoffs, as well as a decrease in investment going towards further expansion.

While this assessment offered a bleak prediction for the executive search industry as a whole, these trends did drive a rise in "employee outplacement" services in the US: dismissals conducted with professional care to achieve successful job transitions and minimise the negative effects for the organisation (Stacho & Stachová, 2015). Based on this analysis, Cornerstone China determined that their "next big thing" would be the provision of employee outplacement services to international businesses in China seeking to reform or reallocate their workforces. This direction would also allow Cornerstone China to leverage its existing expertise in talent sourcing, understanding of the Chinese market and reputation among foreign invested companies in China to become a leader in this emerging market.

Building reputation, capacity and leads: the business-community partnership

With their Plan B identified, Cornerstone China set out to build the capacity and reputation they would need to take advantage of this developing market trend. As the skillset and knowledge required for employee outplacement overlapped with the company's existing work in executive search, talent acquisition to support the new business was not initially a concern. Instead, Cornerstone China took a "learning by doing" approach, allocating a percentage of its current team's time between major projects of retained executive search to developing practical expertise that would grow as the company found outplacement projects. They then focused on establishing the external channels required to generate leads and establish a new client base.

Rather than going local, Cornerstone China chose to build partnerships with global communities of employee outplacement and career transition service providers. One example of these was Career Partners International (CPI), a network covering over 300 locations around the world (Career Partners International, 2022). Connected as a member of these communities, Cornerstone China was not only able to gain leads from other members, but also had access to valuable capability development resources such as career transition coach certification. These would serve to enhance the credibility of Cornerstone China's consultants and the company's ability to adapt to this emerging business. Such practice, known as "business-community partnerships", benefit their members with problem solving, resource integration, exposure, new opportunities, and information exchange. Organisations in a community become "citizens" that both contribute to and receive resources from the community, with this particularly advantageous at a global level (Loza, 2004). As a representative and member of these communities in China, Cornerstone China was able to implement its vision of "global business with local operations", gaining opportunities and exposure internationally while providing a portfolio of outplacement solutions (rehiring, coaching, and training) that evolved alongside the Chinese market.

Evaluation

Cornerstone China's experience reflects a less systematic but more piecemeal application of business theories and frameworks, which is more common in the real business world. In the preparation stage of business change, one highlight is that even for an established global company, entrepreneurial thinking, intuition, experience, and grit in front of uncertainty can make a huge difference when repositioning for a new business. Cornerstone China's case emphasises the importance of grounding business strategies into local market realities, as well as the company's current core competencies and vision. It also shows the advantage of being a global company with local operations: Cornerstone China maintained its global identity and used global networks to acquire key leads and resources to develop a strong client base, but delivered by well-equipped local teams able to satisfy the needs of multinational firms. Such a strategy allowed them to differentiate themselves from both local competitors with no international expertise and international competitors with a limited understanding of the local context.

In terms of implementation, Cornerstone China chose to explore by allocating a small percentage of their resources to a Plan B while maintaining most of their focus on their core business (Plan A). This organic strategy leveraged the company's existing competencies and reputation to build new business, allowing the company and its team to learn by trial and error with minimal reputational or financial risk. Costs were incurred in terms of the re-/up-skilling of personnel and membership to the global business community, but these were far smaller than would have been the case if Cornerstone China had ventured into a new market or hired a new team. This parallel approach, supported strongly by connecting to global networks, allowed the company to build the capabilities of its team, a new client base and a global reputation useful for targeting international companies in local contexts.

Results from such an approach took time to build. In the early 2010s, and as they built their Plan B through trial, error and learning, Cornerstone China serviced an average of 20 executive outplacements per year, with this accounting for around 10% of the company's total revenue per year. Though small in number, these initial outplacement projects served as important practical learning experiences and sources of reputation growth, with many coming from internationally renowned giants, such as world-wide leaders in e-commerce and digital payments. In 2019, Cornerstone China secured its largest outplacement project ever with the China subsidiary of the largest information software and service provider in the world to provide outplacement services for its over 1,300 managers and executives, which made up over 50% of Cornerstone China's total revenue of the year. Furthermore, this invaluable experience provided tools, knowledge and insights that was shared with and benefited Cornerstone group.

Conclusion

This case highlights the importance of a proactive and organic approach to growth based on market and industry trends, particularly in markets with rapidly developing political, technological, and economic environments. Equally important is an understanding of the company's core competencies, how these related to their market and industry, and how these competencies can be leveraged or adapted to take advantage of new growth sectors. While Cornerstone chose a more intuitive and piecemeal approach not entirely based in theory or classic business modelling, their actions and outcomes do align with findings on areas of entrepreneurial practices, business community partnerships, and business transformation.

References

AESC. (2020). *Retained Executive Search vs Contingency: What's the Difference?* Association of Executive Search and Leadership Consultants (AESC). https://www.aesc.org/insights/blog/retained-executive-search-vs-contingency-whats-difference

Allan, C. (2019). *Executive Headhunters vs. Executive Recruiters*. Cornerstone International Group. https://www.cornerstone-group.com/2019/06/18/executive-headhunters-vs-recruiters/

Career Partners International. (2022). *Company Overview*. https://www.cpiworld.com/about/company-overview/

Chenli, R. (2013). *Research on the development of the headhunting sector in China*. Nanchang University.

China National Bureau of Statistics. (2022). *National Data*. https://data.stats.gov.cn/easyquery.htm?cn=C01&zb=A060A&sj=2021

Cornerstone International Group. (2022). *About Cornerstone*. https://www.cornerstone-group.com/about/

Demaris, R., Ries, A., & Trout, J. (1992). Positioning: The Battle for Your Mind. *Journal of Marketing, 56*(1), 122. https://doi.org/10.2307/1252139

Dingman, H. B. (1993). The right fit: Executive search by retained recruiters. *Human Resources, 34*(6), 26–31.

Grundy, T. (2006). Rethinking and reinventing Michael Porter's five forces model. *Strategic Change, 15*(5), 213–229. https://doi.org/10.1002/jsc.764

Harvey, W. S., Beaverstock, J. V., & Li, H. (2019). Common Threats and Managing Reputation in Executive Search Firms. *British Journal of Management, 30*(4), 847–868. https://doi.org/10.1111/1467-8551.12312

Hoffman, R., & Casnocha, B. (2012). *The Start-up of You*. Crown Business.

Lange, D., Lee, P. M., & Dai, Y. (2011). Organizational Reputation: A Review. *Journal of Management, 37*(1), 153–184. https://doi.org/10.1177/0149206310390963

Loza, J. (2004). Business–Community Partnerships: The Case for Community Organization Capacity Building. *Journal of Business Ethics, 53*(3), 297–311. https://doi.org/10.1023/B:BUSI.0000039415.90007.56

Luo, S., Lei, Q., & Li, W. (2020). Investigation on the development of the headhunting industry in South-eastern China—Investigation in Guangzhou, Shenzhen and Changsha. *Enterprise Reform and Management, 6*, 201–204.

Ready, D., & Mulally, A. (2017). How to Become a Game-Changing Leader. *MIT Sloan Management Review, 59*(1), 12.

Sherman, H. J. (2014). *The Business Cycle: Growth and Crisis under Capitalism.* Princeton University Press. https://doi.org/10.1515/9781400862047

Stacho, Z., & Stachová, K. (2015). Outplacement as Part of Human Resource Management. *Procedia Economics and Finance, 34*, 19–26. https://doi.org/10.1016/S2212-5671(15)01596-8

Titleman, G. (1996). *Random House Dictionary of Popular Proverbs and Sayings* (1st edition). London: Random House

Discussion questions

1. Cornerstone China based their new business direction on three main factors: the company's core competencies, emerging market requirements, and vision and core values of the company. When facing a changing market environment and the need to adjust your business offering, what other key factors would you consider, and why?

2. Cornerstone China did not apply theoretical frameworks or business knowledge in a systematic way, which resulted in a piecemeal and intuitive approach. Why do you think it is often challenging to apply business tools or theories in practice? In your own experience, what are the challenges in implementing learning from management education?

3. Companies must take care when deciding on how to explore new business opportunities, as the reallocation of financial and human resources away from the company's core offering can pose a risk to current operations. Do you consider Cornerstone China's Plan A / Plan B strategy a good approach, and why?

4. Cornerstone China benefited greatly by joining a global business community in their newly identified field. Describe these benefits and how your organisations could profit from a similar approach.

CRRC's Management of Foreign Exchange Risk

Juergen Seufert
Honorary Lecturer: University of Aberdeen

Keren Ding
University of Pennsylvania

Abstract

This case study addresses the foreign-currency management of a rolling stock manufacturer and its subsidiaries. We introduce various hedging methods as means to mitigate foreign currency exchange rate risk inherent in long-term service contracts and industry-specific, long cash conversion cycles. This case provides practical insights into the management of foreign exchange rate risks relevant to internationally expanding companies in today's unstable global economy.

Introduction

China Railway Rolling Stock Company Limited (CRRC) is the world's leading rolling stock supplier with large scale, diverse product portfolio with first-class technologies. CRRC ranks among the Global 500 and China's top 100 companies, with products exported to 105 countries and regions. In 2015, state-owned enterprises CNR (China Northern Railway Group) and CSR (China Southern Railway Group) merged to form CRRC Corporation Limited (CRRC 2015) which was subsequently listed in Shanghai and Hong Kong Stock Exchange (Figure 1).

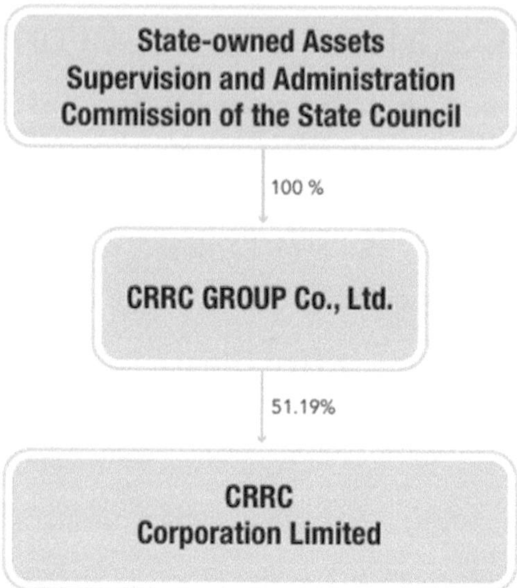

Figure 1: *CRRC's ownership structure*
Source: CRRC (2021a, p.118)

In 2021, the CRRC achieved revenue of RMB225.73 billion and a net profit attributable to shareholders of the company of RMB10.30 billion. As at the end of December 2021, the consolidated total assets of CRRC were RMB426.82 billion (CRRC 2022). (note: China's official currency is the Renminbi, i.e. RMB, of which the principal unit of account is the Yuan, abbreviated as CNY i.e. Chinese Yuan).

For the past decades, CRRC has played an indelible and important role in China's railway market, while expanding globally. By the end of June 2021, CRRC had set up 82 first-tier subsidiaries (Chinese and international including subsidiaries with minority shareholders), 18 Research and Development (R&D) centres, and more than 40 organisations overseas. In 2021, CRRC held more than RMB3 billion (including USD249 million) accounts receivables in foreign currencies and USD327 million short-term borrowing (CRRC 2022).

These international operations are not without risk. Unpredictable changes in the global market, political and economic instability in the foreign countries (e.g., Brazil, Argentina, South Africa, Zimbabwe, USA) long-term contracts common to rail equipment industry, as well as plants and facilities (non-current assets) in foreign countries have exposed CRRC to foreign currency exchange rate risk. Industry specific characteristics make foreign currency exchange rate risk particularly pronounced:

1) Long-term contracts – from signing the contract to the delivery of products or services might take years while the amount denoted in foreign currency is not changing, e.g., USD converted into local currency RMB (Figure 2). For example, in 2014 CRRC Springfield, Massachusetts, was rewarded a USD566 Million contract to manufacture 152 Orange Line cars and 132 Red Line cars, yet these cars were scheduled to enter service between five and nine years later i.e. 2019- 2023.

Figure 2: – *10 years exchange rate chart of Chinese Renminbi (CNY) and US Dollar USD*
Source: XE (2022)

2) Long cash conversion cycles – The cash conversion cycle expresses how long it takes for a company to turn its investment into inventory (raw materials or components) and other resources (e.g. labour) into cash inflows from sales (customer payment). From the construction of a railway vehicle to its delivery and final payment it can take years. Wang (2019) reports an industry (not single contract) average cash conversion cycle of 290-350 days

3) Demand driven markets – Many railway markets are dominated by one or few rail service providers (historically large rollingstock companies which were previously nationalised and combined with their country). Due to their dominant position their negotiation power is strong while competition among rolling stock manufacturers (see Table 1) is fierce and profit margins are limited (EU 2014).

Rank	Company	2019 Revenue ($ Billion)	Country
1	CRRC Corporation	32.4	China
2	Bombardier Transportation	15.8	Canada
3	Siemens Mobility	10.1	Germany
4	Alstom Transport	9.3	France
5	GE Transportation	3.8	US
6	Stadler Rail AG	3.4	Switzerland
7	The Greenbrier Co	3	US
8	Trinity Rail Group	3	US
9	Hyundai Rotem	2	South Korea
10	Hitachi Rail Systems	1.7	Japan

Table 1: *World's largest rolling stock companies*
Source Statistica (2022)

4) High fixed asset intensity - Fixed assets account for a high proportion of a company's total assets while there is high leverage from financing lease liabilities, bank loans and other loans arising from the purchase of production line and manufacturing equipment. It is crucial to manage assets well and ensure the value preservation and appreciation of assets.

Problem statement

While CRRC's 46 wholly-owned subsidiaries (mainly in Mainland China and Hong Kong SAR) are consolidated within the CRRC group (while operating and financing themselves individually, they also compete against each other), these subsidiaries have set up operations abroad and manage foreign exchanges individually. The management of foreign currency cash flows by each individual subsidiary caused suboptimal cash management. That is, some subsidiaries are net receivers of foreign currencies while others are net spenders or in need of foreign currencies for their overseas investments. For example, CRRC ZELC (Zhuzhou Locomotive Co., Ltd) received USD500 million for its service contract with the Turkey Transportation Department in 2018 (CRRC 2018), a maintenance contract of USD84 million with the Argentine Ministry of Transportation in 2021 (CRRC 2020) while CRRC Changchun, in China, spent an initial USD95 million on its Springfield, USA, investment (CRRC (2016).

These asynchronous cash inflows and cash outflows across subsidiaries mean that the total volume of RMB exchanges into foreign currencies and vice versa increased, resulting in more overall cash-holding and higher foreign currency risk exposure. Just in the 3rd Quarter 2020 financial expenses increased by 76.94% compared to the same period of the previous year, which was mainly due to the impact of exchange rate fluctuations and the increase in exchange rate losses (CRRC 2022).

Given the specific industry characteristics (long-term contracts, long cash conversion cycles, demand driven markets and high asset intensity), CRRC's international expansion and the related foreign currency exchange rate risk trigger the questions: How can CRRC minimise its exchange rate risk while still internationally expanding and remaining profitable? Which hedging instruments are available and feasible options for CRRC?

Theory

According to the theory of corporate risk management, the level of hedging (to limit or to qualify risk) depends on various factors:

- **firm size** – larger companies can benefit from economies of scale which allows them to hedge comparatively at lower costs (Nance et al 1993),

- **financial distress risk** - optimal hedging theory suggests that distress risk encourages firms to reduce the variability of their future cash flows, thus reducing probability of bankruptcy (Smith and Stulz 1985),

- **exposure to foreign exchange rate risk** – firms with higher foreign exchange risk exposure tend to hedge more (Gonzalez et al 2010).

- **growth opportunities** – firms with growth opportunities tend to hedge to ensure the availability of funds for future investment opportunities (Myers 1977)

- **level of liquidity** – firms with higher levels of liquidity tend to hedge less, because liquid assets can be a substitute for hedging, and probability of default is less (Nance et al 1993).

Mishkin & Eakins (2019) mention different mechanisms:

1. Forward Market – it allows firms to fix the exchange rate between two currencies (e.g., USD and RMB) for settlement in the future at a fixed future date (up to 10 years later). The forward rate is fixed when the contract is established, and no payments are made until the future value date. Banks commonly trade forward contracts for their clients and themselves.

2. A foreign currency swap – this instrument allows one party to swap a loan's principal and interest in one currency (e.g., RMB) for principal and interest in another (e.g., USD). Commonly, the swap parties borrow different currencies, exchange the receipts, and then settle each other's debt. This eliminates exchange risk and exposure to future currency fluctuations. Another benefit is that sometimes a domestic company can borrow at a cheaper rate than a foreign company.

3. Money Market - the firm exchanges the currency (e.g. RMB to USD) at the current spot rate (today) and invests the proceeds in the money market (trading in very short-term debt investments such as treasury bills, commercial paper, certificate of deposit, trade credit, bills of exchange, promissory notes etc) until they are needed.

4. Direct risk reduction methods – an exporter invoices in their own domestic currency, offsetting payments against receipts in the foreign currency (Matching), setting off intercompany credit against debit balances (Netting).

In the Chinese context hedging developed as shown in Fibure 3:

Figure 3: *The China's foreign-currency management since 1978.*
Source: FRED (2022)

Stage 1 – 1978-1995: After 1978, China's foreign economic activities were dynamic and expanding. In 1980 to prevent "disorder" in foreign currency exchange and circulation of RMB, the Chinese government issued "foreign exchange certificates", which were withdrawn in 1994 and replaced by a managed floating exchange rate regime, ending 16 years of depreciation of RMB. During this period, many enterprises, including CRRC, used foreign exchange certificates as the only means of international settlement. Enterprises in this early stage had not formed an awareness of foreign currency management while their global business accounted for a relatively small proportion of their revenues. Therefore, financial management tools lag behind technological progress, companies lack foreign currency management while China had limited foreign currency reserves and followed conservative policies.

Stage 2 – 1995-Current: China's foreign exchange reserves had expanded as the economy grew. From 2005, China adopted a managed floating exchange rate regime based on market supply and demand with reference to a basket of currencies. After the "811 exchange rate reform" (State Council 2015) in 2015, the fluctuation range of exchange rate further expanded. In 2015, 684 listed companies reported a total exchange loss of RMB51.74 billion, 2.96 times higher than 2014. In the past decade, Chinese enterprises have gradually established foreign exchange risk management with the increase of global business. In addition to the increasing willingness to manage the risks, the State Administration of Foreign Exchange is also strengthening its supervision of the foreign exchange market, and advancing Foreign Exchange Management Regulations.

Actions taken

Firstly, since 2020 due so lower growth in its home- and high-end markets of Europe, America, and Australia, CRRC prioritised Asia, Africa, and Latin America as export markets. It also changed its export mode from single product sales to comprehensive global rail solutions (railroad cars and auxillary services). For example, CRRC (and its subsidiaries) independently established a consortium to win the bidding of a Public Private Partnership project in Mexico (Duran 2020). These actions helped to establish a number of overseas R&D centres. R&D and intellectual property are not subject to exchange rate risk and at the same time provide CRRC with tangible benefits. Thus, CRRC is matching overseas revenues with expenditure to optimise the distribution of overseas resources.

Secondly, direct risk reduction methods. For CRRC's exports, the company's policy requires it to quote foreign business contracts based on the expected value of exchange rate movements over the duration of the contract. For negotiations in foreign business, the range of exchange rate fluctuation and the foreign currency exchange rate risks to be borne by both parties shall be specified in relevant contract clauses (CRRC 2021a).

Thirdly, foreign exchange hedging. For CRRC's import business, subsidiaries are required to settle foreign exchange payables on time (or earlier if the exchange rate is considered favourable) and control foreign exchange risks using forward contracts or swap agreements. Table 2 sets out the sensitivity analysis on foreign currency exchange risk, reflecting the effect of reasonably possible changes in exchange rate of the euro (EUR) against the USD, as well as the impact on net profit under the assumption that all the other variables are held constant.

EUR against RMB		December 31 2021		December 31 2020	
Increase/(Decrease) in exchange rate	in %	9.53	(9.53)	7.49	(7.49)
Increase/(Decrease) in net profit (loss)	RMB'000	(32,154)	32,154	(53,193)	53,193

USD against RMB		December 31 2021		December 31 2020	
Increase/(Decrease) in exchange rate	in %	2.36	(2.36)	8.50	(8.50)
Increase/(Decrease) in net profit (loss)	RMB'000	21,474	(21,474)	87,318	(87,318)

Table 2: *Profit (Loss) sensitivity of changes in foreign exchange rates*
Source: CRRC (2021c, page 218) (Adopted for this case study)

Finally, Table 2 illustrates how CRRC was netting *'Foreign currency financial assets'* against *'Foreign currency financial liabilities'* (both as of 31 December 2021 and 2020) taking into account the maturity of liabilities and expected collection period / liquidity of financial assets, thus matching receivables and payables. About $2.1 billion of "Other non-current assets" were frozen funds held in South Africa, which were placed in custody with a holding subsidiary in July 2021. It will not be included in the scope of the company's consolidated statements. This event also shows that the international business market is exposed to high operating risk.

	31 December 2021 (RMB'000)	31 December 2020 (RMB'000)
Foreign currency financial assets:		
Cash and bank balances	6,592,473	6,773,815
Held-for-trading financial assets	245,095	236,598
Accounts receivable	2,421,400	2,487,950
Other receivables	273,823	447,499
Other current assets	-	392,760
Debt investments	518,686	1,251,587
Long-term receivables	274,081	285,283
Other non-current financial assets	197,647	-
Other non-current assets	-	2,070,791
Total	**10,523,205**	**13,946,283**
Foreign currency financial liabilities		
Short-term borrowings	3,083,909	2,840,607
Accounts payable	3,067,186	3,758,112
Other payables	1,527,707	3,811,546
Long-term borrowings	211,814	220,130
Long-term payable	525	-
Bonds payable	-	2,344,463
Lease liabilities	423,864	-
Total	**8,315,005**	**12,974,858**

Table 3: *Information on financial assets and financial liabilities held in foreign currency*
Source: CRRC (2021c, page 217) (Adopted for this case study)

Evaluation

CRRC identifies exchange rate risks and deals with them in a timely manner, drawing on the three stages of risk disposal:

1. Avoiding risk: CRRC manages its risks from the beginning of the contract. Firstly, when signing the contract, CRRC considers various factors which influence exchange rate risk, including the trend of future exchange rate fluctuation for the settlement currency for vehicles sold, required maintenance costs and other factors to determine the total contract price. Throughout the contract, CRRC optimises its production of goods, effectively controls maintenance and consumables reserves with the aim to reduce unnecessary exchange rate risk exposure. Additionally,

contracts are signed in a hard currency[1]. However, this can be disadvantageous during negotiations because it increases the other party's cost of foreign currency exchange.

2. Hedging risk: CRRC optimises its currency structure of debt:
   - Increase the proportion of RMB debt to control the scale of foreign currency debt and reduce the financial burden when RMB exchange rate depreciation occurs.
   - Adjust the structure of foreign currency debt, repay ahead of expected appreciation of the foreign currency debt, for example repay ahead of schedule the USD debt, increase Japenese Yen or EUR's currency loan which are expected to depreciate to appropriately reduce the exchange rate risk of CRRC's debts.
   - CRRC uses financial derivatives to hedge against currency risk. Financial derivatives include forward market and money market hedges and options.

3. Risk shifting: The risk of currency movements has been shifted from CRRC to the other party.

4. CRRC might allow the other party to pay all or part of the contract price in local currency instead of hard currency (e.g., USD or Euro) but a total value preservation clause must be implemented in the contract. That is, the fixed value of the contract shall be calculated in USD or EUR, which is converted into local currency at the point of settlement. This prevents the exchange rate risk of local currency.

Conclusion

Going global comes with opportunities and risks. This case study emphasises the foreign currency exchange risk faced by CRRC. Rail transit industry is characterised by long cash conversion cycle, long-term contracts,

---

[1] Hard currencies: U.S. dollar (USD), European euro (EUR), Japanese yen (JPY), British pound (GBP), Swiss franc (CHF), Canadian dollar (CAD) and the Australian dollar (AUD) (Bank for International Settlements 2020).

high asset intensity and demand driven markets which determine the need and benefits of hedging against exchange rate risks. Besides these external factors, company specifics such as firm size, financial distress risk, exposure to foreign exchange rate risk, growth and level of liquidity determine the usefulness of managing exchange rate risk by avoiding, hedging, shifting, managing, or retaining risk.

This CRRC case provides insights on how exchange rate risk can be managed by different actions, negotiations, and financial instruments to minimise the financial losses from exchange rate risk. Companies should learn to fully utilise financial tools to maintain the value of their foreign currency denominated contracts and strive to realise value-added from hedging to ensure profit growth and long-term development, while enhancing their international competitiveness within the industry.

References

Bank for International Settlements (2020), Turnover of OTC Foreign Exchange Instruments by Currency. https://stats.bis.org/statx/srs/table/d11.3

CRRC (2022), Financial Report, https://www.crrcgc.cc/g5251.aspx

CRRC (2021a), Annual Report 2020, https://www.crrcgc.cc/Portals/73/Uploads/Files/2021/9-18/637675711244375026.pdf

CRRC (2021b) Semi-annual report 2021, https://www.crrcgc.cc/g4952.aspx

CRRC (2021c) Annual Report 2021 https://www.crrcgc.cc/Portals/71/Uploads/Files/2022/4-1/637844017201521768.pdf (Chinese Version)

CRRC (2020), CRRC signed a maintenance agreement for 709 multiple train units with Argentina, https://www.crrcgc.cc/en/g7389/s10408/t312800.aspx

CRRC (2018), Order of USD 500 Million LRVs for Turkey, https://www.crrcgc.cc/en/g5175/s10162/t297060.aspx#:~:text=On%20October%2026%2C%20local%20time,ISO22163%20international%20railway%20industry%20standard .

CRRC (2016), Topping out" ceremony for $95 million Springfield factory, https://www.crrcgc.cc/en/g7389/s13996/t278169.aspx

CRRC (2015), Chairman's Address, https://www.crrcgc.cc/g6783.aspx

Duran, P., (2020), CRRC to Modernize Mexico City's Metro Line 1 https://mexicobusiness.news/infrastructure/news/crrc-modernize-mexico-citys-metro-line-1

EU (2014), Study on the competitiveness of the Rail Supply Industry, https://ec.europa.eu/docsroom/documents/38025/attachments/1/translations/en/renditions/native

FRED (2022). Chinese Yuan Renminbi to U.S. Dollar Spot Exchange Rate https://fred.stlouisfed.org/series/EXCHUS#

Gonzalez, L., Bua, M., Lopez, S., & Santomil, P., (2010). Foreign debt as a hedging instrument of exchange rate risk: a new perspective. The European Journal of Finance 16 (7), 677-710

Myers, S., (1977). Determinants of corporate borrowing. Journal of Financial Economics 5 (2), 147-175.

Nance, D., Smith, C., & Smithson, C., (1993). On the determinants of corporate hedging. Journal of Finance 48 (1), 267-284.

Smith, C., & Stulz, R., (1985). The determinants of firms' hedging policies. Journal of Financial & Quantitative Analysis 20 (4), 391-405.

State Council (2015). China improves exchange rate formation system http://english.www.gov.cn/state_council/ministries/2015/08/11/content_281475165740232.htm

Statista (2022). Leading rolling stock manufacturers in 2020, by revenue of rail activities https://www.statista.com/statistics/617847/new-vehicle-revenue-rolling-stock-manufacturers/

Wang, B., (2019). The cash conversion cycle spread, Journal of Financial Economics, 133 (2), 472-497

XE (2022). Chinese Yuan Renminbi to US Dollar Exchange Rate Chart, https://www.xe.com/currencycharts/?from=CNY&to=USD&view=10Y

Xiao, H., (2018). CRRC wary of long-term impact, https://global.chinadaily.com.cn/a/201803/31/WS5abef40da3105cdcf65157db.html

Discussion questions

1. Consider the information in Table 3 how could CRRC improve its foreign exchange rate risk exposure?

2. Taking into account *Table 2 Profit (Loss) Sensitivity of Changes in Foreign exchange Rates*, how do you evaluate the foreign exchange rate risk exposure?

3. What are the costs and benefits of managing foreign exchange rate risks for CRRC (or any other company)?

4. What are potential challenges for CRRC to manage foreign exchange rate risks?

5. Is the management of foreign exchange rate risks universally applicable and, if not, why?

6. Which other factors, beyond foreign exchange rate risk, could have an impact on the value of CRRC foreign assets and liabilities?

7. Is there an optimal way of hedging risk for CRRC (or any company)?

8. Referring to Figure 3: How much would CRRC receive (in RMB) and how much would be the profit/loss (in RMB) comparing signing and payment date from a USD100 million contract denoted in USD and signed on April 2015, delivery & payment in May 2017 and October 2019, delivery & payment in January 2021

Customer Perceived Value within China's Digital Commerce Context: Home Appliance at Panasonic

Jing Jiang
Product Manager: Panasonic Appliances China

John Storm
Senior Lecturer: The University of Aberdeen, United Kingdom

Laurie Ann Underwood
Senior Professor of Practice: IESEG School of Business

Abstract

This case exemplifies the first known use of Design Thinking principles within the product development cycle of a household appliance at Panasonic Appliances (China). Themed around timely discussions about the shifting importance of concentrating new product development towards Utilitarian Value or Hedonic Value characteristics, the case reveals steps taken to improve cohesion across a product development team and bring clarity to key internal stakeholders concerning future direction.

Introduction and context

Panasonic is a large Japanese organisation with segments in Appliances, Life Solutions, Connected Solutions, Automotive and Industrial Solutions sectors. Comprising 523 consolidated companies, the Panasonic Group employs over 240,000 people and achieved Fiscal 2021 Net Sales of ¥6,698.8 billion. Appliances account for 34% of Panasonic's recorded sales, with Home Appliances being the largest sub-category (Panasonic, 2021a). Situated within this context, this case study focuses on a particular household appliance herein referred to as 'X Machine' due to sensitivities around ongoing product development. In mainland China, X machine product lines are recording year-on-year growth of 145% (Panasonic, 2021b).

Online shopping platforms provide shoppers convenient access to large volumes of merchandise and relevant information. 24.9% of 2020 retail sales in China were made online, up from 20.7% in 2019 (Statista, 2021). Panasonic has consistently sought to make products that are simple and easy to use, durable and of good quality. However, this utilitarian value perspective towards new product development is beginning to be questioned due to increasingly hedonic value expectations of Chinese customers who, when shopping online, are placing growing attention towards product appearance, packaging, and recommendations from esteemed Key Opinion Leaders (KOL) and Key Opinion Consumers (KOC) (Panasonic, 2021c). Panasonic includes both KOLs and KOCs as KOLs include influencers based upon their existing scope of influence, often from an unrelated background such as being film star, whereas KOCs build their reputation for reviewing products. The audiences are therefore distinct.

House electric appliances in China evidenced significant online sales growth following the outbreak of Covid-19 (McKinsey & Company, 2020). For X machines specifically, 611 responses to a Panasonic survey asking, "Where do you plan to purchase your next X machine?" revealed that 90.2% of respondents intend to purchase online (Panasonic, 2021d). The rapid shift to online sales for products such as X machines raises need for traditional brands to understand what is required to stand out on today's digital platforms. With customer attention needing to be secured within 5 seconds (Ma, 2020), the importance of understanding how customers perceive value within the digital space is of particular consequence for successfully marketing X machines in China. This case study overviews steps taken by Panasonic to improve understanding of value as perceived by target customers of X machines and subsequently feed learning into design processes for new product development.

Research rationale regarding X Machines

Perceived value is the trade-off of the total benefit and total sacrifice anticipated by customers from purchasing a product (Zeithaml, 1988; Dodds et al., 1991; Wood & Scheer, 1996; Cronin et al., 2000; Teas & Agarwal, 2000; Chunmei & Weijun, 2017). Total benefit includes 'utilitarian value', recognised as task-related and rational consumption behaviours that are function, cognitive and a means towards an end; 'hedonic value' recognised as sensory experience relating to pleasure, entertainment and playfulness, and 'social value', recognised as the benefit that a product or service may have in facilitating social recognition or price (Avcilar & Özsoy, 2015; Babin et al, 1994; Kesari & Altukar, 2016; Chunmei & Weijun, 2017; Hanzaee & Rezaeyeh, 2013; Sheth & Mittal, 2004; Rintamäki et al., 2006; Hu et al., 2014; Kang & Kim, 2017). Total sacrifice includes 'monetary type' sacrifices, typically relating to the cost of a transaction in fiat currency terms, as well as 'non-monetary type' sacrifices, typically relating to non-financial factors of expenditure, such as effort and time (Dodds et al., 1991; Grewal et al., 1998; Urbany et al., 1997; Volckner, 2008; Cox, 1967; Zeithaml, 1988; Sweeney et al. 1999; Torkzadeh & Dhillon, 2002). There is a positive correlation between customer perceived value and purchase intention, meaning that new product development (NPD) regularly takes the perspective of maximising perceived value by improving utilitarian value and hedonic value respectively, whilst mitigating Monetary and Non-Monetary Sacrifice to enhance customer purchase intention (Kahneman & Tversky, 1979).

As X machines are a relatively new electronic appliance category for Panasonic, works such as Hartman *et al* (2006) and Chitturi *et al* (2008) suggest that utilitarian value may be improved via educating customers by efficiently highlighting product benefits to gain confidence of practicality – illustrated in Figure 1. It is further noted that customers are paying increased attention towards external product attributes when shopping online (Wheatherell *et al*, 2003; Espejel *et al*, 2007; Brečić *et al*, 2017; Rytkönen *et al*, 2018), leading scholars including Mehrabian and Russell (1974) and Donovan *et al* (1994) to suggest that approaches such as investing in the appearance of a product or promoting a joyous atmosphere when unpacking a new product may lead to improved hedonic value. Exploring the China digital sales context specifically, Chinese online customers attach more importance to the convenience of a purchase, especially with regards to the amount of time investment into obtaining knowledge of a product's core benefits (Assael, 1984; Bloemer & de Ruyter, 1998; Han & Back, 2008; Ryu *et al,* 2008; Han & Kim, 2010). Chinese digital consumers may be characterised as making simple judgements based on common sense or personal preference, such as their personal judgment regarding appearance. Moreover, regarding complex purchasing decisions that require certain high-level knowledge or time to judge, such as product working principle, function and effect comparison, Chinese consumers tend to rely on esteemed KOLs or KOCs (Villanueva *et al,* 2008; Chaudhry & Irshad, 2013; Lu & Zhang, 2020; Zhang *et al,* 2021). Therefore, non-monetary improvements to product attributes facilitating customers to judge a product with convenience and minimal effort may have a positive effect on improving customer perceived value (Ajzen, 1991; Perugini & Bagozzi, 2001; Bagozzi & Dholakia, 2006; Poels & Dewitte, 2008; Prestwich *et al,* 2008; Taylor *et al,* 2009).

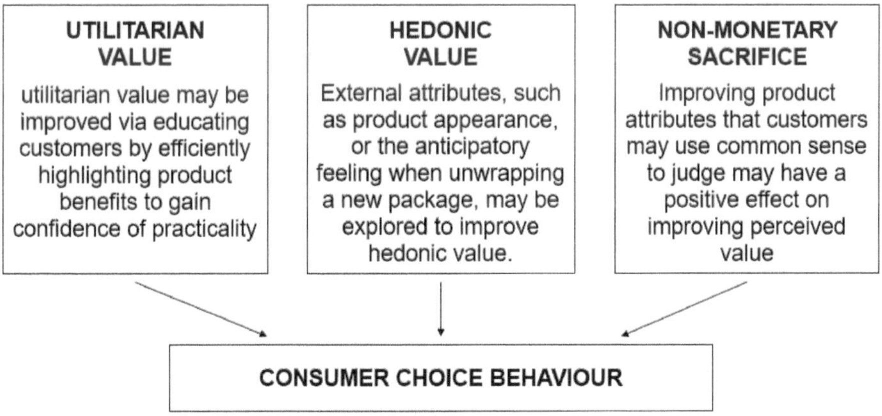

Figure 1: *Improving customer perceived value of RBG machines*

The focus of the project was therefore to improve understanding of how utilitarian value, hedonic value, and non-monetary sacrifice factors may impact customer perception of value of X machines, and feed core learning into the NPD department. Design Thinking was utilised as a framework to direct the project due to its focus on facilitating authentic dialogue with a wide stakeholder base – thus assisting the Project Lead in Panasonic to reduce their inner voice throughout the project.

Design Thinking stage 1 – empathy

The concept of empathy is rooted in a human-centred approach towards research (Johnsson-Sköldberg, Woodilla and Çetinkaya, 2013). Applied within the model of Design Thinking, the aim of empathising with key stakeholders is to gain awareness of varying perspectives towards a given problem and highlight potential risk factors as early as possible (Lockwood, 2009).

Internal stakeholders relating to the development of new X machines at Panasonic were listed and mapped using the stakeholder power / interest matrix (Freeman, 1984; Johnson & Scholes, 1999). Eighteen stakeholders were prioritised and invited to join one of seven focus groups, each focus group focusing attention on a distinct topic of conversation as identified in Figure 2.

Focus groups were held for 1-hour each, providing opportunity for respective parties to raise concerns relating to the development and commercialisation of X machines. In an effort to exercise authentic listening (Storm, 2021), no comment or generalisation toward observations was provided until after all focus groups were completed and only for the purposes of verifying accuracy of notes recorded.

A by-product of the focus groups was their ability to flag the existence of conflicting ideas and priorities between groups in a transparent manner not usually accessible to Product Managers. This was noted as valuable for identifying potential areas of resistance that may arise later in the project. For example, the idea of increasing the volume of X machines' functions to improve customer perception may arguably have been made defunct by Panasonic China's own small-scale surveys that revealed 0 out of 24 respondents as willing to pay more for non-alpha-functions, with respondents regularly revealing that none of them had used some functions at all – such as night-lights, motion sensors or temperature sensors.

It may be highlighted that the stakeholder groups were limited to internal stakeholders only. Given a total project timeframe of 3 months, it was elected to make use of existing research that Panasonic has conducted regarding consumer purchase behaviour and customer preferences towards X machines. Whereas survey and focus group questions on previous studies may not be fully relevant towards the core focus of this project, the access to wider customer base was significantly beyond the resource scope of this project. Additionally, as highlighted in the project aim, the focus is to bring learning into the NPD department at Panasonic, thus ensuring that the voice and perspectives of internal stakeholders are heard in identifying the key areas of internal interest and recognised as most important for ensuring receptiveness internally towards final findings.

Group	Discussion Topic	Participants	Participant Number	Key Observation
1	Business development and planning of X machine for short-mid term	1. General Manager 2. Business Development Manager	2	- Early-stage investment into X machines still not recovered, resulting in increased sensitivity towards financial modelling and return on investment. - Although China market growth is rapid and persuasive, market size remains below critical thresholds perceived to warrant significant new investment. - The suggestion that customers pay more attention towards hedonic value than utilitarian value is not sufficiently quantified in terms of how this translates to sales performance.
2	Product strategy and NPD investment	Product Managers of beauty care products and other related product categories	4	- Whereas hedonic values relating to ceremonial feelings during unpacking, as well as product appearance are noticed as influential, the degree to which these factors motivate customers to ultimate purchase a product is questioned. - Customer Lifetime Value (CLV), which considers factors influencing repeat custom, tend to highlight the importance of utilitarian value factors. - CLV is a priority consideration due to high costs associated with new customer acquisition on digital platforms. Tmall was exampled as costing up to 20 RMB per referral click for beauty products with a conversion rate as little as 1%.

Group	Discussion Topic	Participants	Participant Number	Key Observation
3	Marketing appeal of X machines	Marketing Communication Managers	2	- Reference to Service Dominant Logic (S-D logic) was made, viewing transaction process as a whole rather than a specific point in the experience a critical factor for customers considering repurchase. - Panasonic has 100 years of brand loyalty built upon utilitarian value factors. What would a radical shift mean for brand management and current brand loyalty? - If product development shifted focus, it could not be at expense of utilitarian value factors without risking brand damage and customer loss. - With RGB machines still a new product category for Panasonic, the market is of questionable readiness to sufficiently understand product characteristics. Marketing Communication Managers therefore highlighted preference towards increasing utilitarian value during NPD.
4	NPD of X machines from a technical perspective	Directors from technical engineering department (one for software and one for hardware)	2	- Investing in utilitarian value factors have higher probability to strengthen core competence in related departments. - Although packaging and external hedonic factors were noted as important, they are generally more exposed to imitation. Whereas technical advantages may be protected by intellectual property rights and regulations, thus less open to replication. - Acknowledgement given that the average customer may not cognitively compute the full value and benefit of a given product. - Perceived as easier to improve customer perception by increasing the volume of functions rather than the depth of a single function;

Group	Discussion Topic	Participants	Participant Number	Key Observation
5	Appearance and design of X machines	Designers of Panasonic (Appearance) design centre who are responsible for beauty care products	3	- Investment into hedonic values favoured as opportunity for increased freedom in the appearance design process. - Perception that utilitarian value orientation of Panasonic has often prioritised other functions over the Design Centre. - Hedonic value factors are not only about purchase but may increase the probability of customers sharing their product purchase on social media. The latter therefore indirectly feeds into brand creation and product promotion. - Design Centre hopes Product Managers will liaise with other functions to build awareness of the benefits product appearance may bring.
6	Manufacturing of X machines	Factory manufacturing manager responsible for X machine lines	1	- Significant investment into machinery and operator training made to produce product lines according to existing specifications should not be underappreciated or underutilised. - Adding manufacturing processes to improve product appearance may result in need to hire more trained operators to optimise processes or risk increasing product defective rates. - Some methods of increasing hedonic value (such as minor changes to seasonal packaging) may result in small batch needs that are challenging for factory management and increase production costs. - Desire ROI to be fully considered prior to executing changes.
7	Promotion and sales of X machines	1. Sales Directors 2. Agent Sales Staff	4	- Hedonic value improvement fully welcomed, provided that utilitarian value factors are unchanged and price is not increased. - Increasing levels of competition in the market may raise question about the competitiveness of some product items. - Promotion expenses consistently insufficient for effectively promoting product lines.

Figure 2: *Focus groups with internal stakeholders*

Design Thinking stage 2 – define

The focus of the project has been identified above as 'to improve understanding on how utilitarian value, hedonic value, and non-monetary sacrifice factors may impact customer perception of value of X machines, and feed core learning into the NPD department'. Following engagement with core internal stakeholders, the project aim was optimised through the identification of 3 hypotheses as below:

> **Hypothesis 1:** In China's current digital shopping environment, customers value and are increasingly being influenced by Hedonic Value. Therefore, Panasonic need to rebalance the focus of NPD from improving Utilitarian Value to improving Hedonic Value factors in order to obtain more customers.

If Hypothesis One is not rejected, this research should clarify which product attributes may help Panasonic X machines improve its Hedonic Value from the perspective of NPD when considering return on investment (ROI) and difficulties of factory manufacturing management.

Moreover, part of Panasonic's price premium over competitor products has stemmed from perception towards Utilitarian Value. Therefore, this study must consider the technical feasibility of reducing certain product attributes, while ensuring the overall utilitarian value of Panasonic X machines still meets customer expectations. Thus, the changes must not trigger a loss of loyal customers and damage to the brand image.

> **Hypothesis 2:** Chinese consumers consider the Utilitarian attributes of a product to be valuable whether they are purchased via traditional offline channels or via online e-commerce methods. Although the emphasis on Hedonic Value, such as product appearance, has increased, Utilitarian Value is still the biggest determinant stimulating customer purchase decisions. Thus, future NPD processes should appropriately increase the investment and attention to improve Hedonic Value without reducing focus on Utilitarian Value.

If Hypothesis Two is not rejected, this research must specifically clarify how to balance improvements in utilitarian value and hedonic value, to improve more effectively the overall customer perceived value.

> **Hypothesis 3:** In order to reduce customers' non-monetary sacrifice, we should improve their convenience during online shopping by reducing their burden in terms of the effort needed to obtain knowledge of the product benefits. Since the judgment of Utilitarian Value of a X machine needs certain high-level knowledge or more time and effort, we may try to make the Utilitarian Value of the product more obvious and easily discovered by changing some product attributes. Customers may understand and recognise the product benefits without explanation, thus enhancing their total perceived value of our X machines.

If Hypothesis Three is not rejected, this research should further specify which product attributes should be changed to help improve the expression of Utilitarian Value when considering ROI and reasonable stakeholder burden.

Design Thinking stages 3+4 – ideation and prototyping

Ideation and prototyping are important stages during the Design Thinking process (Lockwood, 2009). Thirteen colleagues from functions involved in related NPD participated in the ideation process, which as identified in Figure 3 orientated around a full day's brainstorming workshop. Participants were consistent with those involved during the 'Empathy' stage, which provided the following three benefits: (1) Understanding of the project from a Panasonic NPD perspective, (2) Understanding of the project as a trial of Design Thinking principles at Panasonic, and (3) Familiarity with the three underlying hypotheses as summarised above.

Prior to testing by means of in-depth customer focus groups, the process required refinement through internal analysis. A key tool during idea reduction at Panasonic is the use of the C = B + I formula (Concept = Benefit + Idea), which includes all attributes relating to a product, such as function, effect, appearance, sense of use, operability, etc. Sorting the 52 ideas generated from the brainstorm session via the C = B + I formula enabled grouping of ideas into categories such as inclusion of a common technology. As testing would include product demonstration and product usage, it was important that prototypes and exhibits would provide sufficient exposure across the full product purchase experience, from first appearance on a digital platform, right through to after purchase usage.

Stage	Participants	Participant number	Summary of steps taken
Idea brainstorming	5x Product Managers 2x Digital Sales experts 1x Marketing Communications Representative 3x Technical Engineers 2x Developers from (Appearance) Design Centre	13	5 stage process combining: - Stage 1 (90 mins): Open brainstorming around topic of how to improve customer perceived hedonic value - Stages 2-4 (70 mins each): Repeat process, but specific towards identified product concept - Stage 5 (30 mins): Wrap up discussion
Idea reduction	Project lead (only)	1	- Formally record output of 52 workable ideas from brainstorming session - Utilise Panasonic's C = B + I (product formula) to reduce ideas down to 6 main choices
Internal prototyping	-	-	- Develop exhibits achieving below: o 13 home electronic skin care technologies o 6 product concepts o 3 mock-ups to show product appearance o 6 CMF (Colour, Material and Furnishing) styles presented by computer graphics

Stage	Participants	Participant number	Summary of steps taken
			o 14 special names for complex beauty technologies and programs o 12 promotional articles o 19 product content descriptions for use on e-commerce platforms - Compile 20 alternatives from Panasonic and rival product lines - Send all prototypes and exhibits to Technical Engineers and Design Centre for analysis

Figure 3: *Key actions taken during ideation and prototyping stages*

Design Thinking stages 5 – testing

The testing stage was developed to achieve two goals: (1) Explore and offer insights into online X machine customer needs and purchase behaviours in relation to Dentsu's (2006) AISAS mode (Attention-Interest-Search-Action-Share), and (2) Observe visual triggers that may indicate perceived value during in-person testing.

Four groups of four target customers were invited to attend 2.5 hours long symposiums. Twelve participants were customers having already purchased an X machine within the past 12 months, with the remaining four participants indicating an interest in purchasing an X machine within the upcoming 6 months. All participants received payment for their time and consented to partake in the study that was conducted by an approved research agency at an off-site venue. Panasonic staff – including the project lead – observed through a one-way mirror, but were out of sight from the test participants at all times. Testing involved the following stages:

1. Survey focusing on understanding individual customer needs

2. Focus group discussion focusing on sharing of methods used and experiences with X machines throughout the purchasing process
3. Invitation to describe priorities and approaches towards purchasing an X machine
4. Ranking of prototypes and exhibits in terms of preference
5. Feedback concerning promotional articles and videos
6. Wrap up, involving participants drawing / listing product characteristics most important to them when picturing the 'ideal' X machines

The testing process was itself trialled internally with 4 Panasonic colleagues to ensure that time was sufficient to complete all desired activities.

Project discussion

Progressing through the project stages, it became noticeable that internal stakeholders were becoming increasingly communicative and supportive towards the process. Rather than limiting contribution according to their own specialised areas, the Design Thinking process was helping participants to visually observe progression from 'their own' simple ideas into a possible reality. There appeared a growing sense of ownership and involvement, with increased understanding towards constraints during NPD. Although not empirically measured, improved cooperation was apparent and generated material time saving as a result of having increased buy-in from key stakeholders who may otherwise have needed more persuasion to trial new ideas.

Upon completion of the testing stage, the project team returned to the underlying hypotheses and reflected on how initial thinking may not be universal or even fully evident when played out. For example, in relation to Hypothesis 1, it was clearly identified during product testing that utilitarian value remains of key importance for customers. This was not only implied during the testing stage, as a question was literally posited to participants to attach more importance to either Utilitarian Value or Hedonic Value factors, through which 15 out of 16 participants chose Utilitarian Value. Equally, all 16 participants noted that their judgement towards Utilitarian Value was primarily influenced by KOL or KOC influencers and not via their own research into product characteristics.

Hypothesis 2 was reinforced by test participants, highlighting aesthetics (not limited to product) as crucial for gaining attraction towards a product, considerably more than descriptions of product functions or effects. Focus group participants revealed that taking longer than 30 seconds to overview product functions would tend to turn off interest in the product, unless specifically regarding a key function that had been highlighted repetitively via numerous sources. These findings reinforced internal thinking that it is important to improve Hedonic Value of NPD, although not at the expense of Utilitarian Value, yet also help keep in check the degree towards change that was initially being proposed by the Project Lead.

A further observation of interest was that customers highlighted that online purchasing was regularly done during fragmented time periods, such as during a commute on the metro. Relating to Hypothesis 3, testing reinforced understanding that making the non-monetary sacrifice of the purchase process as convenient as possible may have material impact on sales conversion. A significant volume of further insights was gathered from the project. However, due to the sensitivity of ongoing product development, not all learning is suitable for public disclosure.

The project exemplifies first use of Design Thinking principles in Panasonic Appliances (China) NPD of X machines. Rather than producing a concrete product idea for implementation, the project has highlighted need for further research and produced a timeline that, with the known buy-in of all key internal stakeholders, aims to offer a holistic strategy involving proposal of a new product to the Managment Board within a 6-month window.

Conclusion

Exampling first use of Design Thinking principles within the product development cycle of X Machines at Panasonic, this project has highlighted direct benefits obtained by bringing key internal and external stakeholder perspectives together, with a primary benefit being improved project team cooperation and cohesion. Themed around timely discussions about the shifting importance of concentrating NPD towards Utilitarian Value or Hedonic Value characteristics, the project has provided improved clarity to key internal stakeholders concerning future direction, whilst simultaneously increasing recognition from all parties with regards to each other's respective contribution. Whilst no new product was proposed as a result of this project, an important deliverable was a concrete action plan, with known buy-in from all key internal stakeholders, that aims to offer a holistic strategy culminating in the release of a new product in the near future.

References

Ajzen, I., (1991) The theory of planned behavior. *Organizational Behavior and Human Decision Processes,* 50 (2), pp. 179–211.

Assael, H., (1984) *Consumer Behavior and Marketing Action,* 2nd Edn. Boston: Kent Publishing Company.

Avcilar, M. Y., & Özsoy, T., (2015) Determining the effects of perceived utilitarian and Utilitarian Value on Online shopping intentions. *International Journal of Marketing Studies,* 7 (6), pp. 27–49.

Babin, B.J., Darden. W.R., & Griffin. M., (1994) Work and/or Fun: Measuring Hedonic and Utilitarian Shopping Value. *Journal of Consumer Research,* 20 (4), pp. 644-656. http://www.jstor.org/stable/2489765 (Accessed on 16 August 2015).

Bagozzi, R.P., & Dholakia, U.M., (2006) Antecedents and purchase consequences of customer participation in small group brand communities. *International Journal of Research in Marketing,* 23, pp. 45–61.

Bloemer, J., & de Ruyter, K., (1998) On the relationship between store image, store satisfaction and store loyalty. *European Journal of Marketing,* 32, pp. 499–513.

Brečić, R., Mesić, Ž., & Cerjak, M. (2017) Importance of intrinsic and extrinsic quality food characteristics by different consumer segments. *British Food Journal,* 119, pp. 845–862.

Chaudhry. S., & Irshad. W., (2013) Opinion leadership and its role in buyer decision making, *Academy of Contemporary Research Journal,* 7 (1) (2013), pp. 7–14.

Chitturi, R., Raghunathan, R., & Mahajan,V., (2008) Delight by design: The role of hedonic versus utilitarian benefits, *Journal of Marketing,* 72, pp. 48–63.

Chunmei, G., & Weijun, W., (2017) The influence of perceived value on purchase intention in social commerce context. *Internet Research*, 27 (4), pp. 772–785.

Cox, D., (1967) *Risk taking and information handling in consumer behavior*. Boston: Harvard University Press.

Cronin, J.J., Brady, M.K. & Hult, G.T.M. (2000) Assessing the effect of quality, value, and customer satisfaction on consumer behavioural intentions in service environments, *Journal of Retailing*, 76 (2), pp. 193-218.

Dentsu Inc, (2006) Digitization Changing the Consumer Purchasing Process: From AIDMA to AISAS

Dodds, W., Monroe, K.B. & Grewal, D., (1991) The effects of price, brand and store information on buyers' product evaluations, *Journal of Marketing Research*, 28, pp. 307-19.

Donovan, R. J., Rossiter, J. R., Marcoolyn, G., & Nesdale, A., (1994) Store atmosphere and purchasing behavior. *Journal of Retailing*, 70, pp. 283–294.

Espejel, J., Fandos, C., & Flavián, C., (2007) The role of intrinsic and extrinsic quality attributes on consumer behaviour for traditional food products. *Managing Service Quality: An International Journal*, 17, pp. 681–701.

Freeman, R.E., (1984) *Strategic Management: A Stakeholder Approach*. Boston: Pitman.

Grewal, D., Monroe, K. B., & Krishnan, R., (1998) The effects of price comparison advertising on buyers' perceptions of acquisition value, transaction value and behavioral intentions. *Journal of Marketing*, 62, pp. 46–59.

Han, H., & Back, K., (2008) Relationships among image congruence, consumption emotions, and customer loyalty in the lodging industry, *Journal of Hospitality and Tourism Research*, 32 (4), pp. 467–490.

Han, H., & Kim, Y., (2010) An investigation of green hotel customers' decision formation: developing an extended model of the theory of planned behavior, *International Journal of Hospitality Management*, 29, pp. 659–668.

Hanzaee, K. H., & Rezaeyeh, S. P., (2013) Investigation of the effects of utilitarian value and utilitarian value on customer satisfaction and behavioural intentions. *African Journal of Business Management*, 7 (11), pp. 818–825.

Hartman, J. B., Shim, S., Barber, B., & O'Brien, M., (2006) Adolescents' utilitarian and hedonic web-consumption behavior: Hierarchical influence of personal values and innovativeness. *Psychology & Marketing*, 23, pp. 813–839.

Hu, T., Kettinger, W. J., & Poston, R. S., (2014) The effect of online Social Value on satisfaction and continued use of social media, *European Journal of Information Systems*, 24 (4), pp. 391–410.

Johnson. G., & Scholes. K., (1999) *Exploring corporate strategy*, 5th Edn, London: Prentice-Hall Europe.

Johnsson-Sköldberg, U., Woodilla, J., & Çetinkaya, M., (2013) Design Thinking: Past, Present and Possible Futures, *Creativity and Innovation Management*, 22 (2), pp.121-146. DOI: 10.1111/caim.12023.

Kahneman, D. & Tversky, A., (1979) Prospect theory: An analysis of decision under risk, *Econometrica*, 47, pp. 263–291.

Kang, H. Y, & Kim, J., (2017) Customer's social value perception and enterprise's sustainability: focus on social enterprise, *Journal of Marketing Thought*, 4 (2), pp. 71–77.

Kesari, B., & Atulkar, S., (2016) Satisfaction of mall shoppers: a study on perceived utilitarian and hedonic shopping values, *Journal of Retailing and Consumer Services*, 31, pp. 22–31.

Lockwood, T., (2009) *Design Thinking: Integrating Innovation, Customer Experience, and Brand Value*, 3rd Edn. New York: Allworth Press.

Lu, H., & Zhang, M., (2020) The impact of perceived risk of online popular goods on Purchase Intention -- A regulated intermediary model perspective, 12, pp. 20-28

Ma, J., (2020) *Live streaming sales techniques, how to introduce product in a live streaming room*, Available at: https://zhuanlan.zhihu.com/p/152187334, (Accessed on 27 November 2021).

McKinsey & Company., (2020) China Consumer Report 2021: Understanding Chinese Consumers – Growth Engine of the World. Special Edition. November 2020.

Mehrabian, A., & Russell J. A., (1974) *An approach to environmental psychology*. Cambridge, MA: MIT Press.

Panasonic., (2021a) *Panasonic Corporation Annual Report 2021*. Available at: https://www.panasonic.com/global/corporate/ir/pdf/annual/2021/pana_ar2021e_a3.pdf (Accessed 23 February 2022).

Panasonic., (2021b) Mid-term strategy of household beauty machine.

Panasonic, (2021c) RFB machine product appearance acceptance interview

Panasonic, (2021d) Customer needs and behavior survey through TMIC

Perugini, M., & Bagozzi, R.P., (2004) The distinction between desires and intentions. *European Journal of Social Psychology*, 34 (1), pp. 69–84.

Poels, K., & Dewitte, S., (2008) Hope and self-regulatory goals applied to an advertising context: promoting prevention stimulates goal-directed behavior. *Journal of Business Research*, 61, pp. 1030–1040.

Prestwich, A., Perugini, M., & Hurling, R., (2008) Goal desires moderate intention-behaviour relations, *British Journal of Social Psychology,* 47 (1), pp. 49–71.

Rintamäki, T., Kanto, A., Kuusela, H., & Spence, M. T., (2006) Decomposing the value of department store shopping into utilitarian, hedonic and social dimensions, *International Journal of Retail and Distribution Management*, 34(1), pp. 6–24.

Rytkönen.P., Bonow, M., Girard. C., & Tunón, H., (2018) Bringing the Consumer Back in — The Motives, Perceptions, and Values behind Consumers and Rural Tourists' Decision to Buy Local and Localized Artisan Food — A Swedish Example, *Agriculture*, 8 (4), p. 58.

Ryu, K., Han, H., & Kim, T., (2008) The relationships among overall quick casual restaurant image, perceived value, customer satisfaction, and behavioral intentions, *International Journal of Hospitality Management,* 27 (3), pp. 459–469.

Sheth, J. N., & Mittal, B., (2004) *Consumer behavior: a managerial perspective,* 2nd Edn, South-Western, USA.

Statista., (2021) *E-commerce share of total retail sales in consumer goods in China from 2014 to 2020,* Available at: https://www.statista.com/statistics/1129915/chinaecommerce-share-of-retail-sales/, (Accessed on 27 November 2021).

Storm, J., (2021) Developing a Design Thinking mind-set to stimulate sustainable development in Chinese SMEs. **In:** *Proceedings of the IIBG Academic-Industry Exchange 2021 Conference on Business as Usual: How do we Turn the New Normal into Normal*. Hong Kong. Proceedings pp.43-67.

Sweeney, J. C., Soutar, G. N., & Johnson, L. W., (1999) The role of perceived risk in the quality–value relationship: A study in a retail environment, *Journal of Retailing*, 75, pp. 77–105.

Taylor, S.A., Ishida, C., & Wallace, D.W., (2009) Intention to engage in digital piracy: a conceptual model and empirical test, *Journal of Service Research*, 11 (3), pp. 246–262.

Teas, R. K., & Agarwal, S., (2000) The effects of extrinsic product cues on consumers' perceptions of quality, sacrifices, and value, *Journal of the Academy of Marketing Science*, 28, pp. 278–290.

Torkzadeh,G., & Dhillon,G., (2002) Measuring factors that influence the success of Internet commerce, *Information Systems Research*, 13, pp. 187–204.

Urbany, J. E., Bearden,W.O., Kaicker, A., & Borrero, M. S., (1997) Transaction utility effects when quality is uncertain, *Journal of the Academy of Marketing Science*, 25, pp. 45–55.

Villanueva, J., Yoo, S., & Hanssens, D. M. (2008) The impact of marketing-induced versus word-of-mouth customer acquisition on customer equity growth. *Journal of marketing Research, 45* (1), pp.48-59.

Volckner, F., (2008) The dual role of price: Decomposing consumers' reactions to price, *Journal of the Academy of Marketing Science*, 36, pp. 359–377.

Wheatherell, C., Treagar, A., & Allinson, J., (2003) In search of the concerned consumer. UK public perceptions of food,farming and buying local. *Journal of rural studies*, 19 (2), pp. 233–244.

Wood, C. M., & Scheer, L. K., (1996) Incorporating perceived risk into models of consumer deal assessment and purchase intent, *Advances in Consumer Research*, 23 (1), pp. 399–404.

Zeithaml, V. A., (1988) Consumer perceptions of price, quality, and value: a means-end model and synthesis of evidence, *Journal of Marketing*, 52 (3), pp. 2–22.

Zhang, Q., Huang, T., & Peng, B., (2021) Research on purchase intention arousal and its influence mechanism in online live streaming - An Interpretation Framework Based on planned behavior theory, *Journal of Shandong Vocational and Technical College of Commerce*, 21, p.6.

Discussion questions

1. The case revolves around the Project Lead's initial idea to increase attention towards Hedonic Value factors during new product development. Individual values and beliefs can significantly impact a project teams outlook and direction. What approaches have you taken to reduce your 'inner voice' and enhance your ability to listen to alternative viewpoints?

2. New forms of Digital Sales, such as the Private Pool Economy or Live Streaming Sales, have gained significant traction in recent years. How do you perceive such sales channels to impact on customer perceived value (including Hedonic Value and Utilitarian Value)? Why?

3. How do you evaluate the role of "Empathy" and "Early co-creation" in cross-departmental cooperation? In your daily work, how may you import the Design Thinking method?

Domestic Airline X: Pandemic, Pilots and Policies

Shenghong Deng

International Pilot: Domestic Airline X

Abstract

All sectors of economies throughout the world have been affected by the Covid-19 pandemic, but some have been affected more than others. The airline industry has been one of the most badly affected and, within it, an unprecedented impact has been experienced by those involved in international flights, not least the pilots. This case study explores the impact of the pandemic on pilots employed by a major domestic airline in China and, in doing so, considers the key issues of motivation and equity.

Introduction

This case considers policies implemented by a domestic airline in China intended to sustain and enhance the motivation of its pilots during the period of the Covid-19 pandemic. In the period since December 2019, the pandemic has inevitably had a profound impact on all countries and all sectors, and not least the aviation industry. However, research to date on the industry, including in China (e.g., Suk & Kim, 2021), has perhaps not given sufficient attention to its impact on pilots, including their morale, volume of resignations and early retirements, seniority of those pilots who have left, and current and future skills shortages.

In China, airlines pilots flying internationally have had to endure lengthy and frequent periods of quarantine when they return to China. This, combined with continued anxiety over job security, has had an understandable impact on the morale of the whole pilot group, including on the airline which is the focus of this case study, referred to here, for reasons of commercial sensitivity and to protect its anonymity, as Domestic

Airline X. Related to this, please also note that, throughout the case, the information given is not from published sources but, rather, has been supplied to the author from departments within Domestic Airline X. Similarly, references to level of morale amongst pilots is not based on in-house surveys but on detailed and extensive discussions with numerous pilots by the author. It is acknowledged here that the author is an international pilot with the Airline and, as such, recognises the risk of allowing subjective views to influence the findings. However, by virtue of the role undertaken, the author can speak authoritatively and objectively about the views of colleagues, not least other international pilots.

The case explores the issue of motivation of pilots employed by Domestic Airline X and comments on policies that have been implemented by the airline.

Context

Perhaps no industry has been more adversely affected by Covid-19 than air transport. Bouwer, Saxon & Wittkamp (2021) state that 'It's difficult to overstate just how much the Covid-19 pandemic has devastated airlines. In 2020, industry revenues totalled $328 billion, around 40 percent of the previous year's. In nominal terms, that's the same as in 2000. The sector is expected to be smaller for years to come; we project traffic won't return to 2019 levels before 2024.' To illustrate the impact, see Figure 1 and Table 1.

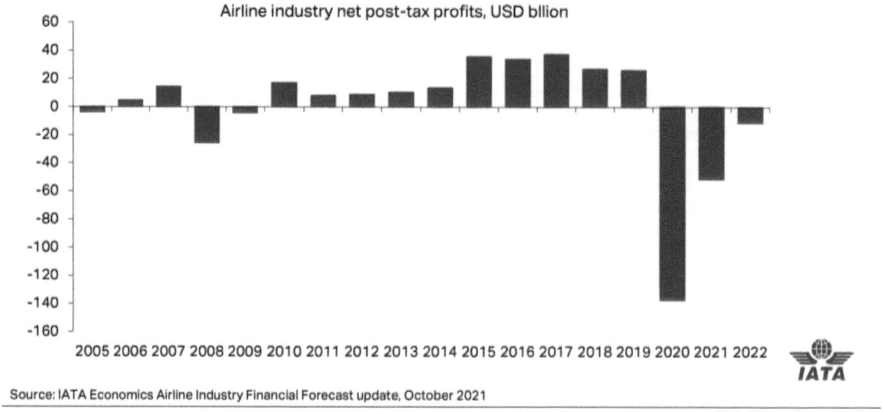

Figure 1: *International airline industry net tax profits 2005-2022*

The data in Figure 1 and Table 1 are in part a function of the downturn in scheduled boarded passengers globally. The numbers increased incrementally from 2bn in 2004 to 4.5bn in 2019 and 4.7bn in 2020 pre-Covid-19 but which then fell to 1.8bn in 2020 post-Covid-19. Though passenger numbers rose in 2021 to 2.3bn this is approximately 50% of the 2019 volume. Note that 'scheduled boarded passengers' refers to the number of passengers who booked and boarded a flight with a commercial airline. Excluded are passengers on charter flights, whereby an entire plane is booked by a private group. In 2019, the Asia Pacific region had the highest share of airline passenger traffic, accounting for one third of the global total (Statista, 2022).

Financial Results

System-wide global commercial airlines	EBIT margin, % revenues							Net profit, $ billion						
	2016	2017	2018	2019	2020	2021E	2022F	2016	2017	2018	2019	2020	2021E	2022F
Global	8.5%	7.5%	5.7%	5.2%	-30%	-11%	-2.7%	34.2	37.6	27.3	26.4	-137.7	-51.8	-11.6
Regions														
North America	13.7%	11.2%	9.1%	9.6%	-32%	-5.2%	4.8%	17.0	17.8	14.5	17.4	-35.1	-5.5	9.9
Europe	6.1%	7.9%	6.2%	4.8%	-32%	-17%	-5.9%	8.5	8.9	9.1	6.5	-34.5	-20.9	-9.2
Asia-Pacific	7.4%	6.3%	4.7%	3.7%	-28%	-14%	-9.1%	7.4	10.5	6.1	4.9	-45.6	-11.2	-2.4
Middle East	2.2%	-3.0%	-4.6%	-5.2%	-21%	-18%	-9.6%	1.3	0.1	-1.5	-1.5	-8.5	-6.8	-4.6
Latin America	5.6%	6.2%	2.7%	2.9%	-34%	-18%	-9.7%	0.4	0.5	-0.8	-0.7	-11.9	-5.6	-3.7
Africa	1.1%	0.8%	1.5%	1.0%	-22%	-13%	-9.9%	-0.4	-0.2	-0.1	-0.3	-2.2	-1.9	-1.5

Sources: IATA estimates for regions. IATA forecast for 2022.
Note: Bankruptcy reorganization & large non-cash costs are excluded. Includes all commercial airlines. Historical data are subject to revision.
Updated: 10/2021

Table 1: *International airline industry financial results 2016-2022*

The importance of the Asia Pacific region reflects the significance of China and, consequently, any downturn or financial distress affecting airlines in China will have a disproportionate impact in the region and globally. With people wary of the infection risk within a confined space and country after country imposing a travel ban and quarantine policy, passenger numbers and airline revenues have plummeted. China's three biggest airlines, Air China, China Eastern Airlines and China Southern Airlines, posted a combined loss of RMB 32.5bn ($5.1bn) in the first three quarters of 2021, after a RMB 42bn loss in 2020 (Reuters, 2022a). Such financial performance reflects the reduction in passenger numbers, from approximately 660m in 2019 to 418m in 2020, a fall of 37% (CEIC, 2022).

However, although passenger numbers have fallen dramatically, there has been a significant increase in freight transport in the world. The International Air Traffic Association (IATA) (2021) reported that: 'In 2021 overall, air cargo volumes rose by 18.7% year-on-year, the second-best yearly performance since our series started in 1990.'

In responding to the pandemic, the Civil Aviation Administration of China (CAAC) has approved a five-year plan to be implemented in two stages i.e., 2021-22 will focus on Covid-19 control and prevention and further support for the sector, 2023-25 will be a period of growth with an expansion in the domestic market and recovery of the international market. The expansion of the domestic market is reflected in the target to have 270 civil airports by 2025 compared to 241 at the end of 2020 (Reuters, 2022b).

However, such recovery depends not only on the control of Covid-19 but also on availability of resources, including the numbers of pilots, for passenger flights and for the significant increase in air cargo flights. Within this context, Domestic Airline X, along with all other airlines in China, has had to respond to the pandemic and ensure it is well-placed for a post-pandemic recovery.

Domestic Airline X – profile

The airline was formally founded in 1986 but in 2002 reformed its share system and formed a new company in collaboration with other companies in China, all of which with one exception were also airline companies. As at March 2022, it had a fleet of 181 aircraft i.e., 178 Airbus passenger aircraft and 3 all-cargo aircraft. The aircraft are of three main types, i.e., the A330, A350 and A320. There is not much technical difference between A330 and A350 other than slight variations in the system operation and their scale. See Table 2.

Type	**A350**	**A330**	**A320**
Passenger capacity when configured all-economy	440	440	180
Passenger capacity when configured three-class	300-350	260-300	N/A
Range (approx. miles)	8,450	7,100	4,100
Max take-off weight (Kgs)	275,000	242,000	89,000

Table 2: *Type of aircraft operated by Domestic Airline X*

The A350 and A330 are practically the same aircraft, therefore pilots are trained and certified for both but, as can be seen from Table 2, the A320 is significantly smaller, functions differently and is mainly used for domestic flights. Because of these differences, and to avoid any confusion which might undermine overall safety, pilots usually fly either the A330/350 or the A320 but not both types.

The Airline operates more than 300 routes covering Asia, Europe, Oceania, North America, and Africa, transporting nearly 30m passengers annually. Up to 2022, it has achieved 36 years of continuous safe flying and was awarded the "Five Star Flight Safety Award" in 2021 by CAAC.

Consistent with a leasing contract with Airbus, the Airline continued introducing new aircraft during 2019 and 2020 but, in response to the downturn in flights as a result of the pandemic, some aircraft have been returned to the leasing company. Since 2020, a new airport in the city in which the Airline is based has opened and the Airline's office buildings, hangars and staff accommodation were built adjacent to it.

The total number of employees as at March 2022 was 18,700 and the number of aircraft was 181, giving a ratio of employees to aircraft of 103.3:1. The ratio of employees and managers is 10:1. There have been no reductions in employee numbers in the period since January 2020 that could be directly attributed to the pandemic. This is due to the industry being state-owned and it benefits from Government protection. Airlines in China were not allowed to lay off, fire or furlough workers as a direct result of the pandemic. The number and breakdown of employees is as shown in Table 3.

Type	Pilot	Maintenance	Aviation Materials	Cabin Crew
Employee to Aircraft ratio	16	14	2.5	33

Type	Marketing	Information	Service C	Service A/B
Employee to Aircraft ratio	3.5	6.5	20.5	4

Table 3: *Domestic Airline X categories of staff as % of total staff as at March 2022*

Service Post-Level A includes Luggage Clerk and Special Vehicle Operation Driver. Service Post-Level B includes Passenger Transportation Clerk. Service Post-Level C includes Administrative Assistant and Station Representative.

With regards to the pilots, there were 2,896 as at March 2022 (16 pilots per aircraft and 181 aircraft), of whom 301 fly the A330/350 aircraft and it is these pilots who have been most affected during the pandemic because they fly internationally.

The impact of the pandemic on Domestic Airline X

In 2020, the outbreak of the Covid-19 caused a serious impact on the civil aviation industry, which experienced the most severe market "winter" since the SARS (severe acute respiratory syndrome) epidemic which began in November 2002. In 2020, losses in the civil aviation industry in China reached RMB 97.432bn, of which RMB 79.446bn is attributable to airlines and, within this total, Domestic Airline X losses in 2020 were RMB 3.6bn. See Table 4.

	2019	2020	2021
	RMB million	RMB million	RMB million
Asset	35,820	41,189	N/A
Turnover	250	150	180
Net Profit	127.5	-3,600	-2,800

Table 4: *Financial performance of Domestic Airline X 2019-2021*

The sporadic distribution of Covid-19 across and within domestic regions in 2021 inhibited the overall recovery of the civil aviation market. The industry remains in a loss-making state as of March 2022. In the fourth quarter of 2021, due to the repeated impact of the pandemic, Domestic Airline X's average daily flight volume has dropped from more than 700 to a low of about 200 and its average daily revenue has dropped from more than RMB 80m to a low of less than RMB 10m, resulting in a cumulative loss of more than RMB 2.8 billion. See Tables 4 and 5.

Items	2019	2020	2021
Number of flights – million	22.1	17.2	18.9
Number of passengers – million	30.64	20.40	22.46
Total flight hours - million hours	54.2	40.7	44.0
Number of international routes	58	4	4 i.e., scheduled passenger flight routes, excluding charter flights, such as passenger-to-freighter
Employee Earnings		Around 30% reduction compared to the same period in 2019 but, in return, there was a guarantee of job security and loss of permanent employees driven by the need to cut costs.	
Increased costs related to epidemic prevention and control[1] RMBm	Not available	40	40+
1 Increased costs related to those associated with epidemic prevention and control e.g., quarantine medical observation, epidemic prevention materials, nucleic acid testing, flight maintenance costs for wide-body aircraft grounded for long periods due to sudden flight reductions etc.			

Table 5: *Domestic Airline X operational and financial information 2019-2021*

Given the unprecedented challenges in operating throughout the pandemic, a need to ensure staff remained as motivated as possible, and not least the pilots, was essential.

Motivation

Motivation can be defined as 'the processes that account for an individual's intensity, direction, and persistence of effort toward attaining a goal' (Robins & Judge, 2017, p236).

There are numerous theories of motivation, two of which are the two-factor theory and equity theory.

Two-factor Theory

Herzberg's (1959) two-factor theory, also known as motivation-hygiene theory, differentiates between factors that make people dissatisfied in their job (hygiene factors) and factors that truly motivate employees (motivators). Hygiene factors are needed to make sure that an employee is not dissatisfied but, in themselves, are not motivators. Motivation factors are needed to ensure employee satisfaction and higher performance levels. The mere presence of hygiene factors does not guarantee motivation, but the presence of motivation factors in the absence of hygiene factors is similarly problematic. See Figure 2.

Figure 2: *Herzberg's Hygiene and Motivating Factors. https://theintactone.com/2019/08/26/ob-u3-topic-3-herzbergs-motivation-hygiene-theory/*

Herzberg's theory is very well-known in the literature but has been subjected to criticisms (see Robins & Judge, 2017) e.g. the methodology was limited because it relied on self-reports (e.g. when things are going well, individuals may wish to take the credit but when not going well they may blame the extrinsic environment), no overall measure of satisfaction was utilised (a person may dislike part of a job but still think the job is acceptable overall) and Herzberg assumed there was a relationship between satisfaction and productivity but actually only considered satisfaction.

Equity theory

'Employees perceive what they get from a job situation (salary levels, raises, recognition) in relation to what they put into it (effort, experience, education, competence), and then they compare their outcome-input ratio with that of relevant others' (Robins & Judge, 2017, p254). If an individual perceives the ratio to be equal to that of relevant others, then a state of equity exists i.e., it is perceived to be fair and just. If, however, the ratio is seen as being unequal, then the individual will feel under-rewarded, leading to a sense of anger. Conversely, an individual may feel over-rewarded, leading to a sense of guilt. The way a person perceives the ratio will influence their response e.g., they may change inputs (exert less effort if underpaid or more effort if overpaid), change outcomes (individuals paid on a piece-rate basis may increase their pay by producing a higher quantity of units of lower quality) or change jobs (see Robins & Judge, 2017).

Equity theory has been questioned in a number of respects. For example, 'inequities created by overpayment do not seem to significantly affect behaviour in most work situations. Apparently, people have more tolerance of overpayment inequities than of underpayment inequities or are better able to rationalise them. It's pretty damaging to a theory when half the equation falls apart' (Robins & Judge, 2017, p256). Similarly, much research on equity theory focuses on pay but equity or inequity may be demonstrated in other ways e.g., job titles and 'status symbols' such as quality and size of offices. Despite these criticisms, it seems reasonable to assume that most employees will have some sense of what is fair or equitable and that such perceptions may have wider implications, including potential impact on morale and motivation.

Domestic Airline X and motivation

From a human resource management perspective, the pilot is the core human resource in airlines and, by virtue of their job, are always expected to display a high level of performance. They are the commanders of each aircraft and are responsible for everything during the flight. Hence, how to motivate them to ensure they remain professional and productive are significant issues for airline managers, and even more so given the experiences of the pandemic, and particularly in the case of those pilots who fly internationally.

From the beginning of 2020, the morale of the whole pilot group, generally and in Domestic Airline X, has been at the lowest level known in the experience of the author and all the pilots who co-operated in this research. Quarantine requirements, involving having to stay in a hotel when returning to China, have been combined with anxieties about employment security. According to the data collection from the Airline's Flight Department, the average of quarantine days per pilot in 2020 was 116. One of the possible negative influences of spending such a total amount of time in quarantine, beyond obvious issues around mental and physical health, is that it could potentially lower pilots' flying skills' proficiency, in turn increasing the risk of unsafe incidents, which, of course, is the last thing wanted by airlines, the overriding priority of which is safety. Before the pandemic, the average hours that a pilot would fly were approximately 900 hours a year. However, during the pandemic period, the average number hours that an A330/350 pilot would fly was around 500.

The negative influence of low morale on pilots could also be seen in schedule planning. The increase of international cargo flights necessarily requires more pilots for these types of flights but, at the same time, a large number of pilots had to undergo quarantine in hotels, leading to a significant pilot shortage and severe difficulties in covering shifts. In addition, some pilots have asked for a long-term leave as they have struggled to cope with having to spend a long time away from home. Operationally, this was the most significant difference between the pilots on A330/350 and the pilots on A320 i.e., pilots on A320 did not particularly suffer the pain of extensive quarantine - 21 days when returning from international flights and could be up to one month in a hotel - as 99% of their flights are domestic.

The structure of the pilots' income consists of three elements: a basic salary; an hourly fee; additional bonuses. This structure means the more hours a pilot flies, the more income will be earned. Since the outbreak of Covid-19, and on the basis of extensive consultation with pilots by the author, the pilots on A330/350 fleet have, on average, lost almost one-third, 30%, of the income they would normally receive. This reduction is largely the result of the extensive quarantine being undertaken, often between two weeks and a month in a hotel, on average 116 days in total in a year based on 2020 data. Such quarantine of course meant they were grounded and unable to fly. See Table 6 for a summary of the data relating specifically to the pilots flying A330/350.

Operational/Financial Item	**Quantity**
Average number of flying hours per year pre-pandemic	900
Average number of flying hours per month pre-pandemic	75
During the pandemic:	
Average number of flying hours per pilot per year	500
Average number of flying hours per pilot per month	41.5
Average number of quarantine days per pilot per year	116
Average loss of income per pilot per year	30%
Average loss of income reflected in:	
Salary	Unaffected
Hourly fee income	Affected - fewer flying hours (average 400)
Bonus – based on flying hours	Affected

Table 6: *A330/A350 pilot flying hours and remuneration structure*

Based on the significant decrease in the pilots' income and the dissatisfaction with the extensive quarantine, Domestic Airline X used measures that reflected hygiene factors within the two-factors theory i.e., the Airline sought, first of all, to make sure that employees were not dissatisfied. Those who were unable to fly as a result of having to quarantine were compensated such that a benchmark of 65 hours was introduced in July 2020 i.e., if any pilot flew fewer than 65 hours, their hourly fee income and bonus would be based on 65 hours and if any pilot flew more than 65 hours, their hourly fee income and bonus would be based on actual hours flown. The 65 hours was agreed between the Finance Department and the Flight Department and represents approximately 87% of the pre-pandemic monthly flying hours (75, see Table 5). This policy reflected assumptions of equity theory, i.e., the pilots, it was assumed, would regard the input-output ratio as being fair and just.

Consistent with the two-factor theory and the removal of dissatisfiers (i.e., addressing hygiene factors), countermeasures have also included offering pilots who fly internationally a fixed income set at the average of the pilot who flies only domestically. In terms of motivating factors, viz. recognition, the company created a video montage of the pilots during these trying times to show gratitude and demonstrate recognition of their achievements, sacrifices and responsibilities. This is an example of the motivation factor of the two-factor theory. However, these countermeasures appear to have been ineffective in general.

The 65 flight hours threshold compensation policy is insufficient to compensate for the loss of income during the pandemic but, importantly, seems to have been regarded as inequitable by the pilots of the A330/350 aircraft when compared to the known income of the pilots on A320. The end result is that the total remuneration of the pilots of the A330/350 is not just below the amount earned pre-pandemic but is far less than a pilot of the A320. Additionally, it is not regarded by the pilots as sufficient acknowledgement of or compensation for the loss of private and family time resulting from the quarantine requirements to which A330/350 pilots are particularly subjected. Humans, of course, are naturally social creatures and this increased isolation in general can adversely affect mental health, potentially causing serious issues and which may remain undiscovered, a particularly dangerous eventuality in respect of pilots. Separation from family can lead to other issues including tension in relationships and in some cases even divorce.

Apart from the ineffective remuneration compensation policy, the video montage countermeasure has also proved ineffective. In the beginning, by placing such videos on social media, it may have had some positive impact on the pilots in that their efforts were being recognised. However, as the pandemic has continued for a long period, with no real end in sight in terms of restrictions in China as at March 2022, this kind of method is hardly likely to have a significant beneficial impact on the pilots. In fact, even though well-intentioned, it could prove counter-productive and be seen as an empty and inexpensive gesture and one which does not remotely address the underlying issues.

In summary, pilots of A330/350 received much lower remuneration during the pandemic than was the case pre-pandemic and had less time with their families whilst having to undergo quarantine and, for both reasons, felt they were unfairly treated relative to pilots of the A320. The measures intended to address hygiene factors and put in place motivators were not regarded as sufficient. Pilots continued to feel aggrieved, and morale was very low. This situation can be related to equity theory as the A330/350 pilots felt their treatment was unfair and, relative to A320 pilots, inequitable.

According to the two-factor theory, an effective motivation measure should always include both valid hygiene factors and motivators. Hygiene factors and motivators go hand in hand. Overall, having a dissatisfied and demotivated team of pilots could be a clear and present risk to any airline. Domestic Airline X prioritises safety but perhaps has failed to appreciate the levels of dissatisfaction and demotivation amongst one group of its pilots. In the meantime, there is an ongoing risk to the company in terms of potential pilot resignations. Foreign pilots, in particular, are not predisposed to endure the extensive quarantine and may easily find a better offer overseas since the international aviation market is recovering quite quickly as at March 2022. There is significant demand for experienced pilots in the overseas market since, internationally, many senior captains were forced to retire at the beginning of the pandemic in order to reduce airlines' costs. In the case of Domestic Airline X, as at March 2022, there were 2896 pilots, of which 2826 were Chinese and 70 were foreign. However, the number of 70 foreign pilots is a reduction of 10 in the 12 months up to March 2022 as they left the company as a direct result of the extensive quarantine requirements and the opportunities elsewhere.

According to CAE (previously Canadian Aviation Electronics) (n.d.), the demand for active pilots decreased significantly during 2020. Airlines and operators initially took short-term measures to offset the impacts of the Covid-19 pandemic, and this resulted in a decrease in the number of active pilots in 2020. This decrease was not just about numbers but also experience and seniority. However, this contraction is temporary as active fleets began to return to service through 2021 and this continued in the first three months of 2022. Analysis indicates that the active pilot population will return to 2019 levels in 2022. Despite this, a significant number of age-based retirements and attrition will continue to reduce the available pilot pool. This is projected to result in a global requirement of 260,000 new pilots over the next decade, including 27,000 at the end of 2021 and beginning of 2022 (CAE, n.d.). See Figure 3.

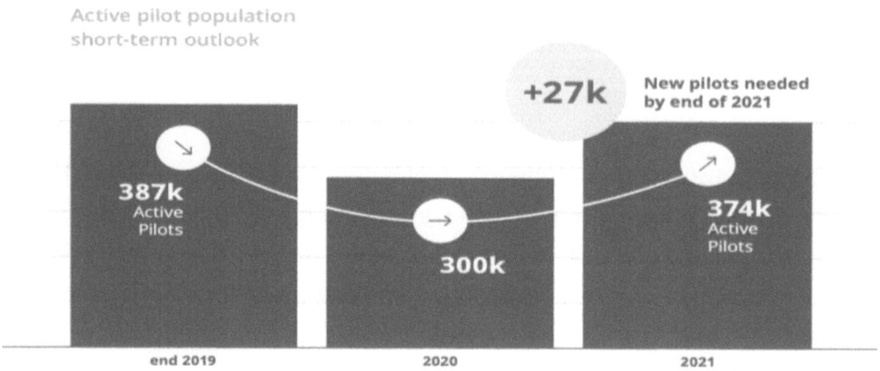

Figure 3: *Active pilot global short-term outlook*

Conclusion

Motivation is the state of mind which pushes all human beings to perform things with the highest spirit and with positivity. Any organisational leader should ensure that every individual in the team and the organisation is motivated. Various motivation theories help in understanding what will motivate people, including a belief in the trustworthiness of the leadership. Robbins & Judge (2017) noted that the three key characteristics which lead us to believe a leader is trustworthy are: integrity; benevolence; ability. As for benevolence, caring and supportive behaviour is part of the emotional bond between leaders and followers, with leaders demonstrating a sincere interest in employee welfare. A failure to do so, a failure to remove dissatisfiers and enhance motivators and a failure to ensure equity can all cause problems in an organisation.

In the case of Domestic Airline X, it should give much more serious consideration to the income differential between A330/350 pilots and A320 and discuss means by which it should be reduced to a minimum. This will help restore a sense of equity. The Airline should also demonstrate it has done everything possible to reduce the number of days of quarantine in a hotel. This will necessitate negotiations with the local governments or Health Commission, taking into account that policies may vary with each city. Although the CAAC has issued the quarantine policy for commercial pilots in airlines since the beginning of the pandemic, each local Government or Health Commission must of course also comply with the local quarantine policy in order to minimise any Covid-19 transmission risk.

Regarding the lessons learned for the post-pandemic environment, it is even more important for airlines to adopt a remuneration structure that is fair to everyone. It is essential to establish a scientific and effective motivation mechanism to encourage employees' recruitment, retention, and motivation. A strong and healthy remuneration system may not depend on or wait for government policies to create a solid airline business.

References

Bouwer, J., Saxon, S. & Wittkamp, N. (2021). 'Back to the future? Airline sector poised for change post-Covid-19' 2 April https://www.mckinsey.com/industries/travel-logistics-and-infrastructure/our-insights/back-to-the-future-airline-sector-poised-for-change-post-covid-19

CAE. (n.d.). *Pilot Outlook Demand - Summary | CAE*. https://www.cae.com/cae-pilot-demand-outlook-2020/

CEIC (2022). 'China Air: Passenger Traffic' https://www.ceicdata.com/en/china/air-industry-overview

Herzberg, F. (1959). *The motivation to work* New York: Wiley

International Air Transport Association (IATA) (2021). 'Air Cargo Market Analysis: air cargo ends a dynamic year on a strong note' December https://www.iata.org/en/iata-repository/publications/economic-reports/air-freight-monthly-analysis---december-2021/

Reuters (2022a). 'China's aviation sector aims for profitability this year – regulator' 10 January https://www.reuters.com/world/china/chinas-aviation-sector-aims-profitability-this-year-regulator-2022-01-10/

Reuters (2022b). 'China targets 2023-2025 for recovery in international air travel' https://www.reuters.com/world/china/china-targets-over-270-civil-airports-by-2025-aviation-regulator-2022-01-07/

Robbins, S. P. & Judge, T. A. (2017). *Organizational Behavior* 15th Edition Beijing: Pearson Education Asia Ltd. & Tsinghua University Press

Statista (2022). 'Number of scheduled passengers boarded by the global airline industry from 2004-2022' https://www.statista.com/statistics/564717/airline-industry-passenger-traffic-globally/

Suk, M. & Kim, W. (2021). 'Covid-19 and the airline industry: crisis management and resilience' *Tourism Review* 76, 4, 984-998

Discussion questions

1. On the assumption that the pilots of A330/A350 aircraft feel very demotivated, and perhaps even more demotivated as a result of the measures intended to improve motivation, what might Domestic Airline X have done differently? In considering this question, take into account the unknown duration of the pandemic and associated quarantine requirements.

2. In your own organisation, what are the main hygiene factors and motivators and to what extent were these influenced by the experience of the pandemic? What evidence do you have for your answer? Outline what your organisation has done or could do to address hygiene factors and enhance motivators.

3. In the case of your own organisation, does equity theory, which seeks to explain how people develop perceptions of fairness in the distribution and exchange of resources, have any relevance in understanding behaviours and levels of motivation?

4. Has the experience of the Covid-19 pandemic enabled any lessons to be learned in relation to perceived equity within your organisation? Give reasons for your answer.

From Surviving to Thriving: The Transformation of a Start-up's HR Strategy

Jiajun Fei

Co-founder & Chief Information Officer: Sequanta

Abstract

This case reviews the transformation of the Human Resources (HR) strategy of Sequanta, a biotech start-up based in Shanghai. Due to macro-challenges, the company went from a period of growth and development to a period of significant turmoil where business almost came to a standstill. Furthermore, the company was adversely impacted by two mandatory Covid-19 lockdowns. Within this context, the company not only managed to survive but retain nearly all its employees.

The case highlights the benefit of implementing continuous and incremental improvements to human resource management during a period of turbulent change. Inclusive and collaborative efforts, from founders to frontline managers, have been instrumental in developing positive outcomes discussed during the case.

Introducing Sequanta

Located in the Shanghai Free Trade Zone, Sequanta Technologies Co., Ltd (herein referred to by its English brand 'Sequanta') is a high-tech company engaged in genome sequencing and multi-omics research services (sequanta.com, 2022). The company has advanced genome sequencing laboratories and owns international certifications, including CLIA (Clinical Laboratory Improvement Amendments), CAP (Certified Authorisation Professional), ISO15189, and ISO27001. It is also one of the leading high throughput Next Generation Sequencing (NGS) labs in China which runs more than 30 Illumina sequencers (ibid). NGS refers to core technologies that serve to assist scientists to characterise cancers by obtaining full genetic information in a detailed manner (Reis-Filho, 2009). The company has established strategic partnerships with multiple international sequencer manufacturers and large drug development companies (sequanta.com, 2022). The revenue for 2021 exceeded 250 million RMB.

As of June 2022, Sequanta had 165 employees. The average employee age is 31 years old. The male-to-female ratio is about 4:5, and the team composition is very diverse. The overall education level of the company's employees is relatively high, with 80% of employees having a bachelor's degree or above and 35% having a master's degree or above. 70% of employees have educational backgrounds in related technologies such as biology, chemistry, medicine, and computer science. The company has a flat organisational structure, as the management team accounts for 25% of the total head count, most of whom are frontline managers. The key management team retention rate has achieved 95% for the past two years.

The HR department is a small team with only two full-time employees and one on-site third-party consultant. The highly effective team assumes responsibility for all HR functions, including recruitment, on-boarding and off-boarding, payroll management, performance evaluation, HR-related communications, people development and training, as well as support with Shanghai residence settlement and other miscellaneous activities.

Company history and the darkest hour

Sequanta was formed in late 2020 as a spin-off during a period of turbulence as documented below. Between 2015-2018, a reputable Contract Research Outsourcing (CRO) company, together with several reputable venture capitalists in China, raised several hundred million dollars to build a global entity 'Group' focusing on genomic information and data analysis. The Chinese subsidiary of this group was the predecessor of Sequanta. By 2018, the Group had 760 employees operating across the world. Within the 'Group', China was the largest subsidiary with 490 employees supported by only 20% of the Group's total investment.

Whereas the Covid-19 pandemic has resulted in public calls for increased cooperation between the United States and China for biosafety (Sachs, 2021), the pre-pandemic situation was quite different. Biotechnology was a point of tension during the US-China trade war. During Trump's presidency, disputes arose between the United States and China over the future of biomedical research, particularly with regards to security concerns and fears around the potential misuse of large volumes of bio data (Lynch, 2017). As a cutting-edge genome sequencing and precession diagnosis company in China, Group was directly impacted by the disputes, ultimately losing 70% of its revenue base as US clients terminated contracts on mass.

The management team at that time tried to adjust the direction to increase the business income in China. They recruited a sales team of hundreds of people and invested tens of millions of Chinese Renminbi (RMB) in anticipation of quickly establishing a clinical business line. The Covid-19 pandemic in 2020 has put everything on hold. After returning from the Covid-19 lockdown in March 2020, the board decided to spin off the China subsidiary and downsize the business. The company's size shrunk from 490 to 110 by May 2020, 380 employees were laid off.

It was the darkest hour for the company, with it almost going into liquidation at that moment.

The new entity, Sequanta, sought new investment and restructured itself to maintain operations. Leadership has focused on domestic business via two primary lines, high-throughput sequencing services, and multi-omics research services. In 2021, Sequanta achieved strong revenues, exceeding 250 million RMB. Through the recent period, it was realised that the success or failure of a strategy depended upon its people. The following sections overview the role of HR during this transformational change process.

Human resource management at Sequanta

As the business reinvented itself following the spin-off, significant energy was invested into transforming the organisation's management of human resources. The basis of coordination and control in start-ups frequently involves different starting assumptions from large established entities (Baron and Hannan, 2002). Born out of a large multinational company, the comparatively redundant, cumbersome, and complex human resource management system was no longer suitable for the actual needs of the new and smaller start-up entity. The existing HR system structure was cut out and the talent management system was transformed. The change may be illustrated via approach towards three challenges; the need to retain, attract and develop talents.

Challenge 1 – To retain talent:

As stated above that 380 employees – 77.5% of the labour force – were laid off during the spin-off process. No formal review process was necessary, the fact that employee morale subsequently hit rock bottom during the restructuring was tangible. As colleagues and friends were let go, many who were retained were known to be looking for alternative job opportunities. There was doubt about the new entity's future. Stabilising the organisation became a priority. Leadership realised that verbal promises would be insufficient; trust needed to be built through practical action.

Action 1 – Pay the year-end bonus.

Accounting for up to 40% of annual earnings nationally, year-end bonuses in China have long been considered one of the strongest motivators for employees in mainland China (Chiu, Luk, and Tang, 2002; Chiu, Tang, and Luk, 2001). Due to historical disputes, Sequanta's parent organisation had not paid out the year-end bonus since 2019. Employees' distrust towards management promises was perceived to be validated by past disappointment. To enthuse excitement towards a new vision, expectation and/or goal, felt like a hallucination. There was a crisis of confidence.

Even though the cash flow was very critical at the time, Sequanta did its best to pay year-end bonuses to all employees. Though pay-out was half a year later than scheduled, the positive action initiated a noticeable turn in perception and earned valuable trust towards the leadership. For all employees, this was a great encouragement and motivation. Everyone recognised the new management's desire to honour on its commitments. This statement of keeping the promise in the problematic situation also laid a solid foundation for the common cooperative struggle in the future.

Action 2 – Build a transparent and efficient organisational structure.

Top heavy administrative structures may reduce an organisation's ability to respond to a rapidly changing environment (Baron and Hannan, 2002). Contrastingly, flat structures have long been associated with higher satisfaction and improved self-actualisation within the labour force (Porter and Lawler, 1964).

Sequanta simplified its structure from 5 hierarchical tiers to 2: first-line managers managing the production team, and second-line managers managing large departments. Every 2 weeks, the CEO sets up a staff meeting with key management figures to review the progress of the operations. The change reduces administrative overheads whilst simultaneously improving transparent transformation throughout the organisation, both factors being crucial amid business transformation. This supported the ability to ensure that everyone understood and worked towards the same new strategic goals.

Action 3 – Establish an equity and option incentive plan.

Share options have received criticism as a long-term motivator as their ability to motivate beyond an organisations stock listing is countered by the fact that they have largely already served to offer their main financial output (Baron and Hannan, 2002). They also only serve purpose if there is belief in an organisation's ability to succeed (Ibid). Regardless, many start-ups have an option incentive plan.

Sequanta leadership viewed options as ethereal as air if the company was unable to demonstrate financial stability. Core management members and technicians were invited to become capital partners. Six months later, as the organisation stabilised, more employees were offered stock options in recognition of their contributions. Membership became something to work towards, keeping talent for the immediate period.

Challenge 2 – To recruit new talent:

The Sequanta team mainly consists of two talent categories: scientific researchers and laboratory operators. The recruitment scenarios for these two types of talent are different. Scientific researchers pay more attention to the company's business field, research direction, and personal development space. Career and study are often complementary to each other for scientific researchers. Compensation, work intensity, and commute distance are often more realistic considerations for laboratory operators. We had challenges in both recruiting scenarios.

Core Issue A: The talent war.

In recent years, the field of precision medicine has shown explosive development. New technologies and start-ups are emerging from diagnosis to treatment. Genome sequencing technology is no longer as promising for a new entrant as it was in 2017. Scientific researchers are more eager to go to newer gene technology-led companies and enter emerging technology fields such as gene therapy, gene editing, and cell therapy.

It is worth noting that the competition for talent not only in the field of scientific research but also in the field of laboratory operators is fierce. A sharp increase in the demand for nucleic acid testing for Covid-19, made PCR laboratory personnel very scarce. Those clinical testing companies hunted experienced lab operators in the industry at the cost of two or three times their salary. Competition over talent is frequently referred to as 'the talent war' (Sarraille, 2020).

Core Issue B: Internet has memory.

The high profile and influence of our company's predecessor in the industry made the layoffs a topical event at that time. The internet has a memory; negative stereotypes proved devastating for Sequanta's recruiting efforts. Over a period, Sequanta became aware of candidates rejecting offers with no reason, but it was not by accident.

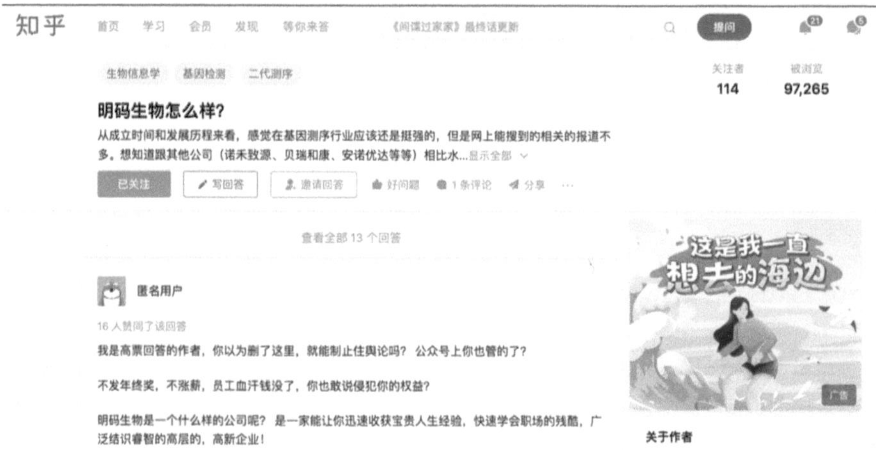

(Anon, 2019)

Figure 1: *A negative review about the company's predecessor on ZHIHU*

There is a Reddit-like Q&A platform on the Chinese internet called Zhihu, and the young generation widely uses it. On Zhihu, it's trendy to discuss the work situation of well-known companies. As exampled in Fig.1, several posts on Zhihu, with more than 100,000 views, gave our company negative feedback because of the predecessor's performance. The memory on the internet has brought great difficulties to our recruitment.

In response to the core issues encountered in recruiting, we have adjusted our HR strategy from a preference for experienced hires to campus hires. 60 new employees were recruited during 2021, 40% being campus hires. We also hire talent from other industries and develop their skill sets to meet our business needs. The following section is going to elaborate on the efforts on people development.

Challenge 3 – To develop talent:

People development is a long-term effort. Sequanta onboarded over 40 new starts who were either fresh from education or from other industries. Representing 25% of the labour force, there is a significant need for learning and development within the HR strategy.

Action 1 – Develop a common HR mindset

Supported by the small HR team, each manager assumed an HR partner role, needing to think and act like HR to ensure that team members get ongoing coaching, evaluation, and development in their day-to-day work. Managers assign a mentor for each new hire to give one-on-one coaching. The mentee's performance is considered a vital measurement of the mentor's year-end goal, and the mentors get rewarded because of their coaching efforts.

Sequanta's HR Director's primary responsibility is to partner with the business teams and help the relevant managers develop their people plan. Both HR and business managers are directly involved in the people development planning and implementation stages. Clear goals and accountability structures for people development for each management role have been established. Tier 1 and 2 managers are not only responsible for the business metrics but also accountable for their employees' development. Sequanta also set staged goals and incentives (cash, salary, promotion) for our employees to encourage their achievement in career development.

Action 2 – Offer opportunities and possibilities

A healthy organisation needs to create enough space to meet employee development needs, especially within a start-up environment (Baron and Hannon, 2002). Sequanta continuously creates opportunities to help our employees realise their potential. Internal applicants are prioritised for management vacancies. Our frontline employees can see their career development goals and set realistic expectations.

In addition to the usual promotions and salary increases, Sequanta encourages employees to try new job opportunities, even cross-skill transfers and received outstanding results through this attempt.

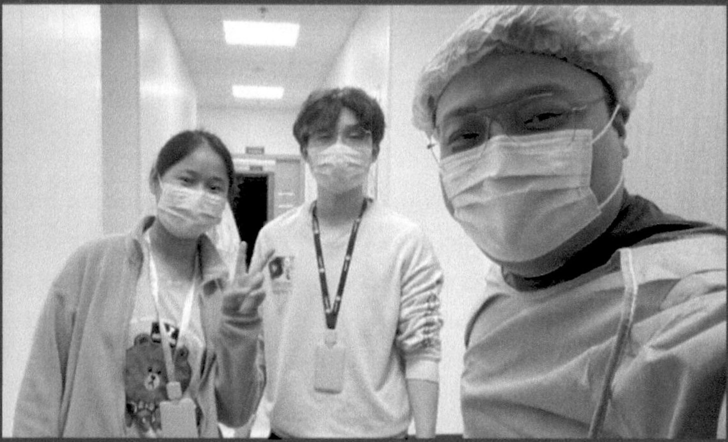

(Image: Fei (left) in Zhoupu lab during the 2022 Shanghai lockdown period)

Fei is Sequanta's production lead at the Zhoupu site, a laboratory that generates 60 million RMB revenue per year. Before being designated to this role, she was a tier 1 manager for a small team. When we opened this branch site, we looked for management candidates inside and outside the company. Fei asked if it was possible to transfer to work there because she lived closer to the branch site. We realised that Fei could be the perfect candidate to manage the site operations and move her to the new branch. It has since turned out to be a sagacious decision. Fei helped to start up the new unit and put it into production ahead of our planned deadline. During the lockdown period in 2022, wherein Shanghai residents were not permitted to leave their place of residence for over 2 months, Fei stayed on the site for 69 days to continue the operation of the Zhoupu laboratory and serve our research partners on their sequencing needs.

Figure 2: *Example of internal promotion and relocation*

> Junjie and Chuang are our sales professionals in research services and pharma business units. Before they took the roles in the field, they were both technologists in the research and development department. Junjie was in charge of the equipment maintenance, and Chuang was the bioinformatics programmer. Their technical backgrounds help them feel confident when engaging the customers.

Figure 3: *Example of role change*

Action 3 – Promote participatory activities

In October 2021, a new initiative entitled 'SEQUANTA AIR' was proposed bottom up from Jun Zhou, Marketing Manager. Leadership supported and invested in the idea which involves weekly broadcasting product and technology training with key business partners. Employees at all levels are encouraged to participate in the live streaming and espouse their knowledge to the audience. SEQUANTA AIR not only provides a mechanism for internal knowledge sharing and empowering of employees by elevating them on a public platform, it has also accumulated over 5,000 subscribers and becomes a primary online go-to-market channel within 9 months of its launch.

Figure 4: *Live on Sequanta Air*

Founding SEQUANTA AIR required leadership to listen to the thoughts and ideas of its employees. A dedicated space, with investment in lighting and recording equipment was also necessary to support the initiative. The initiative exemplifies a non-financial means to communicate value with employees and invest in their personal development. Jun Zhou has continued to demonstrate ability and character, and has subsequently been promoted to Assistant Marketing Director.

Conclusion - The Future is Calling

Throughout Sequanta's HR strategy change, a core factor has been the change in leadership attitude towards employees. Empowering employees and making managers HR partners has fostered an increasing and genuine care across the company. A key learning for the Sequanta leadership may be encapsulated within the Chinese word 真诚, which may be translated as a combination of 'true', 'real' or 'genuine' (真) and 'honest' (诚). Combined, the phrase requires not only being considerate in mind but by pro-actively communicating with integrity, even when it is difficult and inconvenient.

Though this case has emphasised a particular set of actions, attention and effort towards genuine and honest communication needs to be demonstrated across initiatives, great and small. During the Shanghai lockdowns of spring 2022, all employees received full salary, regardless of their ability to work or not. Gift packages with food were also distributed to all employees and their families. Such actions became synonymous with positive leadership in Shanghai during the period.

The reader may note previous reference to Fei, a committed employer who resided in the Zhoupu lab during the lockdown period. In total, 22 employees committed their time to working in the labs throughout the lockdown period. Each employee received an additional financial bonus for every day worked during the lockdown.

Good communication also works two ways. As stated in the company introduction above, Sequanta has a male-to-female ratio of about 4:5, with an average age of 31. At Sequanta, family values and relationships are encouraged. Discussion is welcomed around family planning with the mutual understanding that open communication allows Sequanta to offer support to its female labour force via a combination of shift rotations, workload reduction and/or a generous maternity package. All new mothers have the option of return to their original post on completion of their maternity leave.

The strategic transformation of human resource management is a critical process for achieving business transformation and long-term goals. The core of an enterprise is people. It is difficult for a business to survive without talent and motivation. From the changes in the company's human resource management strategy, it is hoped that this case illustrates the positive driving force of talent development and demonstrates significant benefit for organisations who focus on their employees.

References

Anon., (2019). *明码生物怎么样？* [Online]. Available: https://www.zhihu.com/question/67600571 [Accessed June 2022].

Baron, J. N., & Hannan, M. T. (2002). Organizational blueprints for success in high-tech start-ups: Lessons from the Stanford project on emerging companies. *California Management Review, 44* (3), 8-36.

Chiu, R. K., Luk, V. W. M., & Tang, T. L. P. (2002). Retaining and motivating employees: Compensation preferences in Hong Kong and China. *Personnel review.*

Chiu, R. K., Tang, T. L. P., & Luk, V. W. M. (2001). Hong Kong and China: The cash mentality revisited. *Compensation & Benefits Review, 33* (3), 66-72.

Lynch, D., (2017) *Biotechnology: The US-China dispute over genetic data.* Financial Times. 31st July, 2017. Available from: https://www.ft.com/content/245a7c60-6880-11e7-9a66-93fb352ba1fe. [Accessed 5th July, 2022].

Porter, L. W., & Lawler, E. E. (1964). The effects of "tall" versus "flat" organization structures on managerial job satisfaction. *Personnel Psychology, 17* (2), 135–148. https://doi.org/10.1111/j.1744-6570.1964.tb00057.x

Reis-Filho, J. S., (2009). Next-generation sequencing. *Breast cancer research, 11*(3), 1-7.

Sachs, J. D., (2021). The Origins of Covid-19 and the Urgent Case for US-Sino Cooperation. *Horizons: Journal of International Relations and Sustainable Development*, (19), 122-131.

Sarraille, M., (2020). *The Talent War: How Special Operations and Great Organizations Win on Talent*, Lioncrest Publishing.

Sequanta.com., (2022) *Sequanta.* Available from: https://www.sequanta.com/ [Accessed 6th July 2022].

Discussion questions

1. Several practical actions were taken during the 18 turbulent months following Sequanta's formation. On reflection, which of the actions do you think may have been most troubling for Sequanta's leadership to take? Why may such decisions be difficult? What are the risks for leadership if they make the wrong decision?

2. Two thirds of new appointments made during 2021 were either campus hires or recruits from other industries. Recognising the context being one of transformational change, debate the pros and cons of this decision.

3. Sequanta highlights the positive benefits that can result from managers assuming an HR partner type role. Reflecting on your own workplace, what does your organisation do? What opportunities and/or challenges may result from a shift towards expecting managers to assume this extra responsibility?

How Learning Historical Milestones of Parent Companies may Improve Understanding of a Joint Venture Company: The Case of CRRC and Alstom in China

Tao Tao
Door Production & Process Manager: Jiangsu BIDE Science Shares Co., Ltd

Abstract

CRRC and Alstom are two of the largest rail transit equipment companies in the world. The products of the two companies are very similar, ranging from high-speed trains, metros, monorail, and trams to integrated systems, customised services, infrastructure, signalling equipment, and digital mobility solutions. With CRRC from China and Alstom from France, the author sought to explore differences in the entrepreneurial paths of the two companies by researching into their respective backgrounds. The result however identified the organisations to share a lot of similarities, as the formation of the two companies, major innovation breakthroughs, and today's shareholding structures were each triggered by very similar events.

Introduction and company backgrounds

High-speed rail (HSR) has developed rapidly in mainland China. In January 2020, the length of China's HSR network accounted for 60% of global HSR, with plans in place to expand this by a further 80% - equating to 32,000 kilometres - by 2035 (Zhang *et al*, 2021; Chen *et al*, 2021). This is a considerable feat for a country only launching its first HSR service in 2008. With a network spanning all major cities nationwide, HSR has become the preferred choice for medium-distance travel across the country (He, Wu, and Du, 2021). France similarly has an established HSR network and is well known for carrying significantly more passengers than any other European country by HSR (Crozet, 2013). For both countries, HSR rollingstock have become a symbol of national manufacturing capability. China Railway Rollingstock Cooperation (herein referred to as CRRC) is particularly renowned for manufacturing the G-Series High-Speed Train for China, and Alstom that makes the TGV for France.

CRRC is the largest rollingstock manufacturing company in the world. A Chinese State-Owned Enterprise, meaning that a controlling equity stake of the company is owned by the government, CRRC operates via 46 wholly owned and majority owned subsidiaries (CRRC, 2022). Alstom is a large French rollingstock manufacturer who has joint venture agreements with CRRC to operate in the mainland China market. A brief overview of each company is provided in Figure 1.

Company	**Headquarters**	**Ticker**	**Employees**	**2020 Revenue**
Alstom	Beijing, China	SSE: 601766	180,000	$35.69 billion*[2]
CRRC	Saint-Ouen, France	XPAR: ALO	70,000	$9.70 billion*[3]

Figure 1: *Company profiles*
(Information sourced from CRRC 2021, 2022; Alstom, 2022)

Bamford, Ernst and Fubini (2004) highlight that critical success factors behind joint ventures are rooted back in the parent companies, particularly the strategic priorities, governance mechanisms and economic resources that shape and define an organisation's culture and way of doing things. This report therefore seeks to explore the key historical milestones behind Alstom and CRRC to better understand the existence of similarities and differences in their development that may impact the current day stories and culture in their joint venture entities in mainland China. To better understand the cultural dynamics and attitudes towards strategy from each

[2] Converted into USD for ease of comparison. Converted from 227.66 billion yuan according to exchange CNY to USD exchange rate on 18th March 2022.
[3] Converted into USD for ease of comparison. Converted from 8.8 billion Euros according to exchange EUR to USD exchange rate on 18th March 2022.

respective parent group, the report focuses on three key points: the key figures behind each company's growth opportunity; macro factors presenting opportunity for growth; and attitude towards innovation. Similarities and differences will be tracked accordingly.

Key figures behind the opportunities that built CRRC and Alstom

In 2008, China's first high-speed railway line between Beijing and Tianjin opened. A short distance of 117 km, the line opened at a time when China was attracting increased levels of global attention due to the hosting of the Olympics (2008) and the run up to the Shanghai Expo (2010). Two subsidiaries of CRRC at the time, Qingdao Sifang Locomotive and Tangshan Rail Passenger Car provided the trains for this pioneering line. With the journey speed reaching 350 km/h, cutting the journey time from 2 hours to around 30 minutes, the new line marked the beginning of China's HSR era. The person who started this change was Liu Zhijun, then Minister of Railways (Lawrence, Bullock, and Liu, 2019).

Liu Zhijun was born in 1953 to a peasant family in northern China. Due to the reasons of the times, Mr. Liu only had a junior high school education when he started his work, and he went to graduate school after work. He once served as director of a city railway bureau and worked his way through government roles to become Minister of Railways in 2003. The father of his second wife was a senior general in the army, so his career development will undoubtedly have been favoured due to communist China's favour towards those with esteemed military connections. Mr. Liu may be characterised by his desire for power and initiative.

For people growing up in mainland China, the change in rollingstock quality and standards are easily noticeable. Before HSR, the interior of Chinese trains was known for being dirty and messy, trains had a typical speed limit of 120 km/h, and the methods for buying train tickets was highly cumbersome which – when combined with limited capacity - resulted in large numbers of passengers being unable to travel during peak demand periods such as China's infamous Chinese New Year festival.

However, Liu Zhijun identified these challenges as an opportunity for improvement and saw HSR as part of the solution.

China's economic model features what is known as a 'socialist market economy', meaning that strategic priorities are directly supported by the central government. Privatisation is not essential, but competition is. Through provision of significant funding and partnership opportunity for organisations working towards the identified agenda of the Government, China's planned economy model provides significant growth opportunity for companies that position themselves to align with set direction (McMillan and Naughton, 1992). Railway and infrastructure secured an important position in China's development strategy, enabling Mr. Liu to negotiate with foreign vehicle manufacturers with the aim of advancing the domestic rail system. Through negotiations, CRRC purchased the intellectual property and patents of Kawasaki, Siemens, Alstom, and Bombardier, ultimately contributing towards the launch of China's first high-speed rail line in 2008 (Genin, Tan and Song, 2021). From Mr. Liu's tenure as the Minister of Railways to the opening of the first high-speed railway for 5 years, CRRC – although technically not known as CRRC until a merger in 2015 - took advantage of the opportunity of product innovation to become a manufacturer of high-speed trains and began a rapid development road. Technological transfer in China's HSR has noticeably been politicised from its beginning (Chen and Haynes, 2016).

The development of HSR in France was comparatively early, with the first HSR service launching between Paris and Lyons in 1981 (Crozet, 2014). The first train was provided by Alstom. At that time, the speed of the train reached 300KM/h. Although France's system is comparatively centralised, the HSR train changed the way of travel in France and stimulated the economic development of various regions of France, with the TGV becoming a symbol of modern France. Like CRRC, the man instrumental to France's high-speed rail development, Pierre Sudreau, President of the Federation of Railway Industries, held a significant position of power connecting both industry and government (Dunn and Perl, 1994; Urena, Menerault and Garmendia, 2009).

Pierre Sudreau was born in 1919 into a family of industrialists in Paris, France. He holds a BA from Lycée Carnot. He studied at the University of Paris, where he obtained a law degree, an advanced law degree, and a degree in history. He served in the Air Force and later did intelligence work in the occupied territories. He was arrested in 1943 and released in 1945. After that, he entered politics and served as provincial governor, minister of reconstruction, and minister of national education. He served as chairman of the Railway Industry Federation for 30 years (Buchenwal Memorial, 2012), so he was well aware of the importance of rail transport in a continental country with a large population.

Sudreau was determined to develop the railway network and stated in 1966: *"But we can do even better [than increasing top speed and improving comfort]. Avant-garde technicians are currently developing a formula for ultra-fast trains using the current improved infrastructure and capable of penetrating at high speed into the very heart of agglomerations"* (Pierre Sudreau, 1966). The Société Nationale des Chemins de fer Français (the state-owned rail system of France herein referred to as SNCF) then started the "C03 project" to explore railway possibilities on new infrastructure. This involved significant independent research and development, with the whole process lasting about 10 years. During the research and development process, Alstom was deeply involved in the work of SNCF as an important supplier. In 1976, Alstom won most of the 87 TGV train contracts. With the help of this huge contract, Alstom began to take off.

It can be seen that both CRRC and Alstom participated in innovation when the country launched the high-speed rail era, but neither was the initiator. The railway sector was influenced by a national agenda that provided opportunity and impetus for change. Without which, the design and manufacturing of high-speed rollingstock by either CRRC or Alstom may not have occurred. Interestingly, the key figures behind both CRRC and Alstom's success were politicians with military background who provided the necessary force, direction, and passion to drive change. As Barringer and Ireland (2019, p.37) state, '*Passion is particularly important for both for-profit and not-for-profit entrepreneurial organizations because although rewarding, the process of starting a firm or building either a profit-making corporation or a social enterprise is demanding.*' Neither simply came up with political slogan, but steered and led the innovation. With the expectation and support of the country, the two companies seized this opportunity. One may possibly conclude that the two companies are beneficiaries of a macro change beyond themselves.

Macro factors driving industry change – an opportunity presented

In November 1948, before the founding of the People's Republic of China, for the transportation needs of the war soldiers at that time, a general, Teng Daiyuan, left the army to form the Ministry of Railways and served as Minister. China railway rollingstock manufacturing at that time was a department under the Ministry of Railways called "Factory Affairs Bureau of the Ministry of Railways". The person who made this arrangement was Chairman Mao, the leader of the new country that was formed shortly after the war. This is a defining point in the history of CRRC.

The beginning of Alstom was from the merger of Thomson-Houston and Société Alsacienne de Constructions Mécaniques (SACM), in 1928 (France24.com, 2017). There does not seem to be a political influence here, but we need to note another event from the same period: By a legislative decree of 1937, five leading French railway companies merged and in 1938 officially became the "Société Nationale des Chemins de fer Français" – SNCF. SNCF was a mixed-economy public limited company in which the state-owned 51% of the capital and the remaining 49% belonged to the shareholders of the financial company. This company was created by the government of Camille Chautemps. As mentioned above, SNCF was instrumental in behind the initiation of high-speed railroad in France, ultimately choosing to cooperate with Alstom and provide the pivotal growth opportunity that defines the company we know today (Tikkanen, 2022).

The inference from above is that innovation in large railway companies may be linked with central power structures, and that a government's agenda towards infrastructure and rail specifically may be a key component behind entrepreneurial opportunity. In both countries, government leaders directly participated in the establishment of rail transit companies. The heads of the two governments noticed the importance of this mode of transportation to the country when the proportion of railway transportation was very small and were responsible for driving the development trend. As Barringer and Ireland (2019, p.74) state, *'The first approach to identifying opportunities is to observe trends and study how they create opportunities for entrepreneurs to pursue.'* Interestingly, entrepreneurialism may not be limited to the character of leaders internally, but may be driven largely by key drivers external to the company that gains. Although equally it is noted that the opportunities will have been presented to competitors as well as those who ultimately achieved victory.

As we continue to look at the CRRC and Alstom today, we continue to still see the influence of political forces on them

Exploring shareholding structures

In 2011, Liu Zhijun was removed from his post as Minister of Railways and arrested on suspicion of serious disciplinary violations. In 2013, a Chinese court issued its verdict, sentencing Liu Zhijun to a two-year suspended sentence, which was later changed to life imprisonment and the confiscation of all personal property (Zhu & Wu, 2015, Foo, Wu, and Chin, 2014). It was also during this period that CRRC began its reform path, from being a government department to two private entities – then known as CSR and CNR. These two groups ultimately merged to form CRRC, becoming one of China's State-Owned Enterprises at the heart of today's silk road movement.

Alstom's executive Frédéric Pierucci was arrested by the FBI at JFK International Airport in New York in April 2013 and was not released until September 2018. Alstom settled with the U.S. Department of Justice and paid hundreds of millions of dollars in fines, which ultimately resulted in Alstom's power business being bought by its main competitor, GE in the United States.

Bessant and Tidd (2015, p.154) state, *'In general, the greater the strategic importance, the stronger the administrative linkages between the corporation and venture.'* The outcomes of senior executives behind the growth of both

CRRC and Alstom hold an uncanny similarity. Presumably the inference towards corruption or criminality should not be drawn from Bessant and Tidd. However, it is clear that political forces are closely monitoring and involved in the major developments of large scale rollingstock manufacturers like CRRC and Alstom. This may not be a complete surprise though, given that a nation's railways are of strategic importance to the development of a country.

Innovation and future growth directions

CRRC's innovation is about business strategy. CRRC traded its huge order for the basic technology of the four companies, which is the first and perhaps the last time in the history of high-speed rail. Due to the strong desire of various companies to participate in the transaction, CRRC obtained all the technology of 4 major companies in the world at that time. After purchasing patents and technologies, CRRC also started the road of independent research and development and subsequently developed the CRH380 motor car. Alstom is also continuing to innovate, preparing to produce the Avelia Horizon. Fortunately, the equity changes of the two companies did not affect the company's entrepreneurial and innovative spirit.

Both companies have an internal innovation incentive mechanism, and CRRC distributes a percentage of the amount of profit or savings to those who propose innovations. Alstom sets the "I Love You Innovation Awards" in a similar way. They both understand: *While everyone is potentially creative, they may not choose to deploy their skills in the context of the organization unless they feel it is worthwhile doing so'* (Bessant and Tidd, 2015, p.401).

The competitive environment of CRRC and Alstom is interesting, as though the companies directly compete in many international markets, they equally partner in others. For example, Alstom and CRRC have several joint venture companies in mainland China developing products for the China market. Yet due to IP licensing agreements with terms that limit product manufacturing to certain geographical boundaries, products developed in mainland China are frequently unable to be sold in international markets. Whilst both companies strive for international opportunities, the by-product of political decisions in home companies impacts each company's success overseas.

Relying on the continuous innovation in purchasing technology and the huge market in China, CRRC accounts for over a third of the world's rollingstock manufacturing, firmly establishing it as the world's largest rail rollingstock manufacturer. To compete, Alstom successively completed acquisitions and mergers with Siemens and Bombardier to become the second-largest rail transit vehicle manufacturing company. Equally, whereas China's merging of its rollingstock manufacturers in 2015 was heralded as a national success, efforts of Western brands to merge has been plagued with political opposition, with strong voices fearing monopoly aggression. Regardless, both companies continue to cooperate and compete in many fields in the future, and they are both waiting for new opportunities to come.

Conclusion

Apart from the differences in time and country, CRRC and Alstom have deep similarities in the initial entrepreneurship, innovation of key technologies, and even major events that affect the current ownership structure - the drivers of these major changes are frequently identified as political forces outside the company.

Exploring CRRC and Alstom's high-speed rail manufacturers history is like holding a mirror to both China and France, seeing similarities in places where none may have been expected. One may be led to ponder if shared challenges – that could so easily have become tangling points dogging cooperation and trust – may actually support a shared focus towards eliminating certain negative behaviours in the current joint venture, noticeably with regards to adherence to legal frameworks. Might the shared highs and lows of parent companies contribute towards the fit and success of a joint venture?

These two high-speed rail companies reflect the entrepreneurial and innovative spirit of the two modern countries. For both entities, high-speed rail proved to be the breakthrough product that put each on the world stage. Both CRRC and Alstom are now in their prime and are making steady progress as they prepare for the next new railway era. They may have more opportunities to cooperate in the future.

References

Alstom., (2022) *Key Figures 2020-2021*. Available from: https://www.alstom.com/company/key-figures-202021 [Accessed 18th March 2022]

Bamford, J., Ernst, D., & Fubini, D., (2004) *Launching A World-Class Joint Venture*. Available from: https://hbr.org/2004/02/launching-a-world-class-joint-venture [Accessed 25th March 20220].

Barringer, B., & Ireland, R., (2019) *Entrepreneurship, SUCCESSFULLY LAUNCHING NEW VENTURES,* 6th Edition. Pearson Education Limited, United Kingdom.

Bessant, J., & Tidd, J., (2015) *Innovation and Entrepreneurship,* 3rd Edition. John Wiley & Sons Ltd, United Kingdom.

Buchenwald Memorial., (2012) *Pierre Sudreau 1919 (Paris) – 2012 (Paris).* Available from: https://www.buchenwald.de/en/1257/ [Accessed 18th March 2022]

Chen, Z., & Haynes, K., (2016) A short history of technology transfer and capture: High speed rail in China. Available from: http://dx.doi.org/10.2139/ssrn.2872527

Chen, Z.S., Liu, X.L., Chin, K.S., Pedrycz, W., Tsui, K.L. & Skibniewski, M.J., (2021). Online-review analysis based large-scale group decision-making for determining passenger demands and evaluating passenger satisfaction: Case study of high-speed rail system in China. *Information Fusion*. Vol 69, pp.22-39.

Crozet, Y., (2013) High-Speed Rail Performance in France: From Appraisal Methodologies to Ex-post Evaluation. Available from: https://www.oecd-ilibrary.org/docserver/5jz40rpjlpg0-en.pdf?expires=1647614425&id=id&accname=guest&checksum=B84A0106FCCEEE4DC2FA57E5D880505E [Accessed 18th March, 2022]

CRRC., (2021) *CRRC Annual Report 2020*. Available from: https://www.crrcgc.cc/Portals/73/Uploads/Files/2021/9-18/637675711244375026.pdf [Accessed 18th March 2022]

CRRC., (2022) *About Us*. Available from: https://www.crrcgc.cc/g5141.aspx [Accessed 18th March, 2022]

Dunn, J.A. & Perl, A., (1994) Policy networks and industrial revitalization: high speed rail initiatives in France and Germany. *Journal of Public Policy*, Vol 14 (3), pp.311-343.

Foo, C.T., Wu, W. and Chin, T., (2014) Lessons from China: Fighting Corruption in the Construction Sector. **In:** Governance for China: A multi-method research in corruption studies. *Chinese Management Studies*. pp.59-76.

France24.com., (2017) *Alstom: the key dates of a French industrial jewel.* Available from: https://www.france24.com/en/20170926-alstom-key-dates-french-industrial-jewel [Accessed 18th March 2022]

Genin, A.L., Tan, J. and Song, J., 2021. Relational assets or liabilities? Competition, collaboration, and firm intellectual property breakthrough in the Chinese high-speed train sector. *Journal of International Business Studies*, pp.1-29.

He, N., Wu, J., & Du, X., (2021) Highway Passenger Travel Demand Forecasting under the Development of High-Speed Railway. In *CICTP 2021* (pp. 2213-2220).

Lawrence, M., Bullock, R. & Liu, Z., (2019) *China's high-speed rail development*. World Bank Publications.

McMillan, J. and Naughton, B., 1992. How to reform a planned economy: lessons from China. *Oxford review of economic policy*, *8*(1), pp.130-143.

Sudreau, P. (1966) *"La révolution ferroviaire"*, Transports No. 117, January 1967, p. 19. This text is a declaration delivered before the General

Assembly of the International Association of Railway Rolling Stock Manufacturers (A.I.C.M.R.) in December 1966.

Tikkanen, A., (2022) *Société Nationale des Chemins de fer Français*. Available from: https://www.britannica.com/topic/Societe-Nationale-des-Chemins-de-Fer-Francais [Accessed 18th March 2022]

Ureña, J.M., Menerault, P. & Garmendia, M., (2009) The high-speed rail challenge for big intermediate cities: A national, regional, and local perspective. *Cities*, Vol 26 (5), pp.266-279.

Zhang, Y., Ma, W., Yang, H., & Wang, Q., (2021) Impact of high-speed rail on urban residents' consumption in China – from a spatial perspective, *Transport Policy*. Vol 106, pp.1-10.

Zhu, J. and Wu, Y., 2015. Lessons from China: fighting corruption in the construction sector. *Government Anti-Corruption Strategies: A Cross-Cultural Perspective. Taylor and Francis Group, Boca Raton, FL*, pp.59-76.

Discussion questions

1. CRRC and Alstom have several joint venture corporations in the mainland China market. Why might it be useful for senior managers in a joint venture to be familiar with key historical milestones and stories of the parent companies?

2. Reflect on your organisation's history. How have key milestones and the wider cultural context shaped the organisational culture of where you work today?

3. The case highlights instances where CRRC is unable to take domestically innovated products overseas due to dependence upon technological license gained through joint ventures in mainland China. What does this suggest about the need for a clear legal framework when launching a joint venture?

How Macro-Trends are Urging Change on Top Brands in the China Tyre Market

Jian Huang
Sales Director (China): A Global Top 5 Tyre Manufacturer

John Storm
Senior Lecturer: The University of Aberdeen, United Kingdom

Abstract

Tyre sales at ABC Limited have been negatively affected by declining sales of private vehicles, over-supply in the tyre market, increase in cheaper alternatives, and eroding brand value due to significant quality improvements of domestic competitors. Acknowledging changes to the competitive landscape, combined with growing calls for the tyre industry to explore closed loop supply chains as a mechanism for increasing recycling rates, ABC initiated a project to explore innovative practices that may improve sales performance in the China market.

Introduction

Anonymous Business Corporate Limited (herein referred to as ABC) is one of the leading brands in the global automotive tyre market, maintaining a long and established presence in mainland China. The global automotive tyre market in FY 2020 was calculated to be $116.73 billion dollars (Statista.com, 2021a), with 65.97% of sales revenue being collected by the four dominant brands: Bridgestone, Michelin, Continental, and Goodyear (Statista.com, 2021b). Building on strong international brands, reputation for quality, and volume via a traditionally strong distributor sales model during a period of significant market growth, these brands have managed to occupy an influential proportion of the China market without need for overtly innovating their sales approach. However, the tyre market started to experience a slowdown in 2017 (Bg.qianzzhan.com, 2019) and ABC experienced a noticeable drop in sales volumes. In the instance of one top brand, sales volume of high-end tyres dropped from 2 million to 1 million units, which when coupled with wider industry movement resulted in a drop in market share from 30% pre-2015 to around 10% in 2019 (Chinatiredealer.com, 2021). Recognising the increasingly competitive environment in the China tyre market, this report highlights macro-trends influencing the tyre market in China; provides a case study of an innovation that has introduced Consumer to Manufacturer sales to China's tyre market; and explores the opportunity for ABC to apply lessons from Direct Sales models in America to the China market.

Environmental factors contributing towards the business challenge

Market analysis highlights four core factors that influence tyre sales for the dominant brands. These four factors will be considered within this section in the following order (i) China vehicle market size by sales volume (ii) China tyre market size by production volume (iii) tyre prices in the China market and (iv) market trends relating to tyre replacement, quality, and performance.

i. **China vehicle market size by sales volume:** Annual vehicle sales in China grew from 6.5 million in 2006 to 27.2 million in 2016, a 318% increase (Carsalesbase.com, 2021). Between 2007 and the end of the first half (H1) of 2021, private car ownership increased from 35.3 million to 292 million (Gov.cn, 2008; CHYXX.com, 2021a). In contrast to earlier rapid growth, the 5-year period from 2016-2020 has evidenced a comparative stagnation in annual vehicle sales, with volumes reducing to 23.4 million vehicles in 2020 (Carsalesbase.com, 2021).

   The withdrawal of preferential tax policies will have had a negative impact, combined with wider reductions in macroeconomic growth, reduced consumer confidence levels, and the decision of consumers to retain ownership of current vehicles rather than purchase later models (CHYXX.com, 2021a). Given the natural relationship between vehicle and tyre sales, the slowdown in vehicle sales has had an understandable impact on tyre sale trends.

ii. **China tyre market size by production volume:** Tyre production in China grew from 285 million units in 2006 to 610 million units in 2016, a 114% increase (CHYXX.com, 2020). Acknowledging that production is not exclusive to domestic sales, production volumes have nonetheless exceeded the total volume of vehicle ownership in mainland China by over 120% (CHYXX.com, 2021a). Whereas vehicle sales have dropped since 2017, tyre production volume has continued to increase, thus exacerbating the situation. Assuming the average tyre to last a minimum of 4 years equating to a change of 1 tyre per annum – a favourable assumption to illustrate the significance of the challenge – the supply of tyres far exceeds demand.

Growth in tyre production volume between 2006-2016 was the result of investment from manufacturers to bring new production facilities online and expand capacity (CHYXX.com, 2020b). Prior to 2010, domestic demand outstripped supply, providing favourable conditions for established brands like ABC to enjoy rapid growth whilst charging a price premium. Upon increasing production capacity – predominantly driven by domestic competitors entering and/or expanding in the market – tyre supply has since exceeded demand. As illustrated in Figure 1, CHYXX.com, a leading industry consultancy in mainland China, reveals that tyre production capacity since 2013 has been tapered to between 60-70% of full capacity.

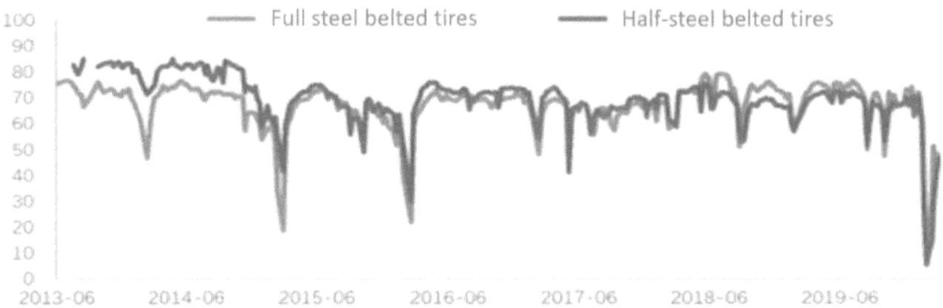

Figure 1: *Production Capacity of Tyre Manufacturers in China*
(Edited from CHYXX, 2020C)

The tapering of production capacity is clear demonstration that the wider sector realises issues with over-supply. However, the timeframe predates domestic downturn, indicating that factors are not purely due to domestic pressures. As Zhou (2021) observes, tensions between China and the US regarding tyre production and trade have been escalating since 2007, culminating in the introduction of tariff rates in July 2015 (Xiong, 2017).

iii. **Tyre prices in the China market:** Influenced by the aforementioned expansion in supply, average prices in the tyre market decreased by as much as 30% (CHYXX.com, 2018). As production capacity and sales volumes have predominantly been attributed towards new market entrants, ABC has found prices on their high-end products have been squeezed by the market with profit margins significantly affected. Relating to international challenges with dumping and tariffs, Urdinez and Masiero (2015) suggest that low tyre prices in mainland China further compound the issue due to China's classification by the World Trade Organisation as a Non-Market Economy. Ongoing international tensions combined with domestic over-supply indicate that tyre prices will remain subdued.

iv. **Market trends relating to tyre replacement, quality, and performance:** Independent agencies are increasingly observing that the quality and performance gap between domestic and international tyre producers is steadily closing (CHYXX.com, 2020c; 360doc.com, 2021). Whilst Chinese consumers appear willing to spend a price premium for the perception of safety that international brands continue to maintain (He,

2020), 6 domestic brands have gained entrance into the official top 15 tyre brands in China. Noticeably, the margin of quality perception formerly enjoyed by international brands is steadily eroding (Icauto.com, 2021).

Analysis of the four core factors influencing the China tyre market has raised concerns for ABC regarding increasing levels of competition, a market slowdown, declining profit margins and eroded brand differential. Combined, ABC is seeking to explore innovative practices to improve sales performance in China.

Problem statement

The dominant tyre brands in China have not been static in their response to the changing market conditions in China. As Bliss and Haddock (2008) highlight, many tyre manufacturers initially entered China for the purpose of exploiting low-cost production and it was Goodyear who pioneered establishing partnerships with outlets to drive sales to the growing market of private car owners in mainland China. Equally, there has been an emphasis on reinforcing quality standards in manufacturing processes and logistical operations. However, considering changes to the competitive landscape as previously raised, combined with growing calls for the tyre industry to explore closed loop supply chains as a mechanism for increasing recycling rates of used tyres (Ebrahimi, 2018; Pedram *et al*, 2017), ABC initiated a project to explore innovative practices that may improve sales performance in the China market.

Overview - approach taken

Innovating a sales model is a significant undertaking, as it not only combines internal stakeholders but also a diverse range of external factors that are outside of a company's control. Furthermore, merely integrating a disruptive practice into one's own business model does not guarantee improved performance (Kim and Min, 2015). In recognition of this, ABC sought to take a transitional approach towards change. A transitional approach views change as a fluid process of specific steps in pursuit of a new future that is an improvement on the current environment rather than a pursuit of changing the fundamentals of a given environment (Roggema, Vermeend and van den Dobbelsteen, 2012; Amado and Amato, 2001). As transitional change involves human perception towards variables (Ambrose, 2001), the project therefore sought not to transform the environment but, rather: consider variables and innovations currently influencing sales channels in the China market; benchmark trends in the China sales models with international best practice; engage with key stakeholders affected by ABC's sales strategy to gauge opinions and perspectives regarding a proposal to adopt international practice to the China sales model.

Case studying changes within China's sales model: The conventional sales model utilised by the dominant tyre brands in China has placed the onus on the role of provincial-level distributors. Distributors would provide stock to wholesalers, to tyre repair / retail shops, and, in turn, for purchase by consumers according to in-store recommendation. Not only has this model raised issues about its impact on tyre recycling rates (Ran and Yin, 2021), the model has also been exposed to innovation in the Consumer-to-Manufacturer relationship. Via the advent of the internet and booming e-commerce market in China, JD.com has proactively developed partnerships with Continental, Goodyear, Pirelli, and Michelin by opening online sales access directly to its 300 million consumers. Via these partnerships, JD.com has sought to disrupt the tyre industry by releasing a new sales model that takes advantage of big data gathered through online sales to feed into tyre supply, utilising JD.com's existing infrastructure to offer services direct to consumers, as well as provide additional convenience to a consumer base that has an increasing habit to shop online with an expectation to have choice and ability to customise their purchase (Goodchild, 2019, Kidron, 2020a; Tyrepress.com, 2017).

Partnership with JD.com's Jaoto initiative (the brand given to JD Auto Services) solves a further issue of price standardisation. This is achieved by facilitating a coordinated distribution mechanism from manufacturer to dealer to car owner that allows price synchronisation (Kidron, 2020b). However, whilst the platform brings together over 7,000 merchants, it also facilitates comparison with domestic competitors and thus provides an opportunity for domestic brands to demonstrate competitiveness, at least on price, with currently leading international brands. Ultimately, the Jaoto case indicates that the China market has an openness to the Consumer to Manufacturer / Direct Sales model. Whereas ABC has not historically engaged in direct sales within the China market, learning may be achieved from benchmarking against practice in other geographical regions.

Benchmarking trends with other geographical markets: Goodyear first launched direct sales services for American consumers in 2015, followed by Michelin in 2016 (Modertiredealer.com, 2020). Strategies for entering into direct sales have been varied, with Bridgestone noticeably using mergers and acquisitions (M&A) to acquire an online-sales provider to facilitate their growth (Bridgestoneamericas.com, 2015). Michelin highlights that for people visiting the websites, online sales brought significant improvements to the experience of consumers in the 35 years and below age bracket. Equally, Michelin's objective was never to become an e-retailer and in April 2020 ceased direct sales, although they maintain an online presence via partnerships (Tirereview.com, 2020).

Whereas Michelin has opted for a partnership approach, third party sites often limit the amount of product information a manufacturer can present. With Forrester Research studies showing that over 40% of consumers want to purchase directly from manufacturers, a growing trend that may have been further affected by Covid-19, Goodyear's perseverance in direct sales in America is resulting in positive press (Dean, 2021).

Within the American markets, the top tyre brands are engaging in direct sales. Consumers may purchase a tyre directly from the brand (or partner) website, the tyre is then delivered to the door by a local dealer, who provides optional services such as tyre removal and installation.

Proposal development: ABC has experience with direct sales in the US, providing an understanding of challenges that may arise during roll out, such as resistance from independent dealers who feel that they may be bypassed in the revised supply chain (Modertiredealer.com, 2020). Jaoto's growth similarly highlights that the China market is increasingly open towards such a model. Equally, ABC needs to be sensitive towards potential for upsetting stakeholders, particularly distributors, who have significant influence over current performance.

The People's Republic of China has an administrative structure comprising 23 provinces, 5 autonomous regions, 4 centrally administered municipalities and 2 special administrative regions. For the purposes of developing business strategy, each of these administrative units may be viewed as being equivalent to a nation state as the variance in conventional economic classifiers is too great to support a single nationwide strategy for all of China. The sheer size and diversity of China inevitably entail each brand having a laggard region in which innovative solutions may be explored towards a large potential market without risk to a strategically important relationship. This is important as a barrier to innovation may be dependence upon relationships in the distributor network, relationships that could quickly turn sour should a tyre manufacturer hint at efforts to go direct to the consumer thus cutting out the distributor.

In the above context, a detailed proposal, including project objectives, target test region, project team, resource requirements and key performance indicator (KPI) suggestions within the context of existing structures was proposed. Due to the ongoing sensitivity of the testing stages as at March 2022, a summary of the proposal may not be publicly disclosed.

Conclusion

Industry change is often a result of external factors. This case has highlighted that some relationships may be explicit and common sensical, such as the relationship between vehicle sales and tyre purchases. Equally, technological development and social change, such as the perspectives and habits regarding how people interact with new technologies, provide opportunity for disrupting traditional approaches towards doing business. For a global leader within an established market, change may not result in a coordinated and instantaneous rollout of an initiative across the globe. Exploring change at a national level, it may therefore prove advantageous to benchmark not only with competitors, but also within one's own company operating in other markets. Not only may this support the negotiation of buy-in internally, but also provide a useful source of change agents to facilitate the planning and implementation process.

References

Amado, G., & Amato, R., Some Distinctive Characteristics of Transitional Change. **In:** Amado, G., and Ambrose, A., eds., (2001) *The Transitional Approach to Change*. Routledge.

Ambrose, A., (2001) An Introduction to Transitional Thinking. **In:** Amado, G., and Ambrose, A., eds., (2001) *The Transitional Approach to Change*. Routledge.

Bg.qianzhan.com., (2019) 2018年中国汽车行业产销量及发展前景分析 预测2019年市场销量将达2810万辆. Available from: https://bg.qianzhan.com/trends/detail/506/190115-8d0fac3d.html

Bliss, C., & Haddock, R., (2008) *Integrating China into Your Global Supply Chain: Lessons Learned from Global Supply Chain Integrators*. Booze and Company.

BridgestoneAmericas.com., (2015) *Bridgestone to Acquire Tireconnect Systems.* Available from: https://www.bridgestoneamericas.com/en/newsroom/press-releases/2015/bridgestone-to-acquire-tireconnect-systems-#

Carsalesbase.com., (2021) *China Automotive Sales Data & Trends – Total Market Volumes*. Available from: https://carsalesbase.com/china-car-sales-data-market/

Chinatiredealer.com., (2021) 中国原配轮胎排行榜|2020.Available from: http://www.chinatiredealer.com/news/show-48078.html

CHYXX.com (2018) 2018年中国轮胎行业供给需求及价格走势分析. Available from: https://www.chyxx.com/industry/201801/605703.html

CHYXX.com (2020a) 2020 年汽车轮胎产业供给侧改革持续推进，破产重组态势愈演愈烈（附中国汽车轮胎工业产销数据及竞争格局. Available from: https://www.chyxx.com/industry/202006/877252.html

CHYXX.com (2020b) 2020 年汽车轮胎产业供给侧改革持续推进，破产重组态势愈演愈烈（附中国汽车轮胎工业产销数据及竞争格局）. Available from: https://www.chyxx.com/industry/202006/877252.html

CHYXX.com (2020c) 轮胎行业分析：2019 年全球乘用车销量下滑，轮胎需求结构变化，中国轮胎产能过剩开始出清，2020 轮胎行业迎来 4 大变局. Available from：https://www.chyxx.com/industry/202006/874325.html

CHYXX.com., (2021a) 2021 年上半年中国汽车产销量、市场竞争格局及未来发展趋势分析. Available from: https://www.chyxx.com/industry/202107/963581.html

Dean, D., (2021) *Selling Direct-to-Consumer is Increasingly an Attractive Option*. Available from: https://www.industryweek.com/leadership/strategic-planning-execution/article/21171121/selling-directtoconsumer-is-increasingly-an-attractive-option

Ebrahimi, S., (2018) A Stochastic Multi-objective Location-allocation-routing Problem for Tire Supply Chain Considering Sustainability Aspects and Quantity Discounts, *Journal of Cleaner Production*. Vol 198, pp.704-720. DOI: 10.1016/j.jclepro.2018.07.059

Goodchild, S., (2019) *Michelin Selling Online in China with JD.com.* Available from: https://www.tyrepress.com/2019/03/michelin-selling-online-in-china-with-jd-com/

Gov.cn., (2005) 中华人民共和国行政区划. Available from: http://www.gov.cn/test/2005-06/15/content_18253.htm

Gov.cn., (2008) 公安部:全国机动车保有量近 1.6 亿汽车驾驶人过亿. Available from: http://www.gov.cn/gzdt/2008-01/04/content_850272.htm

He, H., (2020) 轮胎排名前十名新鲜出炉，固特异稳居榜首. Available from: https://www.pcauto.com.cn/qcbj/2225/22256991.html

Icauto.com., (2021) 中国品牌轮胎排名前十名，中国十大轮胎品牌排行榜. Available from: https://www.icauto.com.cn/zdm/66/669820.html

Kidron, E., (2020a) *JD Brings Popular Italian Tires to the Chinese Market*. Available from: https://jdcorporateblog.com/jd-brings-popular-italian-tires-to-the-chinese-market/

Kidron, E., (2020b) *JD Wins Influential Domestic Auto-aftermarket Award*. Available from: https://jdcorporateblog.com/jd-wins-influential-domestic-auto-aftermarket-award/

Kim, S., & Min, S., (2015) Business Model Innovation Performance, *Strategic Entrepreneurship Journal*. Vol 9 (1), pp.34-57. DOI: 10.1002/sej.1193

Ministry of Public Security., (2020) *National Car Parc 2020*. Sourced from the National Bureau of Statistics. Available from: https://www.mps.gov.cn/n7944517/n7944597/n7945888/c7478950/content.html

Pedram, A., Yusoff, N., Udoncy, O., Mahat, A., Pedram, P., & Babalola, A., (2017) Integrated Forward and Reverse Supply Chain: A Tire Case Study, *Waste Management*. Vol 60, pp.460-470. DOI: 10.1016/j.wasman.2016.06.029

Ran, W., & Yin, W., (2021) Effect on the Model of Government-Subsidized Dual-Channel Closed-loop Supply Chain: Taking Automobile Tire Recycling as an Example. **In:** *IOP Conference Series: Earth and Environmental Science*. Vol. 820 (1). DOI: 10.1088/1755-1315/820/1/012013

Roggema, R., Vermeend, T., & van den Dobbelsteen, A., (2012) Incremental Change, Transition or Transformation? Optimising Change Pathways for Climate Adaptation in Spatial Planning. *Sustainability.* Vol 4, 2525-2549. DOI: 10.3390/su4102525

Statista.com., (2021a) *Size of the Global Automotive Tire Market from 2019 to 2027*. Available from: https://www.statista.com/statistics/1228044/global-automotive-tire-market-size/

Statista.com., (2021b) *The World's Largest Tire Producers in FY2020, Based on Tire-Related Revenue*. Available from: https://www.statista.com/statistics/225677/revenue-of-the-leading-tire-producers-worldwide/

Tirereview.com., (2020) *Michelin Ceasing Direct-to-Consumer PLT Tire Sales.* Available from: https://www.tirereview.com/michelin-ceasing-direct-to-consumer-plt-tire-sales/

Tyrepress.com., (2017) *Goodyear Partners with Key Chinese e-Commerce Player JD.com*. Available from: https://www.tyrepress.com/2017/12/goodyear-partners-with-key-chinese-ecommerce-player-jd-com/

Urdinez, F., & Masiero, G., (2015) China and the WTO: Will the Market Economy State Make Any Difference After 2016?, *The Chinese Economy.* Vol 48 (2), pp.155-172. DOI: 10.1080/10971475.2015.993228

Xiong, B., (2017) The Implications of US Punitive Tariffs on Chinese Tires for Rubber Exports from South-East Asia, *Journal of the Asia Pacific Economy*. Vol 22 (4), pp.575-586. DOI: 10.1080/13547860.2017.1312073

360doc.com,., (2021) *8 Tires were Tested Comprehensively, and the Results of Domestic Branded Tires were Unexpected.* Available from: http://www.360doc.com/content/21/0411/18/72465772_971701875.shtml

Discussion questions

1. The report mentions that tyre brands have been experimenting with a direct sales model in the American market since 2015. Given that mainland China is widely considered a leader with regards to consumer adoption of e-commerce behaviours, what factors may have influenced ABC to decide not to transition sales model at any earlier point of time?

2. The report makes reference towards production facilities having typically operated at a 60-70% production capacity for several years. Recognising that Property, Plant and Equipment (PP&E) assets are expected to generate an economic return, it may be assumed that the financial ratios evaluating PP&E performance may be below original forecasts. What impact may this have when considering future large scale investment decisions in the tyre market?

3. The report highlights that transitioning too quickly to a direct sales model may risk upsetting relationships with distributors who hold a significant influence over regional sales. What suggestions do you think may have been included in the proposal submitted to ABC leadership to mitigate against such risks?

Izivat Survives a Strategy Pivot Triggered by Covid-19

Laurie Ann Underwood
Senior Professor of Practice: IESEG School of Business

Abstract

When French start-up IZIVAT launched its new app – which allowed overseas shoppers to redeem their VAT (value added tax) refund digitally – it was exactly the wrong time. Targeting Chinese consumers, with a soft launch planned for February 2020, the launch coincided exactly with the outbreak of the covid-19 pandemic. Overnight, Izivat's business model changed from promising to impossible. The company's dramatic and successful pivot to an entirely new strategy led Izivat to not only survive the pandemic but to win first place at the Top Start-up Awards for 2021 from Tecom Shanghai (Izivat, 2021).

This case study tracks Izivat's 180-degree shift in business model from a Business-to-Consumer (B2C) model targeting individual travellers to a Business-to-Business (B2B) model targeting cross-border wholesalers. The change required transforming the operating model, altering key legal aspects, and developing an entirely new IT platform – while simultaneously maintaining employee morale and investor confidence. In our analysis, we update Lewin's 3-step change model, tweaking the "thaw-move-refreeze" format into a modern variation.

Introduction

In 2019, three colleagues at a French bank began dreaming of launching a start-up business which could leverage their collective China expertise. Focusing on China's then booming outbound tourism business – in 2019, Chinese travellers made 155 million outbound trips (Xinhua, 2020) – the three entrepreneurs sought to address a long-running "pain point" for

Chinese shoppers in Europe: collecting the Value Added Tax (VAT) refund. While travellers have the legal right to the refund of 20% – which represents a substantial amount for shoppers who purchase luxury items such as designer bags or wine – the traditional paper-based process could require up to 10 hours of queueing and form filling (Izivat website, 2022), frequently followed by a wait of four or even six months to receive the refund (ASD Group, 2018).

Armed with a self-proclaimed mission to "make tax-free shopping global and digital" (Izivat website, 2022), the company developed a user-friendly mobile app allowing overseas shoppers to easily and quickly redeem VAT. Specifically targeting Chinese shoppers, the app invited users to follow three steps: snap it (upload photos of purchase receipts), stamp it (use the Izivat kiosk at French airports for fast validation), cash it (receive a digital refund by Alipay or WeChat within 24 hours). The process had two advantages over traditional competitors including Global Blue and Planet Payment: first, Izivat's app was designed to be entirely digital; second, it allowed users to shop tax free in all French shops, without having to reach a minimum purchase amount per store.

With these benefits in mind, Izivat SAS was launched as a French-registered private company in 2019. In pilot studies conducted in summer of 2019 with more than 20 test users, Izivat's speedier refund was largely deemed worth the fee of 15% of the refund value (which was less than many competitors). With all this in mind, Izivat Go app was launched in November 2019. At the time, Izivat founders planned to use the Christmas 2019 and Chinese New Year 2020 holidays as a soft launch for the app.

However, Izivat's launch plans suddenly and completely derailed. In early January, international media began reporting on a strange and deadly virus in Wuhan, China, triggering a global health scare. By late January, the World Health Organisation announced that Russia and Japan had imposed travel restrictions against China; by March, 45 nations had done so (BBC, 2020).

Problem statement

"For us, it was pretty brutal. It was our industry – travel – which shut down," remembers Izivat co-founder Wody Keita-Stemper. Because Izivat's business model relied heavily on Chinese tourists using their VAT refund app, the ban on travellers from China entering key markets (especially France and other European destinations) made the original strategy impossible. As the company's LinkedIn site states, regarding this time period: "It was clear that we had to innovate or die."

The fact that two of Izivat's three founders, as well as most of the other 7 full-time employees, were based in China during this time of turmoil turned out to be a benefit. Keita-Stemper explains: "From Day 1, we realised the seriousness of the situation…. Seeing the problem was easy because it was in our face." Thus, the founders quickly agreed to prepare (operationally) for "up to one year" without revenue from the original business model – a prediction which was considered "very pessimistic" at the pandemic's start.

The only solution was to find an entirely new operating model, and fast. Keita-Stemper describes the heady period redirecting the business in this way: "I didn't have the luxury to ask myself whether Izivat would survive. Once we decided to move, we just had to move – and plan to learn along the way. It was more about not being stuck." She also advises that it was the sense of continued motion, the energy of launching an alternative business model, which motivated the Izivat team during this time. She attributes the team's sharp focus on the alternative operating strategy with maintaining positivity among most employees despite the challenges caused by Covid-related business uncertainties as well as the mental and emotional strain caused by lockdowns and working from home.

Theory

Lewin's three-step change model (Lewin, 1951) has for decades offered managers a trusted construct for leading organisations through change. The model continues to offer business leaders a useful framework for managing change, especially when, research shows, the model is combined with active knowledge sharing during the first two phases and when active employee involvement is achieved in each of the three phases (Hussein, et al, 2016).

However, in today's VUCA business environment (i.e., characterised by volatility, uncertainty, complexity, and ambiguity), the model's stages – thaw, move, refreeze – have been criticised for no longer matching business realities (Bywater & Lewis, 2019). More recent research findings have emphasised that, after the change is 'completed', business leaders must continue to collect and react to staff feedback (Barrow et al, 2021.) Thus, in this case study, we seek to correct misinterpretations of Lewin's model by referring to the final stage as "chill" rather than "refreeze."

In the case of Izivat, the company passed through the three stages of change rapidly, along this timeline:

Thaw stage: March 2020: Izivat founders realised that the covid-19 pandemic had made cross border travel-based shopping for individuals impossible. Thus, the company had to switch from its original service to a new concept: wholesale cross-border shopping services. This required changing the business model from a legal standpoint, developing a new IT platform, and changing the marketing direction to shift away from individual shoppers to wholesalers. Specifically, the new target user would be Chinese ecommerce wholesalers selling imported product to Chinese consumers now unable to travel.

Move stage: June 2020: As Izivat completed the transformation of its business model, legal structure, and sales targets (to focus on B2B instead of B2C clients), the IT team was busy adapting the IT platform to include an entirely new element -- delivery services. This involved developing and testing several different beta systems. By early summer, the company was satisfied with the IT functionality.

Chill stage: September 2020: Izivat issued its first official communication to attract B2B cross-border customers. The new operating model was launched, including an in-built system of constant evaluation and tweaking as a regular and permanent part of the revised business strategy. Although the company initially lacked any pre-existing partners or customers in this new field, the sales team efficiently located small-scale ecommerce wholesalers with clientele seeking goods from abroad. Izivat tapped into China's growing community of cross-border ecommerce wholesalers serving consumers who sought foreign products during the nation's ongoing travel bans.

Actions and evaluations

Action 1: Brainstorm worst case scenarios in advance

One critically important action taken by Izivat leaders during the transition to a new business model was an exercise called "What If". Before launching in November 2019, Izivat founders had undertaken an activity with its accelerator in which the team created a "map" of their business model showing their core services in the centre surrounded by all critical stakeholders – such as consumers, business partners, and internal teams. The team then used the map to brainstorm a full range of 'worst case scenarios' disrupting the business model. They asked, "What if we don't get funding?" and "What if the laws change." Remembers Keita-Stemper: "Because of that exercise, we had already asked ourselves: 'What if our customers can't travel?' It seemed very unrealistic back then, but it actually became a reality."

When the pandemic hit, the team remembered this exercise – and used the outcomes of the brainstorming session as a starting point for the new business model. Recalls Keita-Stemper: "This helped us because we already had something on paper." During the exercise, the team had already decided that, if consumers cannot travel, then Izivat could still help them shop online by facilitating cross-border purchasing and delivery. "We already knew that cross-border would fall into the same business scope as our initial operating model. The alternative to our original business model was already there for us. So, it was more about figuring out the legal frame and the process and the IT platform."

Action 2: Address employee morale

When Izivat began shifting to the new business direction in March 2020, one key challenge was the widespread lockdowns under way in both areas of business operations: China and France. Thus, Izivat employees had to work from home at the time when the company had lost its original business model. "It's not easy to keep people motivated," remembers Keita-Stemper. "We found that working from home, especially for more senior employees, leaves people even more scared of the prospects." For some senior employees, losing the ability to work face-to-face exacerbated the sense of insecurity. Thus, some key personnel quit during this time – a challenge that Keita-Stemper says "put a light on the fact that we were not stable. That time period was not easy for those looking for stability."

As a way to retain staff, Izivat managers introduced specific tools designed to boost morale. In April 2020, they launched "Weekly Wows" in which all employees shared at least one "wow" – something which made them very happy -- from the week previous. Says Keita-Stemper: "Our normal work meetings are very intense -- scheduled, results driven. On top of that, being online, we lost any informal place to know our colleagues. We lost coffee breaks. So, the weekly wows really helped to keep people close." After finding that the sharing of personal highlights from family life, or sports, or hobbies helped to forge bonds and relieve stress, Izivat founders have continued the ritual even after the company has shifted toward more face-to-face operations post-pandemic, as many employees value the exercise. Says Keita-Stemper: "When we started, people were a bit shy. But now they are freely talking, showing photos and videos. It has helped to counteract the tension of the business situation."

Action 3: Frequent, effective internal communication

Another useful tool introduced by Izivat was daily "Standups" – ie, short daily meetings to share urgent observations. The standups were especially useful and effective as the new IT platform was being developed and tested. During these meetings, employees stand (not sit) as the meeting should take around 15 minutes. Each employee quickly updates the team on any feedback for the IT platform – what is working well, what is not working. "Each person goes around and mentions whatever bug is happening or whatever IT changes that need our input (from the founders) Are you stuck somewhere? Do you need help?" The meeting happens every morning at 8 AM French time, still now.

Conclusion

Overall, Izivat founders say the experience of managing radical change during covid-19 has reinforced their belief in the philosophy of: "think slowly but act quickly." Because the business strategy was thoroughly researched before the launch, including brainstorming worst case scenarios challenging the business model, they had done the homework needed to allow them to "act quickly" when the pandemic hit.

As of mid-2022, Izivat leaders feel they have weathered the worst of the storm – in terms of avoiding staff layoffs, not acquiring debt, and attracting new investors over the past two years. Building upon this new base, company founders say they will 'definitely' maintain cross-border trade as the focus of the business but will also gear up to add individual shoppers back into the mix. In fact, during summer 2022, Izivat began reactivating the travel-based services. "We can handle both," says Keita-Stemper. "Today, we view the customer as one group, needing two services. For us, the cross-border trade is still accelerating but we hope to see individual travel bringing the same level of excitement very soon."

The new dual business track again illustrates Izivat's continued flexibility since the company has had to shift its focus away from Chinese travellers (due to continued restrictions on outbound travel) to travellers from the UK and Middle East. Thus, the start-up's "refreeze" period is characterised by constant evaluation, tweaking, and adapting to various VUCA aspects of business operations.

References

ASD Group (2018). "How do you recover VAT in France?", 14 March Retrieved from: https://www.asd-int.com/en/how-do-you-recover-vat-in-france/

Barrow, J.M., Annamaraju, P., & Toney-Butler, T., (2021). "Change Management," StatPearls Publishing LLC.

BBC (2020). "Coronavirus: US and Australia close borders to Chinese arrivals," 1 February Retrieved from: https://www.bbc.com/news/world-51338899,

Bywater, J., & Lewis, J., (2019). "Leadership: What competencies does it take to remain engaged as a leader in a VUCA world?" Assessment & Development Matters, Vol. 11 No. 3

Hussein, S.T., Lei, S., Akram, T., Haider, M.J., Hussain, S.H., & Ali, M., (2018). "Kurt Lewin's change model: A critical review of the role of leadership and employee involvement in organizational change, *Journal of Innovation and Knowledge,* Volume 3, p. 123-127.

Izivat, LinkedIn, posted July 2021. Retrieved from https://www.linkedin.com/feed/update/urn:li:activity:6804938136569823232/

Izivat, website. Retrieved on April 13, 2022: https://www.izivat.com/en/about-us https://www.izivat.com/en/about-us

Lewin, K., (1951). Field theory in social science: selected theoretical papers (Edited by Dorwin Cartwright.).

Xinhua.net (2020). "China reports growth in outbound tourists in 2019" November 11 Retrieved from: http://www.xinhuanet.com/english/2020-11/11/c_139509342.htm

Discussion questions

1. Izivat benefited from conducting the "What if" brainstorming exercise before its launch, identifying and developing a plan to handle all conceivable possible scenarios disrupting its initial business strategy. Consider extra-ordinary factors that may impact your business and then discuss how much time you consider is reasonable to grapple with each one.

2. The loss of the original business model and a prolonged lack of revenue coupled with the isolation and stress caused by working from home left some employees (especially senior professionals) feeling insecure. Izivat found that ensuring a sense of constant motion toward the new business model, including setting short term goals when long term goals proved unclear, help employees feel 'unstuck' and motivated. In addition, the launch of "Weekly Wows" offered an opportunity to strengthen intra-employee bonding and to create a sense of comraderie during remote working. What initiatives may your organisation do that brings people together, without being a distraction or drain on resources?

3. In highly dynamic periods, such as during the beta testing of Izivat's new IT platform, the company used daily "stand up" meetings effectively. These short, focused meetings, in which participants literally stand to enforce brevity and focus, offer an excellent method of efficiently collecting relevant feedback from team members to identify and eliminate bottlenecks and to ensure that the change is evolving correctly. What simple tools and techniques are you aware of that encourage efficiency and effectiveness during team meetings?

Perspectives on CSR from Chinese PV Manufacturers

Senior Executive
Top 5 PV Manufacturer

Abstract

The solar photovoltaic industry is growing at significant speed. Dominated by Chinese enterprises who account for over 80% of global production, this report recognises that operating within an environmentally orientated sector does not make a company or industry environmentally sound. The author has interviewed eleven senior executives from five Chinese solar photovoltaic manufactures to explore attitudes towards corporate social responsibility from organisations with the largest footprint. The report concludes with recommendations for further improvement.

Background of Chinese enterprises in PV industry

Supported by favourable government policy and aspirations for reduction in carbon emission volumes across the globe, the solar photovoltaic (PV) industry has experienced significant growth (Jia, Sun and Koh, 2016). Jackson, Lewis, and Zhang (2021) highlight that at a value of $7.8 trillion, investment in renewable energy by 2050 is anticipated to outpace investment into fossil fuels by 270%. From this, the PV industry is forecasted by the International Energy Agency (2019) to account for a significant majority of this growth. China, which makes up for over 80% of the worlds' supply of solar panels (Wu, 2021), is therefore of vital importance to the future of the industry.

As shown in Figure 1, Chinese enterprises are not exclusively manufacturing PV units for the China market, but may be viewed more as the engine for the globe. Favourable government policy and competitive pricing have been significant drivers behind the rise of China's PV manufacturers (Zhang *et al*, 2021). China's expansion into renewable energy has provided significant financial returns. Equally, there is expressed concern regarding the model and footprint in overseas markets, with local communities questioning Chinese enterprises ideas and concepts of CSR (KPMG, 2013).

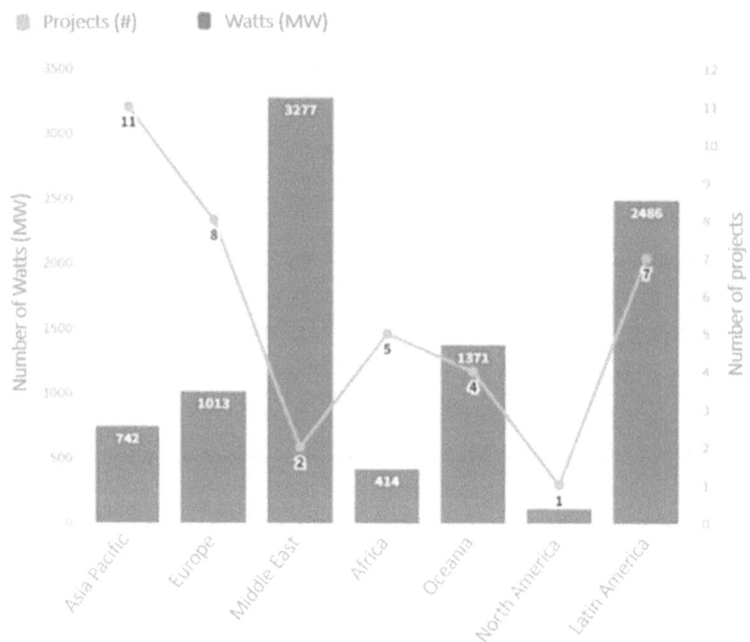

Figure 1: *Chinese overseas solar PV investments by area (2012-2020)*

Perspectives towards CSR

Although not exclusive to solar panel manufacturers, a study by Brunswick conducted at 300 Chinese Enterprises and 90,700 international firms highlighted significant differences regarding perspectives towards CSR – ultimately concluding that leadership at Chinese firms viewed CSR as primarily a governmental issue (Brunswick, 2021). Whereas Western businesses are increasingly highlighting need towards taking a multi-stakeholder perspective towards business, Chinese enterprise leaders are noticeably prioritising shareholder returns (Brunswick, 2021). When asked to rank importance of shareholders, Chinese business leaders focus on

Government (60%), Investor Profits (59%), Customer Value (47%), Fairness to suppliers (37%), Employee investment (33%), Community (33%) (Brunswick, 2021). Simply operating within renewable energy space does not make a company conscious towards sustainability, with some concluding that there is a gap between CSR initiatives that Chinese enterprises are doing and what the market and communities are expecting (KPMG, 2013). As Maon, Lindgreen and Swaen (2010) stress, CSR is not only about removing an organisation's negative impact on a society, but requires strategic effort to contribute and make a positive difference.

This study will help those Chinese Renewable Energy Corporations realise the inadequacy and shortcomings in terms of CSR from global market demand and encourage them to minimise the gap with its counterparts from developed nations (Ray, 2008).

Stakeholder analysis

Stakeholder perspectives are important to the discourse of CSR (McWilliams & Siegel, 2001). Figure 2 highlights core stakeholders for a Chinese PV manufacturer. Although most stakeholders for PV manufacturers may be considered external, the relationship and value alignment between executive management and stakeholders are important in setting a united direction (Freeman, Wicks, & Parmar, 2004). Therefore, understanding attitudes towards CSR internally at Chinese PV manufacturers is an important starting point before offering recommendations.

Stakeholders	Internal / External	Related requirement	Activities provided by company
Customers	External	High quality products Quality services	New product launches Attend events and summits Satisfaction surveys
Authorities	External	Strong governance systems	Optimised compliance mechanisms Disclosure of information
Investors	Primarily external	Long term profitability Returns to shareholders	Financial reporting Investor calls
Suppliers	External	Green supply chain Socially responsible	Supplier code agreement Supplier training
Employees	Internal	Career development Health & safety at workplace	Training and education Social activities
Community	External	Environment safety	Activity support
Industry	External	Technology exchange	Collaborative innovation
Government	External	Industry development Pay taxes Compliance	Provide jobs Technological innovation Compliance with laws and regulations
Media	External	Environment safety	Information disclosure
NGOs / 3rd Party Organisations	External	Environment safety	Industry association member

Figure 2: *Core stakeholders for Chinese PV manufacturers*

Stakeholder research

To understand awareness of CSR at Chinese PV manufacturers, interviews were conducted with ten senior directors from five Chinese enterprises. All interviewees had over ten years of related experience, were at a senior position from which to comment, and stemmed from functions as follows: 5x Sales Director, 1x Marketing Director, 1x Finance Director, 1x Public Relations Director, 1x Legal Director, 1x Supply Chain Director.

Semi-structured interviews were conducted, with core feedback from responses summarised as below:

1. Is CSR equal to philanthropy?

Only the Public Relations interviewee recognises CSR as larger than philanthropy. The Supply Chain Director did highlight that CSR criteria were impacting supplier selection, but was not aware of how this filtered into wider corporate strategy.

2. What is the biggest challenge in terms of CSR you faced so far?

Nine interviewees stated that they were unaware of any CSR challenges arising during their careers. Two interviewees – both working at the same company – had experienced a significant incident in 2013. A chemical leak at a factory in Haining, Zhejiang Province, coincided with the company's listing on the New York stock exchange. This generated significant international press and share price performance suffered as a direct result. Both respondents were therefore aware of the potential for failure to achieve CSR requirements to generic negative publicity.

3. What do you think of the importance of CSR to your work?

Nine respondents linked CSR to compliance, such as working hours, health and safety requirements, equality for female workers etc. One respondent highlighted studying CSR as part of an MBA, with the final respondent saying that he had never heard of CSR before the interview.

4. Who makes decisions relating to CSR issues?

Respondents unanimously assumed that CSR decisions would be taken by their enterprises' leadership respectively. One respondent raised that this should not be surprising given that corporate structures in listed Chinese enterprises have traditionally been dominated by a few individuals who assume multiple governance roles, and where relatives account for over 50% of senior management (The Economic Observer, 2007). Decision making is therefore often limited to a few individuals, and top-down decision making is widely accepted as common practice in mainland China.

5. Who are the main stakeholders in your company?

Priority stakeholders mentioned included traditional media, banks, traders, financiers etc. Noticeably, all stakeholders mentioned orientated around finance, compliance, or general image of the company.

Overseas expansion has also raised importance of building a solid supply chain. With external pressures including trade wars, some aspects of manufacturing have also been employed overseas. Respondents mentioned that arguably the motivation has been financial rather than desire to bring employment opportunities to other community regions.

6. Is CSR a function strategy or a corporate strategy?

All respondents mentioned that aligning with Western practice is increasingly important as enterprises increase their international exposure. All implied that CSR may therefore be considered a part of corporate strategy.

7. Is CSR a moral or legal obligation?

All respondents highlighted that CSR should be considered both a legal and a moral obligation. Respondents further noted that challenges exist due to lack of awareness, as well as emphasis on economic performance. However, it was also raised that on 30th July 2020, the China Corporate Social Responsibility Evaluation Criteria, initiated by China Enterprise Evaluation Association, were released in Beijing. The result is that by 2025, China Enterprise Evaluation Association will carry out the evaluation of "500 excellent Chinese corporate social responsibility reports" and excellent case analysis based on the standard 2.0, therefore providing a ranking and thus incentive to improve CSR activity (Economy.cn, 2021).

8. Do you understand your corporation's own CSR content?

Respondents revealed that none of them had read any published document regarding CSR in their company – such as an annual CSR Report. Most mentioned a general awareness of the concept, but that CSR remains far from their daily work.

9. What do you think about content in CSR reports?

Here, interviewees were given a copy of Jinko Solar's 2020 CSR Report (Jinko Solar, 2021). Following a brief read, respondents all agreed that CSR was more strategic and should be included in management tools than they had initially thought.

10. Do you take CSR into consideration when negotiating deals with your customers or other regular work activities?

Respondents highlighted that conversation often involves themes that overlap with CSR, but that conversation is not necessarily strategic or intentionally focusing on CSR. An example was provided by one, who mentioned that during negotiations with a new supplier, the supplier may comment on carbon emissions during their production process as being part of their value. Compliance around supplier selection (e.g., healthy working conditions for labour, training provision for labour etc) are also related to CSR and part of conversation around supplier selection, but these are not pro-active in effort to drive improvement.

Discussion

From interviews, the incident for Jinko Solar in 2013 highlights that CSR compliance can have material impact on a company. Respondents have evidenced that compliance is an important feature, with examples about the need for integrating supply chain into required standards being clearly raised. Chinese enterprises account for over 80% of the worlds' supply of PV panel manufacturing, largely as a result of its cost and performance advantages. Whilst these factors present advantage for bidding against competition, a potential byproduct is that this focus overshadows attention towards CSR initiatives – particularly when placed in direct comparison with Western multinationals operating within the same area.

The lack of proactive attention from respondents towards CSR was surprising, particularly when no respondent confirmed ever reading a document on CSR. This does raise concern about the embeddedness of CSR values in Chinese enterprises. Equally, findings from Brunswick Group's (2021) study clearly imply that the global public is willing to listen to the vision, mission, and value pitch of a Chinese enterprise, not prioritising investment decisions purely on financial performance. There therefore is opportunity for Chinese enterprises to improve. Local communication strategies, fairness of local employees and local environment are therefore important to local stakeholders.

Research findings are limited to the experiences and perspectives of only eleven Directors at five firms, therefore not representative of the full industry. Given assumptions that CSR is more of an issue for enterprise leadership, the interview process is also limited by not including any CEOs in the study. Exposure to a larger group of stakeholders may also have added more value to the report. However, from the authors experience in the PV industry, significant deviation from current findings would not be expected.

It is proposed that Chinese PV manufacturers have the concept of CSR in their mind and also to be the key part of their business strategy in a long term as well as a more specific functional business in a short run. The following suggestions may be considered:

(a) Strengthen compliance management and stick to the risk bottom line: This may involve benchmarking according to recognised pillars, such as the United Nations Sustainable Development Goals in order to align discussion with global approach and widely used frameworks.

(b) Pay attention to community development and obtain social permission: This may involve participating in local summits providing opportunity to increase connection with local stakeholders.

(c) Recognise CSR platforms as a bridge: CSR is a common discussion point at global forums, Chambers of Commerce and other high-profile events. Involvement with prominent players to develop new standards can lead to knowledge sharing, organisational learning, risk prevention and improved branding for Chinese enterprises.

(d) To implement green supply chain management in the whole life cycle: Improved supply chain management may strength cultural and conceptual recognition of environmental protection between suppliers and the enterprise.

(f) Engage with latest international governance standards: ESG frameworks and standards are varied and constantly changing. Conforming with internationally recognised standards may help improve communication of key metrics.

(g) Engage with ESG investment products: Communicate with investor groups about ESG metrics to get inclusion into growing range of ESG theme index. This will help build awareness of CSR within investor community.

(i) Consider green promotion opportunities: China is proactively involved with global green finance, providing sponsorship opportunities for green companies.

(j) Introducing the concept of responsible investment into charitable funds: It is clear that charitable organisations should not make investments that violate the purpose of the organisation and may damage their reputation. Attracting investment from charitable funds may offer win-win for increased share demand, whilst also increase investor awareness of CSR needs.

Conclusions

The solar PV industry is an important component of global transitioning to renewable energy sources. Dominated by Chinese enterprises who account for over 80% of global production, this report has recognised that operating within an environmentally orientated sector does not make a company or industry environmentally sound. The author has interviewed 11 senior executives from 5 Chinese PV manufactures, revealing a surprising lack of recognition towards the importance of CSR or how it relates to operational work. Recommendations are therefore provided with the hope of broadening discussion of CSR away from only compliance and finance, to become more strategic in the companies.

References

Brunswick Group., (2021) *国际视野中的中国企业*. Available from: https://www.brunswickgroup.com/media/7175/%E5%8D%9A%E7%84%B6%E6%80%9D%E7%BB%B4_%E5%9B%BD%E9%99%85%E8%A7%86%E9%87%8E%E4%B8%AD%E7%9A%84%E4%B8%AD%E5%9B%BD%E4%BC%81%E4%B8%9A-2020%E5%B9%B45%E6%9C%88.pdf [Accessed 14th March 2022]

Economic Observer., (2007) 120 家中国私营企业调查. Available from: http://www.eeo.com.cn/2007/0228/45378.shtml [Accessed 20th September 2021.

Economy.cn., (2021). *中国企业社会责任评价准则 CEEA-CSR2.0 在京发布*. Available from: https://economy.gmw.cn/2020-07/31/content_34047527.htm [Accessed 1st October 2021]

Freeman, R. E., Wicks, A. C., & Parmar, B., (2004) Stakeholder theory and "The Corporate Objective Revisited, *Organization Science*. Vol 15, pp.364-369.

International Energy Agency., (2019) *IEA Renewables 2019 Market Analysis and Forecasts to 2024*. Available from: https://www.iea.org/media/presentations/Renewables-2019-Launch-Presentation.pdf [Accessed 14th March 2022]

Jackson, M., Lewis, J., & Zhang, X., (2021) A green expansion: China's role in the global deployment and transfer of solar photovoltaic technology, *Energy for Sustainable Development*. Vol 60, pp.90-101.

Jia, F., Sun, H., & Koh, L., (2016) Global solar photovoltaic industry: an overview and national competitiveness of Taiwan, *Journal of Cleaner Production*. Vol 126 (10), pp.550-562.

Jinko Solar., (2021) *2020 CSR Report*. Available from: https://www.jinkosolar.com/uploads/2021%20Jinko%20CSR%20Report-en.pdf [Accessed 1st October 2021].

KPMG., (2013) *中国企业的 海外绿色运营*. Available from: https://assets.kpmg/content/dam/kpmg/pdf/2013/10/China-enterprises-green-globalisation-201310-c.pdf [Accessed 14th March 2022]

Maon, F., Lindgreen, A., & Swaen, V., (2010) Organizational stages and cultural phases: a critical review and a consolidative model of corporate social responsibility development, *International Journal of Management Reviews*. Vol 12 (1), pp.20-38.

McWilliams, A., & Siegel, D., (2001) Corporate social responsibility: A theory of the firm perspective, *The Academy of Management Review*. Vol 26 (1), pp.117-127.

Ray, C., (2008) *A Cross-Cultural Comparison of Corporate Social Responsibility Practices: America and China*. University of Tennessee. Available from: https://trace.tennessee.edu/cgi/viewcontent.cgi?referer=https://www.google.com/&httpsredir=1&article=1522&context=utk_gradthes [Accessed 14th March 2022]

Wu, H., (2021) *The United States can't afford the brutal price of Chinese solar panels*. Available from: https://foreignpolicy.com/2021/07/14/us-chinese-solar-panels-green-tech-strategy/#:~:text=In%202019%2C%20China%20made%2080,coal%2Dpowered%20electricity%20in%20Xinjiang. [Accessed 14th March 2022].

Zhang, X., Zhang, L., Feng, K., Rangaiah, G., & Ng, K., (2021) Product design: impact of government policy and consumer preference on company profit and corporate social responsibility, *Computers and Chemical Engineering*. Vol 118, pp.118-131.

Discussion questions

1. The case references that simply operating within the renewable energy space does not make a company automatically conscious towards the broader concept of sustainability. Are there different degrees of awareness and adoption toward sustainable practice? If so, what are they? (*Note: The cited article of Maon, Lindgreen and Swaen, 2010, may provide useful context for this discussion*).

2. To what degree might you expect awareness and / or focus on CSR initiatives to be influenced by an individual's job role? For example, may job role direct attention towards a particular theme of CSR, or should attention towards CSR be more broadly mandated across all functions at a company?

3. Many interviewees in the case appeared to indicate that CSR was not directly relevant to their daily job responsibilities. Why do you think this may be the case?

Should Successful or Unsuccessful Promotions be the Focus of a Manager's Attention? A Case Study of a Higher Education Provider in China

Lionel Huntley Henderson

Abstract

Employee promotions have been used by some organizations to reward good behaviour, cultivate talent, enhance organizational commitment, and ensure employee retention. With only one, or a handful, of successful applicants per promotional round, most employees are unsuccessful in advancing their position within organizations despite in some cases being exemplary employees. Promotions are particularly important in academia and represent an increasing body of experience and achievements (e.g., research publications, administrative oversight, recognition for inspirational teaching, voluntary practices, etc.). This case study raises the question of where management should place their attention (e.g., candidates who were successful or unsuccessful in promotion rounds) to assist the organizational performance of a not-for-profit higher education provider. Employee retention, motivation, and development are core elements taught in undergraduate and graduate business management programmes, as are decisions related to promotions for practising managers. This business case draws on a 5-year period (academic years 2016-17 to 2020-21 inclusive) from a transnational education (TNE) provider (*The Educational Provider*) and demonstrates the impact of informal policies, strategies and action for unsuccessful promotions and recommends human resource departments, in higher education institutions (HEIs) and more generally, to consider such initiatives in their organization.

Organizational Profile

This case is based on *The Educational Provider*, a small to medium sized enterprise (SME) located in Shanghai, China, with the purpose to prepare undergraduate students for studies abroad. *The Educational Provider* has enjoyed a significant track record of success over the past 10 years (i.e., since 2012) with a strong student alumni and market reputation. It has 60 full time academic staff (all expatriate staff holding the rank of either Lecturer or Assistant Professor) and enrols over 2,000 full time undergraduate students annually. The annual turnover, derived exclusively from tuition fees, is proportionally comparable to other SME HEIs in the education sector. Many information technology (IT) resources and campus facilities have been upgraded in and since the 2016-2017 academic year as part of the annual summer renovation development plan. It has enjoyed a reasonable staff retention rate over its 10 years of operations considering the ratio of expatriate staff who typically leave every 3 – 5 years given they are not employed in their home nation (see employee, tenure, and promotion figures below in Table 1). In May 2016 a decision was taken to implement with effect from September 2016 a promotional development scheme. *The Educational Provider* adopted a formal promotions scheme, with the 5th academic year of operation giving 5 years of data being timely to review and inform the case. Despite the results of the scheme, they are still considered in need of maturity and development upon reflection - reasons given below in the case. Separately, it is difficult for HEIs to implement promotional and development schemes in China that reflect those in Western countries and from where they are, in the main, attempting to recruit staff – reasons being different labour laws, a lack of institutional maturity and cultural differences in terms of employer/employee power distances. The mission of *The Educational Provider* is to prepare students and to assist their educational progression abroad (at affiliated partners) viz. preparatory knowledge and skills for undergraduate degree studies – which is only possible based on the recruitment of staff with education and academic experience at such partner programmes abroad. The schemes were intended to underpin the mission, but management realised they were in further need of revision to remain attractive as an employer in an increasingly competitive higher education market.

Problem Statement

Increasing competition (see Sharma, 2021) faced by *The Educational Provider* to retain their staff forced senior management to re-think whether the promotion scheme (introduced in the year 2016) was sufficient – or even helpful – when most applicants would be unsuccessful in achieving a promotion and with abundant employment opportunities provided by the overall educational sector. A re-think occurred in 2022 by which time 10 long-term staff members had left and sought employment at competing HEIs (see *Environment* section). Their exit was viewed as a problem because of the long-term institutional knowledge they had, which was an invaluable contributor to the daily operations of *The Educational Provider*, particularly underpinning a healthy staff and student experience. The realisation is that not all who received promotions were necessarily going to stay and, further, that most of the staff who did not receive a promotion were essential for the operations of *The Educational Provider*. With much praise associated with traditional promotions and many unsuccessful yet valuable staff members at risk of leaving, the following question was asked:

Should successful or unsuccessful promotions be the focus of managers' attention?

In this case a successful promotion is defined as one where an individual who applied for promotion as part of a promotions scheme was promoted. An unsuccessful promotion is defined as one where an individual who applied for promotion as part of a promotions scheme was not promoted. The case argues for the importance in managers' attention to unsuccessful promotion to ensure employees are committed, engaged, and motivated as well as to ensure *The Educational Provider* has confidence in its distributive justice and procedural justice to assist the organization to achieve its goals.

Promotion Scheme Preparation

The scheme was initially discussed in 2015 in order to address the lack of a formal promotion system at *The Educational Provider* and formally began a year later by a process which introduced the aspects of role growth, development, and responsibility for the staff. The objectives of the promotional scheme as defined in the official documentation were intended to serve interests of staff, students, support departments (e.g., human resources) in both tangible (e.g., staff profiles and surveyed staff and student experiences) and non-tangible (e.g., goodwill, responsible leadership) aspects, to increase the retention of staff (to re-sign a multi-year contract) and students (for the duration of their undergraduate degree). Specifically, the problem of an increasingly competitive environment for the recruitment of academic talent needed to be addressed through the promotion scheme to ensure compliance with accreditation bodies and international quality standards, despite enjoying a reasonable staff retention rate. Further, the promotion scheme was intended to enhance the attractiveness of joining *The Educational Provider* and enhance employee commitment and retention rates - with the aim of retaining all academic talent from an entry position to what would eventually be reviewed to that of a full Professorial post - to be achieved a decade out from the start date of the promotion scheme. The decision making that approved the promotion scheme was exclusively by senior academic administrators. There was no cap placed on the number of successful applicants promoted and a healthy budget to resource a no-cap promotions policy. A successful promotion scheme – with success defined on the basis of having no cap and in alignment with promotional criteria and outcomes of the foreign partners, was subsequently approved within the 2015 academic year. The profile of the promotion scheme included Lecturer to Assistant Professor promotions and Assistant Professor to Associate Professor promotions. Further plans for Associate Professor to Professor were intended to happen in the future with appropriate research contributions made to demonstrate the title. The sensitivity of the mixed success of the promotion scheme itself (specifics available in the end section of *Theory*) prevents further information/evidence being made available in this case.

Tenure (years)	Number of Employees	Instances of Successful Promotions *
10	3	3
8	15	3
7	10	1
6	7	5
5	5	1
4	10	4
3	10	1

Table 1: *The years of tenure, the number of employees and the instances of successful promotions from 2016 - 2021.*
** Instances of successful promotion are defined as a promotion per individual staff member. Each staff member receiving no more than one instance of promotion.*

Higher education environment in China

The higher education sector in China has experienced a significant massification and maturity (e.g., the ongoing improvement in quality of staff, systems, research output, student experience) – demonstrated by their rising rankings in world universities (Clark, 2021), resulting in a competitive market to hire and retain academic staff. Goodman's (2014) publication *Class in temporary China,* demonstrates the massification with undergraduate enrolments in higher education growing from 856,000 in 1978 to 23,085,078 in 2011. Currently, as part of a second phase of university massification, both private and public universities are now fiercely competing for staff, particularly in Guangdong province (Sharma, 2021). Staff recruitment and retention being constraints for success towards successful TNE programmes and partnerships towards 2030 was forewarned by Henderson's (2019) visions of successful Sino-Foreign University partnerships. *The Educational Provider* has lost 10 staff (approximately 17% of total staff) who all had tenure of 10 years e.g., in the three-year period April 2019-March 2022 to competing universities in Mainland China (note: staff currently no longer employed by *The Educational Provider* are not included in Table 1). All staff indicated competitive packages were reasons for leaving. It also raised more questions to the management about salary and conditions rather than promotions and professional development as drivers for departure (exit interviews were undertaken and information was retrieved for the motivations to leave *The Educational Provider*). Separately, border restrictions and exceptionally costly Covid-19-related international airfares into Mainland China since 2020 have caused a smaller pool of available candidates – with employers almost entirely recruiting academics from within Mainland China's borders – the recruitment market is more dynamic and complex due to the restrictions put in place to form a zero-Covid-19 policy.

Promotion Scheme Review

The promotions and professional development schemes adopted six years ago (September 2016) has resulted in the minority of applicants being successful (over 50 people applied with 18 people successful – no caps were applied to the number of successful applicants). Staff were also guided on how to apply. Separately, efforts have been made by the management since the Covid-19 pandemic to ensure staff have a good work-life balance that is family oriented and caters to an average staff profile (i.e., mid-career academic, full time Assistant Professor status) with a single child in primary school. Despite such efforts being made a hybrid work environment (e.g., working offline/online at the office and at home) is a constant discussion piece at informal management meetings to keep staff engaged. To achieve all operational targets, such as satisfactory student experience reviews and student award standing (i.e. a year on year improved percentage of good degrees) upon graduation from *The Educational Provider*, all staff must be committed: "*the first important element that any employees must have in order to boost productivity and efficiency of any organization*" (Salleh et al., 2016, p. 140), engaged: "*a state including vigor, dedication, and absorption, and describe the results of qualitative studies on the manifestation of engagement*" (Bakker, 2008, p. 2) offering extended office hours/support/review classes for students, and motivated: "*a management process of influencing behaviour based on the knowledge of what make people think*" (Salleh et al., 2016, p.139). Whether or not the current promotion scheme improved or worsened commitment, engagement and motivation was a question of *The Educational Provider.*

Theory

The topics of human resource policy and promotions are well published among both academic and practitioner journals. The published literature of unsuccessful promotions is an aspect not sufficiently discussed by evidence of the absence of published articles relating to the topic and is deserving of more attention given the impact (both positive and negative) employees can exert on organizational performance. A search on Google Scholar utilising the keywords *promotions* and *unsuccessful* yields Hofman (2005) research of incorrect promotions – i.e., an individual received a promotion yet did not have the competencies needed for the position, that Hofman (ibid) described as unsuccessful promotions. Note: Hofman's (ibid) definition differs from that of this case study (see definition on page 2, problem statement section). Separately, the work of Gustafsson and Swart (2020) profiles cases of individuals with narratives of their professional career progression and promotion – not all of which are positive experiences for those who are successfully promoted. The lack of voice given to individuals unsuccessfully promoted (see definition in page 2, the problem statement section), and their contribution to organizational performance targets – needs attention. Similar thoughts were brainstormed by the senior management of *The Educational Provider* that imagined the competitive ability of an organization if all staff were promoted to fulfilling potential. The conclusion was that unsuccessful promotions should be the focus of management's attention and a staff survey was issued to capture their views of the promotion scheme.

In addition to staff engagement, commitment, and motivation, the staff survey focused on perceptions of the distributive justice, being "*the economic, political, and social frameworks that each society has – its laws, institutions and policies etc. result in different distributions and benefits and burdens across members of the society*" (Stanford Encyclopedia of Philosophy, 2017) i.e. -survey questions regarding an equivalent application received the same outcome – either for both successful or unsuccessful promotions and procedural justice: "*people's perception of fairness is strongly impacted by the quality of their experiences and not only the end result of these experiences*" (Yale Law School, N.D.) - (i.e.. – survey questions regarding whether staff members have confidence in the governance and outcomes of the promotional system) to assess the overall fairness in the promotion scheme. The survey also focused on the exploration of non-applicants and their level of satisfaction with their current responsibilities, their confidence in the system and viewed worth of any increased responsibilities (e.g., equity theory: "*the perception of equitability and inequitability*" (Al-Zawahreh & Al-Madi, 2012, p.158) for a promotion. The survey findings suggested that perceptions had a 50% confidence rate in both distributive and procedural justice at *The Educational Provider*. The findings of non-applicants were equally mixed with satisfaction and dissatisfaction of distributive justice, procedural justice, and equity theory and that the increased responsibilities created worthiness for a promotion at *The Educational Provider*. Action was then taken in collaboration with the staff to improve their perceptions of *The Educational Provider*.

Actions taken

In response to the 10 long-serving staff members leaving and the survey results, the organization provided development opportunities with priority going to unsuccessful promotions as appropriate. The opportunities were a result of focus groups held and led by all the staff. These opportunities as suggested by the staff included the following:

- External engagement, including paid membership/tickets, or a platform to speak at such external events and raise *The Educational Provider* profile (e.g., American Chamber of Commerce Committee memberships).
- Research opportunities as well as conference attendances supported by appropriate financial funding.
- The adoption of Whitney and Trosten-Bloom's (2010) appreciative inquiry in all staff appraisals that are linked to a successful promotion, whereby all staff should not be assessed critically, but from a positive lens to contribute to organizational performance (e.g., focusing on the positive actions/potential of staff rather than their weakness/areas of development).

- The inclusion of the staff voice through initiatives such as staff surveys, interviews with individuals not promoted (as well as successful promotions post completion of the probation period for their new job). A staff survey was issued post academic year 2021-2022 to get further input (post-implementation of the promotion scheme.) The outcomes of the survey suggested *The Educational Provider* was viewed as making improvements as a caring employer in part due to the attention provided to those who were not promoted.
- A 360-degree annual appraisal on *The Educational Provider* led by the staff.
- A communication feedback loop for all initiatives to ensure transparency and understanding.

The actions taken were in part individually applied to staff members (at date August 2021 – including those who had informally indicated they had plans to leave *The Educational Provider*). The lack of formal promotion programme for the first five years of operations for *The Educational Provider* has been a needed area of development – with staff who have fulfilled in some cases ten years of commitment to the institute with a lack of career progression (reasons for staying varied but included family and the increasing qualification requirements for employment at other HEIs, and reasons for not getting promoted included the changing requirements for staffing and research outputs as required by accreditation bodies). The actions taken were now made by the senior managers with insight of the staff, their talent and potential.

Evaluation

The formal actions taken by the senior academic administrators have to date retained staff - defined as *"the effort by an employer to keep desirable workers in order to meet business objectives"* (Frank et al., 2004, p.13) and kept them engaged – defined as *"the emotional commitment the employee has to the organisation and its goals"* (Krause, 2012) – for renewal (to renew another short-term contract) in the most recently completed academic year (i.e., 2020-2021). There was a realisation that more actions and procedures were imperative in the longer term yet would need to be led by the staff themselves and would require significant research and resources to be effective in alignment with the broader goals of assisting organizational performance. More actions linked to procedures discussed included: linkages within appraisal schemes; a policy document devoted to unsuccessful and non-applicants; the participation of all staff in drafting such policy documents. Any other actions were open to discussion as it became apparent the concept of promotional policies may change as broader expectations of social behaviour (e.g., staff presenteeism and teamwork engagement), institutional norms in the public, private and voluntary sector become increasingly complex, and change as competition intensifies.

Conclusion

Promotional schemes are deeply embedded artifacts to drive employee retention, engagement, and organizational performance. Managers should be warned of the disadvantages of poorly implemented promotional schemes and should consider the impact of not paying attention to unsuccessful applicants. It is also important for managers to be optimistic about the ability of staff and integrate a management philosophy of appreciative inquiry in daily management practices and actions that build up and represent the broader promotions scheme (Whitney & Trosten-Bloom, 2010). Promotional schemes should be designed to capture the broader contributions made by staff.

References

Al-Zawahreh, A., & Al-Madi, F. (2012). The utility of equity theory in enhancing organizational effectiveness. *European journal of economics, finance, and administrative sciences*, *46*(3), 158-169. https://www.researchgate.net/profile/Faisal-Al-Madi/publication/267783009_The_Utility_of_Equity_Theory_in_Enhancing_Organizational_Effectiveness/links/59387072a6fdcc58ae5968bf/The-Utility-of-Equity-Theory-in-Enhancing-Organizational-Effectiveness.pdf

Bakker, A. (2008). Building engagement in the workplace. In *The peak performing organization* (pp. 96-118). Routledge. https://www.isonderhouden.nl/doc/pdf/arnoldbakker/articles/articles_arnold_bakker_204.pdf

Clark, E. (2021, August 16). Chinese higher education lays foundation for brighter future. *China.Org.Cn*. Retrieved from: http://www.china.org.cn/opinion/2021-08/16/content_77695653.htm

Frank, F.D., Finnegan, R.P., Taylor, C.R. (2004). The race for talent: retaining and engaging workers in the 21st century. *Human Resource Planning*, 27, (3), 12-25. https://citeseerx.ist.psu.edu/viewdoc/download?doi=10.1.1.514.4132&rep=rep1&type=pdf

Goodman, D. S. (2014). Class in contemporary China. John Wiley & Sons.

Gustafsson, S., & Swart, J. (2020). 'It's not all it's cracked up to be': Narratives of promotions in elite professional careers. *Human Relations*, 73(9), 1199-1225. https://core.ac.uk/download/pdf/210587673.pdf

Henderson, L. H. (2019). Envisioning Successful Sino-Foreign Universities in 2030: Considerations for Current and Prospective Partnerships. *In Futures Thinking and Organizational Policy* (pp. 201-223). Palgrave Macmillan, Cham. https://doi.org/10.1007/978-3-319-94923-9_10

Hofmann, P. B. (2005). Responsibility for unsuccessful promotions. Inappropriate promotions result in ethical and personal costs to people and their organizations. *Healthcare executive*, 20(1), 32-33.

Krause, K (2012, June 22). *What is employee engagement?* Forbes. Retrieved from: https://www.forbes.com/sites/kevinkruse/2012/06/22/employee-engagement-what-and-why/?sh=d4908347f372

Peter, L. J., & Hull, R. (1969). *The peter principle* (No. 04; RMD, PN6231. M2 P4.). London: Souvenir Press. https://keinding.com/onewebmedia/The%20Peter%20Principle%20%28%20PDFDrive%20%29.pdf

Salleh, S. M., Zahari, A. S. M., Said, N. S. M., & Ali, S. R. O. (2016). The influence of work motivation on organizational commitment in the workplace. *Journal of Applied Environmental and Biological Sciences, 6*(58), 139-143. https://www.researchgate.net/profile/Suzila-Mat-Salleh/publication/305637762_The_Influence_of_Work_Motivation_on_Organizational_Commitment_in_the_Workplace/links/606e8c58299bf1c911b6422f/The-Influence-of-Work-Motivation-on-Organizational-Commitment-in-the-Workplace.pdf

Sharma, Y. (2021, March 13). So many new universities – Where will the staff come from? *World University News*. Retrieved from: https://www.universityworldnews.com/post.php?story=20210310102053217

Stanford Encyclopedia of Philosophy. (2017, Sept 26). *Distributive Justice.* Retrieved from: https://plato.stanford.edu/entries/justice-distributive/index.html

Whitney, D. D., & Trosten-Bloom, A. (2010). *The power of appreciative inquiry: A practical guide to positive change*. Berrett-Koehler Publishers. https://positivechange.org/wp-content/uploads/2014/04/Why-AI-Works-2010-22-pgs.pdf

Yale Law School. (N.D.). The Justice Collaboratory. Procedural Justice. Retrieved from: https://law.yale.edu/justice-collaboratory/procedural-justice

Discussion questions

1. How do your organization's customers benefit from your employee promotion scheme(s) and what evidence do you have in answering the question?

2. In addition to the points made in the business case,
   - how could promotional schemes be counterproductive and what are the implications for an organization's performance?

3. What are the benefits and limitations of internal (i.e., the employees and senior management) and/or external (e.g., customers, suppliers, investors, etc.) stakeholders getting involved in the development/review of promotional schemes?

4. Utilise the three forms of benchmarking to brainstorm examples of promotional schemes.
   - Internal benchmarking – a comparison of practices within a single organisation (e.g., customer service reviews for a McDonald's franchise in London to one in Shanghai).
   - External benchmarking - a comparison of practices within an industry to competitors (e.g., customer service reviews for McDonalds compared to Burger King).
   - Best practices benchmarking- a comparison of practices across all industries for an ability that is world renown (e.g., customer service reviews comparison of McDonalds to Ritz Carlton).

5. What can organisations do to counter the Peter Principle, the concept where individuals are competent in roles and continue to be promoted to roles until they are unsuccessful in a role (i.e., incompetent) at which point promotional opportunities cease (Peter & Hull, 1969).

6. Will and should organizations in the future prioritise internal promotions?

Strategies for Attracting TikTok Customers: A Case Study of Online Calligraphy Courses

Yuanyuan Zhang
Entrepreneur: Xifan Laoshi Jiaoxiezi

John Storm
Senior Lecturer: The University of Aberdeen, United Kingdom

Abstract

Micro-entities are vulnerable to being inadvertently impacted by policy shifts that seek to bring change in what may appear an unrelated area. Set in a context of turbulent change, this case examples how Design Thinking and AISAS models may be applied to facilitate the transition of a traditionally offline business model to gain a growing online presence on the TikTok platform.

Introduction and context

Xifan Laoshi Jiaoxiezi (herein referred to as Xifan) is a micro-entity delivering calligraphy training workshops to students in Shanghai, comprising a single entrepreneur, Western scholars may characterise Xifan as being part of the gig economy due to it offering services part-time as a means of diversifying income streams beyond stable employment. Interpretation of China's labour law is less clear however as 'independent contractor' status does not exist in China (Wei and MacDonald, 2021), with factors such as content ownership, control of materials, responsibility for social security provisions and the degree of subordination of labour to capital being important defining points for one's 'permanent' employment status (Wang and Wang, 2018; Wang, 2017; Wu *et al*, 2019).

Whereas transmitting information is the fundamental purpose of writing, calligraphy seeks to expand the information beyond words on a page to convey a greater sense of emotion (Halimi, 2021). Recognised as a visual art, calligraphy is a medium of artistic expression that allows one practising it to cultivate and communicate their ideas of morality, personality and thinking as creators of text (He, 2018). The long lifecycle of calligraphy reveals distinct periods of evolution and change that allow readers to understand the characteristics of a particular era in time (Halimi, 2021).

Formal study of calligraphy has not been a core component of curriculums in Chinese schools. Within a culture that prioritises formal study perceived to enhance financial or career prospects, this not only limits interest for learning calligraphy, but also reduces sources of stable employment for calligraphers. Art education as a genre in China is itself complicated. As Chang (2005) comments, art is a component of cultural identity, and given China's extensive 5,000 years of history there is a trade-off regarding focus points for educators. The trade-off has been further complicated since Deng Xiaoping's 'Open Door Policy' resulted in a significant influx of Western ideas and philosophies that need to be balanced with local ones. The outcome may be an appearance of apathy, with art educators in China being accused of teaching in a perfunctory manner (Dou, 2015). The result is that calligraphy is regularly perceived as an extra-curricular activity that may be integrated into a wider art programme delivered via off-campus training institutions. For Xifan, as at Q1 2021 this business model has placed dependence upon external partners that recruit 70% of Xifan's clients yet claim 50% of associated gross revenues. Furthermore, integration into a larger programme exposed Xifan to regulatory changes that came into effect in July 2021. The resulting clampdown on institutions offering non-traditional educational packages saw this business model – irrespective of its own challenges – cease to be a legitimate option. Although small in size and scale, this paper overviews key trends impacting the calligraphy training sector and studies pro-active actions that Xifan has taken to grow during this period of turbulent change.

Formulating the problem

In July 2021, the Ministry of Education of China issued new regulations to reduce various pressures on students and parents associated with societal expectations to engage in costly extra-curricular activities (Bishop, 2021;

Ministry of Education, 2021a, 2021b). Training institutions across China were impacted, with many closing down. Whilst calligraphy was not targeted within the Government mandate, calligraphy workshops had regularly been integrated into larger programmes that were cull victims. This resulted in Xifan losing 70% of its client base.

Government policy may sometimes be favourable for calligraphy providers. From August 2011, the Ministry of Education has issued several opinion pieces on calligraphy education with the explicit view that calligraphy education should be reinforced as a core foundation in the basic education stages (Wu *et al*, 2021). From 2019, writing proficiency has received increased emphasis in elementary school tests, with handwriting being a noticeable component (Shanghai Education Bureau, 2019). Whilst elementary school children have not been a target market for Xifan, policy change has created a stimulant that may indirectly drive demand for calligraphy classes at this age demographic. Equally, targeting this different end consumer would require a shift in delivery methodology to cater for the different needs and learning styles of a significantly younger audience.

China's online education market has gained noticeable traction in recent years (Zhou *et al*, 2020), providing commercial opportunities for the 75 million people in China who view digital platforms as a source of work (State Information Center, 2019). The single platform, TikTok, is China's largest online social media platform with 800 million active daily users (Bain & Company, 2021). As highlighted by Feigua Data (2021), the ability for TikTok to link content to a large number of potential users provides significant opportunities in e-commerce. One function in TikTok is the ability for content creators to sell courses and related products upon accumulation of 1,000 confirmed fans.

Following the drop in clientele caused by regulatory change, online revenue streams had grown to account for 10% of Xifan's monthly revenues as at July 2021. This reveals that whilst Xifan had not been absent online, online presence had not been a focal point. However, following significant changes as detailed above, growing online sales gained importance as a medium for attracting new customers to compensate for the loss of traditional clientele. Illustrated in Figure 1, Michael Porter's Five Force Framework was utilised to kickstart exploration into the business case for investing time, effort, and finances into TikTok. Although Five Forces may only facilitate a surface level analysis of a business case at a specific point of time (Lynch, 2006), it highlighted the scope of opportunity available. It was also noted that whilst regulatory change may push more content creators on to platforms like TikTok, lack of videography skills within the aging supplier base would limit this risk. Contrastingly, Xifan founders' experience in having studied courses in video editing offers a potential advantage, as it would reduce the influence of one of the main barriers to entry.

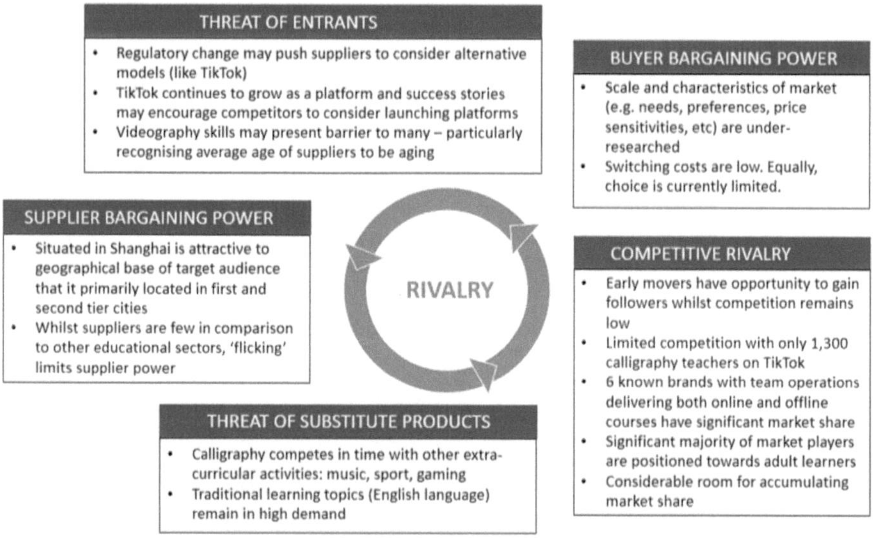

Figure 1: *Applying Five Forces to TikTok*

Supported by Government policy and pushed into everyday lives by the pandemic, online learning took significant leaps forward during 2020 (Zhou et al, 2020). Specifically pursuing TikTok as a platform for acquiring new online customers is merited by the significant growth of the platform. In May 2020, TikTok daily playback volume was 100 million videos. By August 2020 the daily playback volume had multiplied tenfold to achieve 1 billion videos (Bain & Company, 2020). With only 1,300 content creators competing in the market, project questions formulated as following: what are the needs of online target customers? What are the characteristics of an attractive online course? What are the characteristics of an attractive online persona? How to operate a TikTok account effectively to increase fanbase and important performance metrics, such as number of comments, frequency of shares, number of fans, etc?

Combining the core questions, the project aim therefore became, how might we develop the best strategy for attracting TikTok customers (aged 5-8) to take Xifan calligraphy courses online?

Application of theoretical frameworks

The project revolved around the application of two theoretical frameworks. Developed by Dentsu Corporation in Japan and comprising 5 steps 'Attention, Interest, Search, Action and Share', the AISAS model facilitates understanding of user purchase behaviour by supporting research and problem-solving in the internet era (Xu, Hao, and Han, 2017; Zhang and Tan, 2020). AISAS orientates itself towards understanding consumer engagement and interaction with online content. This is facilitated through analysis of consumer comments, feedback, and transfer of content (which may for example be demonstrated by sharing a link). This is not entirely dissimilar to evaluating teaching quality, which is determined by exploring the degree of response, feedback and sharing of students on provided content. AISAS therefore offers a model that may align with conventional methods of evaluating teacher performance, but most importantly offers a model that may be applied in the internet age. This is achieved via the 'Share' component, which is a continuation of action equivalent to the traditional word-of-mouth effect and thus an important metric for measuring consumer engagement, interest, and perception of value (Javed, Rashidin and Xiao, 2020).

As a framework to steer stakeholder engagement during the project, Design Thinking was used. Consisting of the 5 core phases, 'Empathy, Define, Ideate, Prototype, and Test', Design Thinking offers a framework for exploring creative solutions to an ambiguous problem. It presumes that core facets of a problem scenario are not known, and that understanding of a complex issue may only be achieved via first gaining an in-depth understanding of perspectives across a range of stakeholder groups –

enveloped by its distinctive first phase 'Empathy' (Storm, 2021a, 2021b; Luka, 2014). Carlgren, Elmquist and Rauth (2016) highlight several barriers when implementing Design Thinking within an institutional context, particularly relating to challenges in adopting new ideas within a group setting where mindset and perception towards risk may vary. However, within a context of an individual initiating a project within a new landscape and expecting to encounter new perspectives and ways of thinking, several of these perceived barriers offered a comparable reassurance in the given context.

Actions taken

During August – December 2021, the following actions were taken to address the challenge:

- Seven hypotheses were developed to direct primary research that explored the needs and characteristics of the opportunity.
- Parents were identified as a key stakeholder group due to their position as decision maker for what their respective elementary child would study out of school. Twenty parents known to have interest in calligraphy lessons for their children responded to a survey, with a further eight parents being interviewed to explore findings at a deeper level. Two calligraphy teachers were also interviewed to explore observations and trends that they may have noticed from their relevant clientele.
- Findings were analysed and key learning points reflected on. An example observation was that parents discussing price in-person communicated comfort with a price range ten times higher than parents who responded anonymously to the survey.
- 5 videos were developed to prototype different teaching styles in effort to incrementally edge towards the most 'attractive' delivery. Variables within the prototype video included: degree of linkage with elementary school textbooks; use of story-telling tools to animate character development; degree of emphasis on stroke and font structures; use of split screen verses regular screen viewing; degree of emphasis shown towards evaluating standards;

perception towards video length; type of clothing worn during presentation, etc.

- Performance of uploaded videos was quantified by likes, comments and shares. Upon reflection with AISAS model and relating observations with previously received feedback, a proposed format was ready for testing.

Evaluation

Twenty new videos were published over a ninety-day period in Autumn 2021 that resulted in the following metrics – visualised in Figure 2. (1) increase in TikTok account fans from 586 to 2058, equating to a higher fan base than 93.3% of similar creators. (2) Most viewed video during the month of November was played 6,671 times, stated as being higher than 85.77% of similar creators, and (3) over 50% of viewers were aged 31-40, indicating that the videos are appropriately positioned towards those of elementary child' parent age.

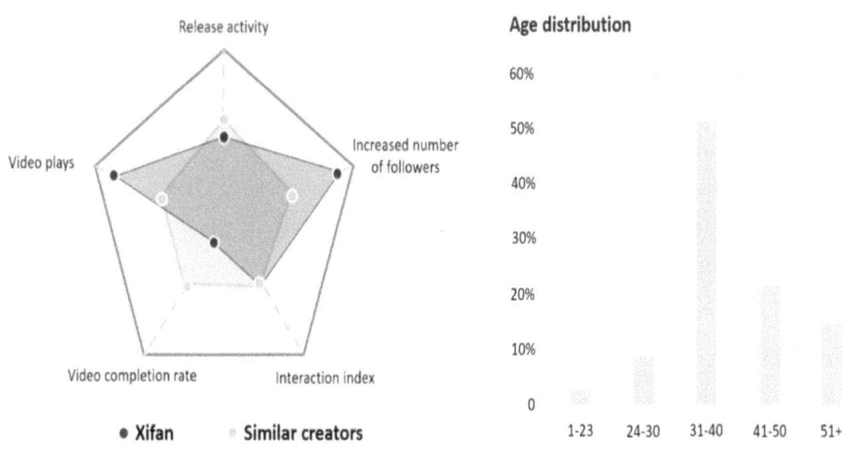

Figure 2: *Activity performance shown by TikTok backend*

Equally, TikTok revealed that other content creators are posting more regularly and that viewers are more consistently completing their videos. Upon reflection, it was noted that Xifan's usage of the AISAS model may have focused attention towards 'attracting' viewers, but not necessarily holding viewer focus. With some viewers flicking to another channel within just 5 seconds, the findings highlight need to make the first 3 seconds more stimulating to maintain '*Interest*' beyond gaining initial viewer '*Attention*'.

The initial goal of achieving 1,000 fans to enable commercialisation of course material on TikTok was achieved and doubled at an unexpected pace. Whilst recognising limitations during the implementation period, this has been interpreted as demonstrating the effectiveness of the taken approach - steered by use of the AISAS and Design Thinking models. In the 3 months following this project, Zhang Yuanyuan, founder of Xifan has consulted for another TikTok channel and supported growth to 3,000 fans by applying the same models. The importance of bringing value to the audience, as perceived '*by*' the audience, has been an essential learning point during the project process.

The final key learning from the project was that stakeholder engagement should neither be rushed nor focused on volume of contributors. Quality of contributor, combined with thoughtful analysis that follows up initial rounds of primary research to explore early findings to a deeper level is critical to determine meaningful results and the underlying assumptions behind observations. The circular process of returning to key stakeholders throughout information gathering and several rounds of prototyping, although giving the appearance of being intensely time consuming, provides opportunity for generating an effective output that could not have been reasonably expected without the initial time investment.

Conclusion

Micro-entities are more vulnerable than larger companies to being inadvertently impacted by policy shifts that seek to bring change in what may appear an unrelated area. Set in a context of turbulent change, this case has exampled how Design Thinking and AISAS models may be applied to facilitate the transition of a traditionally offline business model to gain a growing online presence. Whereas scholars have critiqued the limitations of these models when applied in larger organisations with thousands of employees, they facilitate a quick and responsive framework for incremental improvement that may be viewed positively for micro-entities that face less institutional resistances. Equally, as revealed by the over-emphasis towards '*Attention*' in the AISAS model, project teams with viewer voices may over-emphasise a particular aspect of a model, thus failing to utilise the full value of a given approach. Ultimately however the approach taken not only enabled Xifan to achieve the project goal, but to double the targeted output within a very short period of time, therefore advantageously positioning Xifan ahead of competitors seeking to transition their models to a similar mechanism for replacing lost sales.

References

Bain & Company., (2021) *FACT 经营矩阵 激发兴趣电商新增量 – 2021 抖音电商商家经营方法论白皮书*. Available from: https://www.bain.cn/pdfs/202105190303414094.pdf (Accessed 21st March, 2022)

Bishop, R., (2021) Burden of Homework and Off-campus Training on Students in Compulsory Education Stage. Available from: https://www.appinchina.co/government-documents/opinions-on-further-easing-the-burden-of-homework-and-off-campus-training-on-students-in-compulsory-education-stage/ (Accessed 21st March, 2022)

Carlgren, L., Elmquist, M., & Rauth, I., (2016) The Challenges of Using Design Thinking in Industry – Experiences from Five Large Firms, *Creativity and Innovation Management*, Vol 25 (3), pp.344-362.

Chang, R., (2005) Culture and Art Education in China, *International Journal of Education through Art*. Vol 1 (3). DOI: 10.1386/etar.1.3.225/1.

Dou, X., (2015)The Problem and Reform of Art and Design Education in Colleges and Universities in China, *Creative Education*. Vol 6 (20). DOI:: 10.4236/ce.2015.620227

Feigua Data., (2021) *2021 上半年：短视频及电商生态研究报告*. Available from: https://www.bj-xinghe.com/wp-content/uploads/2021/08/2021%E4%B8%8A%E5%8D%8A%E5%B9%B4%E7%9F%AD%E8%A7%86%E9%A2%91%E5%8F%8A%E7%94%B5%E5%95%86%E7%94%9F%E6%80%81%E7%A0%94%E7%A9%B6%E6%8A%A5%E5%91%8A.pdf (Accessed 21st March, 2022)

Halimi, N., (2021) From Written Word to Art / Calligraphy, *PHILOSOPHICA International Journal of Social and Human Sciences*. Vol 15, pp.78-86.

He, W., (2018) Research on Calligraphy Teaching Reform under Quality Education in China. **In:** 8th International Conference on Education,

Management, Computer and Society (EMCS, 2018). Available from: https://webofproceedings.org/proceedings_series/ESSP/EMCS%202018/EMCS15202.pdf

Javed, S., Rashidin, S., & Xiao, Y., (2021) Investigating the Impact of Digital Influencers on Consumer Decision-Making and Content Outreach: Using Dual AISAS Model, *Economic Research-Ekonomska Istraživanja*, pp.1-28. DOI: 10.1080/1331677X.2021.1960578

Luka, I., (2014) Design Thinking in Pedagogy, *Journal of Education Culture and Society*. No.2, pp.63-74.

Lynch, R., (2006) *Corporate Strategy*, 4th Ed. Harlow: Pearson Education Limited.

Ministry of Education., (2021a) *中共中央办公厅 国务院办公厅印发《关于进一步减轻义务教育阶段学生作业负担和校外培训负担的意见》*. Available from: http://www.moe.gov.cn/jyb_xwfb/gzdt_gzdt/s5987/202107/t20210724_546566.html (Accessed 10 November 2021).

Ministry of Education., (2021b) *教育部办公厅关于进一步明确义务教育阶段校外培训学科类和非学科类范围的通知*. Available from: http://www.moe.gov.cn/srcsite/A29/202107/t20210730_547807.html (Accessed 10 November 2021).

Shanghai Education Bureau., (2019) 2019 年写字等级考试考生信息上报通知. Available from: https://kszx.qpedu.cn/qsxx/jtks/331764.htm (Accessed 17 February 2022).

State Information Center., (2019) *中国共享经济发展年度报告(2019)*. Available from: http://www.sic.gov.cn/News/557/9904.htm (Accessed 17 February 2022).

Storm, J., (2021a) A Design Thinking Workshop to Kickstart Sustainability Initiatives: For Entrepreneurs and SME Leaders. **In:** *EdMedia+ Innovate Learning*. Online. Proceedings pp.407-412.

Storm, J., (2021b) Developing A Design Thinking Mind-set to Stimulate Sustainable Development in Chinese SMEs. **In:** *Proceedings of the IIBG Academic-Industry Exchange 2021 Conference on Business as Usual: How do we Turn the New Normal into Normal*. Hong Kong. Proceedings pp.43-67.

Wang, Q., (2017) Pre Limitations Thinking on Labor Employment Forms and Labor Relations Under the Background of "Internet +". *China Labor*. Vol 08, pp.7– 8.

Wang, Q., & Wang, Q., (2018) The Labor Relationship Identification and Rights Protection of my Country's "Online Hire Workers", *Law Science*. Vol 04, pp.57– 72.

Wei, W., MacDonald, I., (2021) Modeling the Job Quality of 'Work Relationships' in China's Gig Economy, *Asia Pacific Journal of Human Resources*. https://doi.org/10.1111/1744-7941.12310

Wu, S., Wang, J., & Wan, X., (2021) Construction and Implementation of Calligraphy Course in Normal Universities From the Perspective of Aesthetic Education—Taking Leshan Normal University for Example. **In:** *7th International Conference on Social Science and Higher Education (ICSSHE 2021)* (pp. 415-419). Atlantis Press.

Wu, Q., Zhang, H., Li, Z., & Liu, K., (2019) Labor Control in the Gig Economy: Evidence from Uber in China, *Journal of Industrial Relations*. Vol 61(4), pp.574– 596. https://doi.org/10.1177%2F0022185619854472

Xu, C., Hao, Q., & Han, G., (2017) Research on the Marketing Strategy of the New Media Age Based on AISAS Model: A Case Study of Micro Channel Marketing. **In:** Li, X., & Xu, X., (eds) Proceedings of the Fourth International Forum on Decision Sciences. Uncertainty and Operations Research. Springer, Singapore.

Zhang, C., & Tan, T., (2020) The Impact of Big Data Analysis on Consumer Behavior. *Journal of Physics: Conference Series*. Vol 1544 (1). IOP Publishing.

Zhou, L., Wu, S., Zhou, M., & Li, F., (2020) 'School's Out, but Class is On', the Largest Online Education in the World Today: Taking China's Practical Exploration During The Covid-19 Epidemic Prevention and Control as an Example, *Best Evid Chin Edu*. Vol 4(2), pp.501-519. DOI: 0.15354/bece.20.ar023.

Discussion questions

1. The key disruptor impacting Xifan was change to a national policy that was not intended to harm companies like Xifan. What can small-to-medium sized businesses do to keep themselves informed of government policy and insulate themselves from being negatively impacted by policy change?

2. The above case mentioned that Design Thinking may incur several barriers if applied withing an institutional context, particularly with regards to drawing consensus between a large and diverse group of stakeholders. Does the size of a team / number of stakeholders engaged really impact the usability of a framework like Design Thinking? Justify your opinion.

3. Models such as AISAS and Design Thinking may assist project teams with structuring their processes and way of doing things. Equally, as revealed in this case, a project team may become overly focused towards a particular stage in a model in a way that is not always constructive or positive. What can project leads do to ensure a balance between effectiveness and optimal efficiency?

The Gradual Demise of a Global Entity

H W D Gunaratna
Senior Executive: Top 5 Technology Company

Abstract

This case explores the gradual demise in China of a well-known European brand, anonymised as Technology Business Corporation Limited (TBC or TBC Ltd), that held a 40% market share in key technology sectors. A reactionary decision to a policy change of China's government triggered widespread discontent amongst expatriate employees within a strategically important department. As China's macro-landscape changed from being a centre for export manufacturers towards a maturing market with its own demands and increasing volumes of local competitors, core talents were poached by competition who reversed established advantages of TBC.

The case highlights how business failure is often unattributable to a single decision but may result from a series of events that has negative consequence. Focusing on events within China and wider Asia, the case further highlights challenges for multinational firms including: the need to balance local needs with global pressures; maintaining investment to adapt locally versus reduced domestic market share; how local competitor pressures mature as a local economy develops; and how multinational firms may be caught out by paradigm shifts that transform the historical norms of how an industry behaves.

TBC Ltd, a global technological company

At the turn of the century, TBC Ltd was a prominent European technological products developer with more than 40,000 employees (Figure

1)[4]. TBC's product portfolio was wide and deep, with customers from multiple industries such as manufacturing, telecom, railways, oil, aviation, and emerging technologies. TBC held significant market share across global information technologies sectors and its brand was positively associated with robust and long-lasting products.

TBC	Turnover (£Bn) 2003	Turnover (£Bn) 2004	Market Share	Number of Employees
Global	13.5	14.1	~41%	42,000
China	2.9	3.1	~40%	10,200

Figure 1: *TBC Global and TBC China turnover, market share, and employees 2003-2004*

Human capital, referring to the knowledge, skills, abilities, and other characteristics of employees that generate value within an organisation, is particularly important within technology firms where innovation and technology management are essential to maintaining long-term success (Banerjee, 2013).

Employee satisfaction at TBC was generally high, and employees from specific research and development specialisms were frequently mentioned at prestigious technical events, such as ITU Telecom World and 3GSM World Congress. As internally developing key employees can foster a positive culture towards innovation and continued learning (Banerjee, 2013), senior research and development leaders graduated to become business leaders, and engineering was perceived a core strength at TBC. The company's unwritten values were hard work, commitment and passion, and employees were clear about those values. Successful long-term employees who became figureheads and leaders demonstrated these behaviours through their working practices and style.

---

[4] To maintain anonymity, the company is referred to as 'TBC'. Several items of data are drawn from company reports as well as from the personal experiences of the author and other individuals close at hand. However, sources are only provided when able to maintain anonymity.

The Asia Pacific headquarters of TBC was based in Beijing, with branches focusing on the China market present in several provinces. The company also maintained five corporate hubs worldwide, and the Asian corporate hub was in Shanghai, alongside a large manufacturing plant. The Shanghai region corporate hub was a large campus that supported regional business development, training, demonstration centres, research and development labs and testing centres. The corporate hub was a familiar location to expatriates throughout Shanghai, foreign employees, and contracted consultants.

When establishing a presence within mainland China, important things to consider include situation in a trade zone, trade policy, connectivity with national transportation infrastructure and local government relationships (Ambler *et al*, 2016; Atherton and Smallbone, 2013). These factors were critical criteria for TBC, who invested significant financial capital in Shanghai's corporate hub with long-term prospects in mind.

The 90s to mid-2000s – China

It has long been recognised that leadership performance is impacted by situational variables and that change in a performance metric as a result of leadership decision may lag quite significantly beyond the time a decision was made (Lieberson and O'Connor, 1972).

In the mid-90s, TBC'S leadership team identified prospects and challenges in respect of the China market and decided to establish a unique legal structure to manage China operations. As visualised in Figures 2 and 3, the structure consisted of functional areas that were either composed from TBC Global or through local partnerships. As a legal entity, TBC was the major shareholder. Products, corporate and research functions were led by TBC and local leaders managed sales - and human resource-related functions. TBC-China President's role was primarily ceremonial and nominated by majority shareholders, with the President also as leader of the board of directors. Furthermore, TBC Global appointed a Managing Director (MD) who was accountable for TBC China's performance. The MD was also a member of the board as a non-voting member.

Shareholder	Percentage
TBC Ltd	45
Local partners	41
Employees	14

Figure 2: *TBC China's legal and shareholder structure*

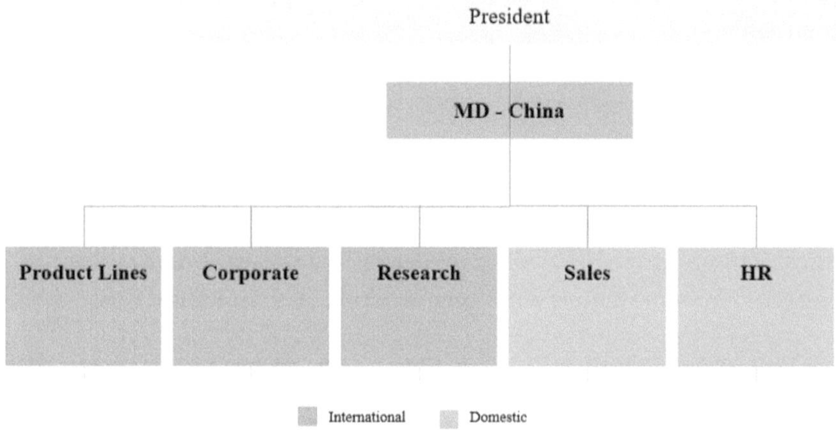

Figure 3: *Organisational structure*

Annual growth rates in China's economy heated up in the early 2000's, raising from 8.5% GDP growth in 2000, peaking at 14.2% annual growth in 2007 (Worldbank, 2022). During this period, local markets started to expand and transform. Products from local Chinese competitor organisations gained increasing presence in competitive biddings. Legacy factors such as an established brand, trusted leadership and reputation for know-how supported TBC amongst an increasingly competitive environment. However, 2007 evidenced the beginnings of an enduring economic downturn (IMF, 2009). As a multinational entity, TBC was significantly impacted by global events. TBC's China manufacturing plant recorded lower orders and the global predicament gained priority attention from leadership. Conversely, the Chinese economy was still growing – albeit at a slower pace (Worldbank, 2022) – and local companies continually improved their business models to become increasingly resilient and competitive.

Undisturbed by global events, local competitors had distinct advantages from political, economic, social, and grounded technical ecosystems (CKGSB, 2014; Froese *et al*, 2021). For example, they were able to concentrate on and be focused towards a single market. They were also able to capitalise on localised relationships with key domestic decision makers in finance and policy. Alongside China's rapid economic growth, consumer markets similarly matured. This resulted in consumers increasingly expecting features distinct from other market geographies, which for TBC resulted in increased engineering cost for local unit sales as units could not be easily sold to other regions. Furthermore, local quality standards emerged, resulting in increased costs relating to product development, intellectual property, and production processes.

With costs mounting, TBC found itself forced to either reduce margins or suffer from reduced price competitiveness, the end result being that TBC started to lose market share and important large-scale deals. As challenges grew, the China sales teams started complaining about the growing disparity of product requirements and pricing. Customers continued to demand additional features and standards at the same time as they were expecting prices to remain competitive, exacerbating bottom line pressures. Even though TBC continued to invest in China, global leaders were also losing confidence in future returns.

For large organisations with repute, changing environments may lead to high-level debates internally with increasing frequency of tussles between regional and global leadership (Blazejewski and Dorow, 2004). For TBC, growing market uncertainty, lack of clarity and inability to foresee the importance of investing into core technical areas of the business resulted in serious performance issues for the organisation.

Triggering future woes

Within the Shanghai Regional Hub, there were two main classifications of internal employees: local and foreign. In 2009, the proportion of foreign employees was between 4-5%, and they faced challenges in healthcare, children's education, housing, and living costs. For example, local schools did not accept foreign passport holders, and international school tuition fees were expensive (St. James's Place Wealth Management, 2018). There were also communications and treatment issues from local hospitals. Foreigners preferred English-speaking doctors but the number of hospitals and clinics employing English speaker doctors was few and tended to be expensive (Expatfinancials, 2021). Within this context of rising costs of each foreign employee, the TBC leadership team offered individual healthcare insurance to foreign employees from an early stage. Children's education benefits were limited to higher grade employees.

Although foreign employees represented a small percentage of TBC's workforce, they were not representative of average employees. Foreign employees in China may be stereotyped as highly incentivised and highly skilled talents, not easily replaceable within domestic talents pools. They either demonstrate ability within a critical technical function or assume a senior management position.

For decades, TBC had a slogan, "*our people make the most powerful products*" on their customer presentations. This slogan was envisaged to inspire all employees and to recognise employees' contribution to each of TBCs products that made it to market. The following section exemplifies how organisational statements can quickly become disconnected from reality.

In November 2009, the Director of Human Resources (HR) sent an email to foreign employees giving an update about healthcare benefits. The email (replicated to be anonymous in Figure 4) mentioned that the existing health insurance policy had to be cancelled due to government regulations. Instead, an alternative insurance plan was introduced with drastically reduced benefit packages. Emails were sent to individual employees, which were interpreted as forcing the employees to accept the proposed insurance plan.

EMAIL	
To: all foreign employees	From: Human Resources Director
Priority: High	Date: 2009-11-12
Re: update about healthcare benefits	

Dear all,
Initially, the PRIME health benefits package was introduced to foreign employees working in China. Last month HR leadership team decided to replace the PRIME health benefits package with a local insurance services provider from Jan 01, 2010. Based on HR understanding, locally established companies cannot offer foreign insurance benefits such as PRIME health benefits.
New insurance agents will reach you next week for your details, and there will be a briefing session about the new insurance plan on Nov 20, 2009.

Best,
Director – HR
TBC - China

Figure 4: *Director of Human Resources email to all foreign employees*

The reception of this change may be exampled through the case of Mathew[5], a solution designer from the cloud technologies department of TBC China. Mathew was a key contributor to the Asian region business development. Married and with three children, he was deeply disappointed about the situation alluded to in the email (Figure 4). He replied to the Director of HR requesting a discussion and clarification

[5] Matthew represents a real individual employed at TBC. His name has been changed for anonymity.

around some key questions. There was no reply to his email, nor to those from several other foreign employees also asking for more details.

Two months after the Director of HR's email, the Compensations and Benefits Director provided additional information, saying that insurance costs were escalating due to the strengthening of the Chinese Yuan (CFA Institute, 2017) and explained that HR had decided to reduce the total insurance costs by transitioning to a local insurance partner.

When communicating around sensitive topics, timeliness of communication, honesty and empathy would directly influence the satisfaction of those engaged (Strong *et al*, 2001) and it seems reasonable to assume this should have been particularly appreciated by those working in technology and telecommunications.

Ultimately, slow communication and sense of exclusion from decision making resulted in demotivation amongst the expatriate staff, who started to discuss informally within their own groups away from management. Some significantly impacted employees escalated complaints to higher level management. However, no immediate solutions were proposed. Management indicated the company budget forecast was closed for the year. Local HR had no further clarification or communications. Finally, expatriate employees were forced to accept reduced insurance benefits, and HR were able to reduce their costs.

Internal problems coincide with growing competition

Mathew, introduced above, had started his career in Germany with TBC as an intern and felt a strong emotional connection with the company. New Competing Entity Limited (NCE), an anonymised emerging competitor within the industry, had recently attempted to headhunt Mathew. On discussing his thought to leave TBC, his manager had successfully persuaded Matthew to stay by negotiating a counteroffer that included attractive long-term prospects – although no solutions to health insurance concerns. However, Mathew had become frustrated and believed that the company's values were no longer consistent with his own. Matthew reconnected with NCE and moved. In 2010, over 20 talented and experienced employees resigned and moved to NCE Ltd. Within TBC's Emerging Technologies Department, 40% of employees resigned to work with competing firms (Figure 5). They were known to be creative, skilled, experienced, and well-travelled professionals – highly attractive to upcoming competitor organisations.

Emerging Department (talent pool)	2009	2010
Senior Solutions Designers	10	6
Senior Business Devlopers	5	3
Junior Solutions Designers	12	7
Other roles	20	12

Figure 5: *Emerging technologies department talent pool*

The specific case of the Emerging Technologies Department is particularly important. Reduced capacity and specialist expertise started affecting TBC's ability to resource its emerging technologies – frequently viewed as the growth engine for technology firms within a mid- to long-term horizon. As commented above, there tends to be a lag between leadership decision and performance. The downward trend for TBC's ability to bid for projects in Asia involving emerging technologies was therefore foreseeable. By 2011, NCE Ltd had started its emerging technology business in Asia and, within three years, had become a prominent player in emerging technologies in Asia.

Understanding market behaviour in technology industries

The following section introduces the key concepts of market references and incumbency advantage, which are key factors for gauging long-term performance of a technology firm. Exampled within the context of Cloud technologies, an emerging technology that underwent significant demand during the same period of internal turmoil as previously introduced, the case demonstrates how challenges from one department (in this case HR, with a decision originally derived from an external government policy change) may result in further challenges in other critical areas of a business:

Market references:

Market references are recent wins in a certain technological area. If the reference is related to a specific customer who is a technology leader in a particular industry, it can have great value. Vendors may advertise those wins as success stories and become technology partners of leading customers (HP, 2020). When it comes to new technologies, market references are essential. Customers like to follow peers and success stories of implementations and turnarounds. At the same time, new vendors desire to get market references to prove their capabilities.

Company	Market references in 2010	Market reference in 2011	Market References 2012
TBC Ltd	8	4	1
Local Players	3	4	5
NCE Ltd	0	3	9

Figure 6: *TBC Ltd market references*

Sourced from internal records of TBC, Figure 6 illustrates a comparison of market references in emerging technologies in Asia. Noticeably, TBC's prominence as market leader radically reversed within a 2-year period. As new product development cycles radically changed from 10–15-year cycles to 2–5-year cycles (Biglairser *et al*, 2019), this sudden reversal of performance in market references suggested that TBC's assumed position as market leader may be quickly threatened.

TBC incumbency in the technology industry:

Existing installed-based of clientele (often referred to as incumbency) is critically vital to technology players. A common strategy for technology firms is to enter into agreements with customers with long-term intentions. Technology firms would seek to expand their footprint with the customers, growing presence within large markets over a period to expand revenues and profits. From the customers' point of view, it is equally easy to work with a reliable partner who is also a leader in emerging technologies (Biglaiser *et al*, 2019).

TBC had been a player in the technology field where market norms were traditionally slow to update. As emerging technologies entered markets, incumbency advantage facilitates early sales amongst an existing client base (Biglaiser *et al*, 2019).

> **Exampling an Emerging Technology - Cloud Technologies:** Cloud technologies in simple form refers to the ability to access files, data, programs, and 3rd party services from a web browser via the internet, hosted by a 3rd part provider (Kim, 2009). Publicly conceptualised by Google in 2003, with Amazon's commercial services marking a milestone when they entered market in 2006 (Qian *et al*, 2009), cloud technologies, by 2010, were widely believed to be a central technology for reshaping the entire information technology industry (Dillon *et al*, 2010). As shown in Figure 7, Cloud services had become a prominent and the most collaborative technology among emerging technologies.

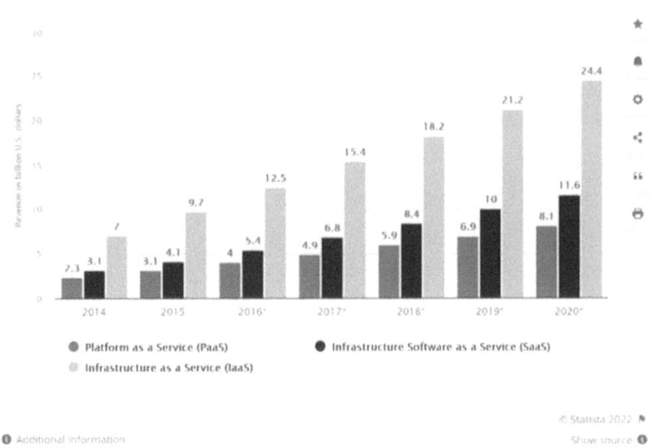

Figure 7: *Forecast of cloud computing as a service market revenue worldwide from 2014 to 2020, by type*
(Sourced from Statista.com, 2016)

TBC ceased being at the forefront of new technology development and failed to secure prominence in new technologies such as Cloud technologies. Market references dropped and incumbency advantage reduced.

In the information technology industry, established players focus on market share. This strategy will help them bring sustainable custom, synergies between operations, and a strong bottom line. By 2012 TBC market share across its various business units in China dropped below 25%, a reduction from 40% a decade earlier.

Outcome

Underlying challenges outlined above continued to mount, resulting in significant financial struggles. In 2016, TBC was acquired by a technology company with comparatively limited product lines. Following the acquisition, TBC went through a rebranding, recognised in this report as 'New Business Corporation Limited', or NBC[6]. NBC's presence in China continued to dwindle as core challenges remained unresolved. With growing pressure from local competitors, NBC's market share in China dwindled to around 5% by 2019. Corporate functions were relocated to Thailand, Singapore and India, and foreign experts were reluctant to join. NBC's workforce transitioned from being young minds at the forefront of technology development to a noticeably less ambitious workforce. NBC China's management team increasingly focused on protecting market share than expanding. In contrast, the Chinese technology market rapidly outpaced NBC (Figure 8). Several potential new players entered relevant markets and built relationships with local customers.

---

[6] NBC is a pseudonym for ongoing anonymity.

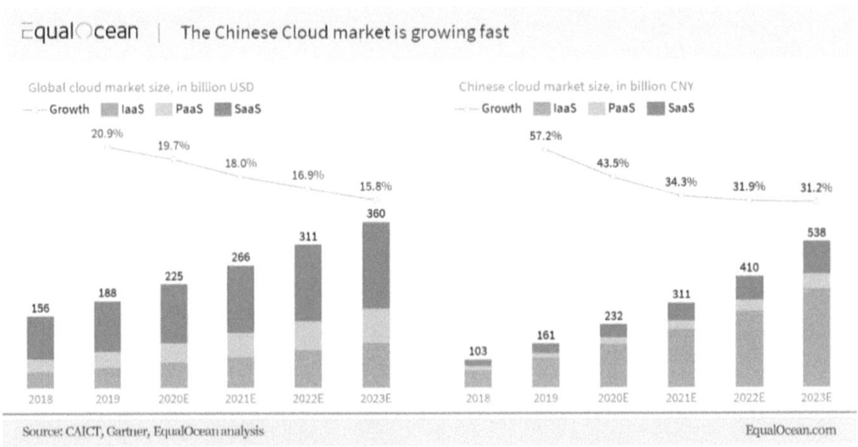

Figure 8: *Chinese Cloud Market*
(Sourced from prnewswire.com, 2021)

Discussion and conclusion

Around the turn of the century, product development processes underwent noticeable change as product cost, quality and time-to-market became increasingly important characteristics of successful enterprise (Minderhoud and Fraser, 2005). The stages from idea to large scale production that previously would typically take 10-15 years were shortened to 2-5 years (*ibid*).

Gartner (2009), a leading technology research firm, releases a technology hype cycle to illustrate the "time to mainstream" and expectations of the technologies. As illustrated in Figure 9, the exampled case of Cloud technologies showcased particularly high expectations and shortened time to market.

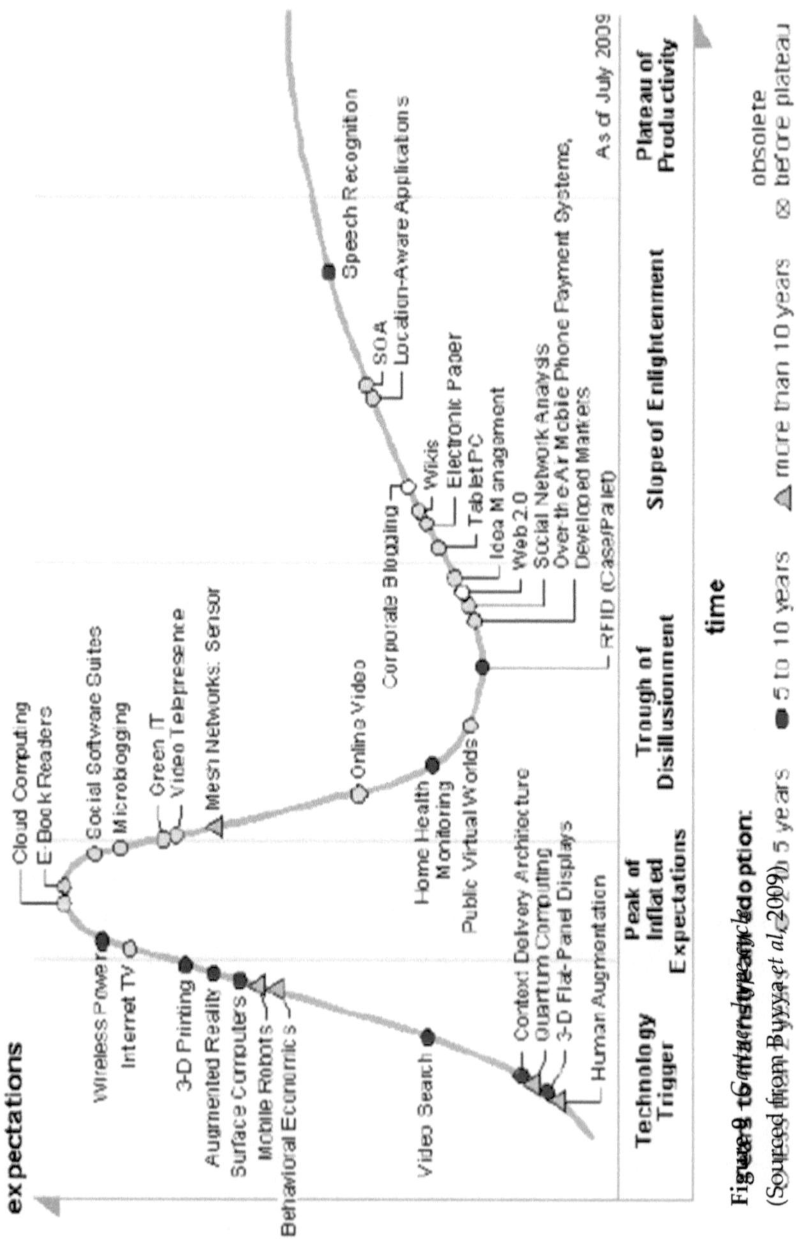

Figure 9-16 Gartner hype cycle
(Sourced from Buyya *et al.*, 2009)

Critically, as industry norms and new product development paradigms changed, TBC experienced significant turmoil within its emerging technologies department. Key human capital was lost, investment reduced, vital market references declined and the market outlook for the entire corporation increasingly suffered.

Simultaneously, China was transitioning its global position as a centre for manufacturing to becoming a core market for consumption and innovation. The Chinese market has high expectations regarding technology adaptation (HBR, 2021), investment into research and development is key to domestic growth opportunity (Fidelity, 2018), and, as local competitors grew, Chinese customers increasingly wanted multinational companies to demonstrate long-term commitment through strategic investment – a tough ask when multinationals may also be balancing demands of other geographical markets during a period of economic uncertainty on a global level.

The decline of TBC draws out several important learning points for senior executives:

- In the technology industry, incumbency is critical to continue stable market share, yet equally insufficient by itself. Since technologies are dynamically changing, continuous development and investment in promising technologies are vital.
- Established large companies are facing challenges in dynamic changes in the market. Agility and flexibility of policies and structures are critical to rapid changes in the market. Larger companies may struggle to adjust their human resources strategy to fit changing business environments.
- Employees with high-end technological skills with solid experience are not widely available in the market (Fong, 2011). Therefore, people strategy is very important. In addition, high-tech companies introduced employee-friendly human resources policies and set a dynamic workplace culture to protect competitiveness (Jolly, 2005).
- Large scale business failure may seldom be attributed to an individual error. As exampled above, failure may be seen as a series

of events, each with a knock-on effect that produces further negative decline.

- Whereas multinational firms may have significant resources that give them weight when entering a new market, they may equally find themselves caught out of sync with change in that same market. As attention may remain fixed on global strategy, individual regions, even significant ones like mainland China, may find themselves under-resourced and eventually outpaced by local competitors.

References

Ambler, T., Witzel, M., & Xi, C., (2016). *Doing business in China*. Routledge. Chapter 4.

Atherton, A., & Smallbone, D., (2013). Promoting private sector development in China: the challenge of building institutional capacity at the local level. *Environment and Planning C: Government and Policy*, *31*(1), 5-23.

Banerjee, P. M. (2013). Sustainable human capital: Product innovation and employee partnerships in technology firms. *Cross Cultural Management: An International Journal*.

Biglaiser, G., Calvano, E., & Crémer, J. (2019). Incumbency advantage and its value. *Journal of Economics & Management Strategy*, *28*(1), 41-48.

Blazejewski, S., & Dorow, W. (2004). Conflict in multinational corporations: An integrative framework. *Vortrag beim*, *20*.

Buyya, R., Pandey, S., & Vecchiola, C. (2009). Cloudbus toolkit for market-oriented cloud computing. In *IEEE International Conference on Cloud Computing* (pp. 24-44). Springer, Berlin, Heidelberg.

CFA Institute., (2017) *An annotated history of the USD/CNY exchange rate*. Available from: https://blogs.cfainstitute.org/investor/charts/an-annotated-history-of-the-usdcny-exchange-rate/

CKGSB., (2014) *The Going Gets Tough for MNCs in China*. Available from: https://english.ckgsb.edu.cn/knowledges/the-going-gets-tough-for-mncs-in-china/

Dillon, T., Wu, C., & Chang, E. (2010). Cloud computing: issues and challenges. In *2010 24th IEEE international conference on advanced information networking and applications* (pp. 27-33). IEEE.

Expatfinancials.com., (2021) *Challenges Expats faced in China.* Available from: https://expatfinancial.com/5-challenges-for-expats-in-china/

Fidelity., (2018) *China's R&D spending is rising rapidly.* Available from: https://www.fidelity.com.hk/en/articles/investment-spotlight/2018-08-17-technology-adoption-in-china-624362441

Fong, M. W. L. (2011). Chinese SMEs and information technology adoption. *Issues in informing science and information technology, 8,* 313-322.

Froese, F. J., Sutherland, D., Lee, J. Y., Liu, Y., & Pan, Y. (2019). Challenges for foreign companies in China: Implications for research and practice. *Asian Business & Management, 18*(4), 249-262.

Gartner., (2009) *Gartner Hype Cycle.* Available from: https://www.gartner.com/en/research/methodologies/gartner-hype-cycle

HBR., (2021) *How Tech Adoption Fuels China's Innovation Boom.* Available from: https://hbr.org/podcast/2021/05/how-tech-adoption-fuels-chinas-innovation-boom

HP., (2020) *HP Helps Japan's SOFTBANK MOBILE Build Online Content.* Available from: https://www.hp.com/us-en/hp-news/press-release.html?id=1263869#.Ys5E0s7isbA

IMF., (2009) *IMF World Economic* Outlook. Available from: https://www.imf.org/en/Publications/WEO/Issues/2016/12/31/World-Economic-Outlook-April-2009-Crisis-and-Recovery-22575

Jolly, D. R. (2005). human resource management in high-tech companies. *Int. J. Technology Management, 31*(3/4), 197.

Kim, W. (2009). Cloud computing: Today and tomorrow. *J. Object Technol., 8*(1), 65-72.

Lieberson, S., & O'Connor, J. F. (1972). Leadership and organizational performance: A study of large corporations. *American sociological review*, 117-130.

Minderhoud, S., & Fraser, P. (2005). Shifting paradigms of product development in fast and dynamic markets. *Reliability Engineering & System Safety*, *88*(2), 127-135.

Prnewswire.com., (2021) *A glimpse into China's burgeoning edge cloud market.* Available from: https://www.prnewswire.com/news-releases/a-glimpse-into-chinas-burgeoning-edge-cloud-market-301265027.html

Qian, L., Luo, Z., Du, Y., & Guo, L. (2009, December). Cloud computing: An overview. In *IEEE international conference on cloud computing* (pp. 626-631). Springer, Berlin, Heidelberg.

St. James's Place Wealth Management., (2018*) Cost of International Education in Shanghai.* Available from: http://www.austchamshanghai.com/application/files/4615/8330/3455/Cost_of_International_Education_in_Shanghai.pdf

Statista.com., (2016) *Forecast of cloud computing as a service market revenue worldwide from 2015 to 2020, by type.* Available from: https://www.statista.com/statistics/526029/worldwide-cloud-computing-revenue-by-type/

Strong, K. C., Ringer, R. C., & Taylor, S. A. (2001). THE* rules of stakeholder satisfaction (* Timeliness, honesty, empathy). *Journal of Business Ethics*, *32*(3), 219-230.

Worldbank.org., (2022) *GDP growth (annual %) – China.* Available from: https://data.worldbank.org/indicator/NY.GDP.MKTP.KD.ZG?end=2021&locations=CN&start=1998

Discussion questions

1. This case exemplifies how failure stemmed from a series of events. What factors do you think prevented TBC from identifying and tackling the core challenge(s) before decline became so engrained?

2. TBC fell victim to several challenges happening simultaneously, from policy change, global-economic instability, increasing competition in China, etc. What might leadership at TBC have done differently to combat these multiple pressures?

3. The case highlights that domestic competitors who focus locally (at least initially, even if they later grow and expand internationally themselves) may have benefits such as concentrated focus, closer ties with local influencers, increased adaptability, and responsiveness to local market changes etc. What does this mean for multinationals in general when competing within a maturing overseas market such as China?

4. TBC's legal structure identifies the human resources department as being run via a local partner. How may this have impacted the communication approach around the initial challenge raised? Discuss the pros and cons of this decision.

5. When making important decisions – often viewed as important due to their anticipated impact on the bottom line – what factors of human capital would you recommend large entities take into consideration?

The Start-up Factory in Kunshan: A Case Study of Entrepreneurship in China

Anselm A.M. Vermeulen
Senior Lecturer: Donghua University

Abstract

This case explores the launch and ongoing development of the Start-up Factory in Kunshan. Delivered as a narrative following the key founder, Mr. Bernd Reitmeier, the case exemplifies how entrepreneurial ambition is not necessarily inherent as a reflex reaction; highlights the importance of location when establishing a new entity in mainland China; reveals that not all opportunities are planned; demonstrates the ongoing need for entities to reinvent themselves as they grow and mature within a vibrant environment, and illustrates the importance of consolidating a responsible leadership team to govern current and future business strategy.

Introduction

'Start-up' is a term referring to the emergence of a new organisation into being (Carter, Gartner and Reynolds, 1996), often associated with efforts to do something differently, quickly and / or responsively to the status quo (Blank, 2000). Accelerators and incubation centres, with core features including the provision of educational workshops, mentorship, and network building, offer much needed support for start-ups as they strive to mature and achieve financial independence (Cohen *et al*, 2019). When we think of incubation centres, our mind may turn to young entrepreneurs in casual clothes tapping away on their high-end laptops, sipping on coffee, and inventing the next big app. However, the Start-Up Factory in Kunshan (SUFK) is very different. It is not an incubation centre for the common start-up, it is in the business of incubating factories. Actual factories that build physical products.

This case explores the launch and ongoing development of the Start-up Factory in Kunshan. Delivered as a narrative following the key founder, Mr. Bernd Reitmeier, the case exemplifies how entrepreneurial ambition is not necessarily inherent as a reflex reaction; highlights the importance of location when establishing a new entity in mainland China; reveals that not all opportunities are planned; demonstrates the ongoing need for entities to reinvent themselves as they grow and mature within a vibrant environment, and illustrates the importance of consolidating a responsible leadership team to govern current and future business strategy.

The venture begins - alone

Mr. Bernd Reitmeier arrived in Shanghai in the year 2000 to commence a new employment opportunity at the German Chamber of Commerce. During the preceding years, China had undertaken significant structural reform (economically and politically) that had propelled it from being one of the poorest countries in the world to one of the worlds' largest economies (Lin, 2011; Yueh, 2010). The rapid pace of growth and constant process of change required a keen vigilance to keep up to date with the macro business landscape. Forward growth projections had transformed China to become the second largest recipient of foreign capital in the world (Ho, 2004) and demand for people with understanding of both Chinese and German culture was on the increase. Tasked to "promote and advance Sino-German business cooperation" (China.ahk.de, 2022), Reitmeier threw himself into learning about the intricacies of doing business in China with thoroughness and enthusiasm. Through years of learning by doing, Reitmeier gained a valuable skillset in navigating the vast bureaucracy and regulatory frameworks governing the setting up on a manufacturing unit in mainland China.

As the process of learning continued, it evolved into innovation. Through brainstorming with entrepreneurs and discussions with local officials, Reitmeier developed a business model that he hoped the German Chamber of Commerce may swiftly adopt. Krueger, Reilly and Carsrud (2000) highlight that starting a new business is not necessarily a natural reflexive action upon encountering a problem or opportunity. Similarly, Reitmeier had, at the time, never given a thought to starting his own venture.

However, when he finally made his presentation to the Board of his organisation back in Germany, it received a somewhat less than enthusiastic response. It seemed that the wheels of bureaucracy in his own organisation were slow to grind and prone to friction. He returned to China rather disappointed.

Disappointed he may have been, but disheartened, it seemed, was not a word to be found in his dictionary of life. He decided, with the characteristic aplomb of a man of action, that if no one wanted to invest into his brainchild, he would simply have to do it himself. Reitmeier's attitude, beliefs and experiences had convinced him towards action in a manner characteristic of Ajzen (1991)'s theory of planned behaviour. With sentiment towards his current job cooling, he parted from the German Chamber of Commerce and invested financially, emotionally, and mentally into realising his own idea.

Location – getting it right can make or break a new venture in China

SUFK specialises in nurturing assembler manufacturers, repair service providers, and on-the-job shop trainers. With a typical incubation period of 2.5 years, SUFK distinguishes itself by offering vital hardware within its high-quality production premises in Kunshan – approximately 50 kilometres from the heart of Shanghai (startupfactory-china.de, 2022). Housing production companies, SUFK gives the full appearance of being a factory of factories, hence the rationale behind Reitmeier's christening his venture as the 'Start-up Factory'.

Initially finding a suitable facility to house the Start-up Factory, however, represented a significant first hurdle. Although office space is easy to find in Shanghai, factory space is another kettle of fish entirely. When he mooted the idea of setting it up in the Waigaoqiao area in the city, he found out that the city government was rather lukewarm to the idea of having more factories in the city. From 1992, Shanghai officials had launched a series of initiatives to reclaim Shanghai's position as Asia's pre-1949 status as the most cosmopolitan city in Asia. Priority was given towards ventures projecting the desired image of progress and advancement (Tianshu, 2011).

Reitmeier took his proposal to Taicang, a city near Shanghai with an established reputation for hosting German companies. However, he was again met with a somewhat apathetic city government whose response was not to his expectations. Finally, he found a sympathetic ear in the government of Kunshan, which already had several factories, but mostly from the USA or Taiwan Province. They were helpful, and excited at the prospect of this new concept and its focus on German companies joining their industrial base. Local government support is important when founding a new entity in China as government plays a more direct role in the country than many Western nations, such as with support for access to land, facilities, funding, introductions to influential decision makers etc. Local government support can thus significantly influence the opportunities available to a company (Ambler *et al*, 2016; Atherton and Smallbone, 2013). Kunshan's support was, in the end, the pivot on which Reitmeier's decision to locate there was made, and the Start-up Factory (SUF) morphed into the Start-up Factory, Kunshan (SUFK). Launched in 2011, it bears the same name to this day.

Not all opportunities are planned

Cash flow is a vital component behind the success of a business, especially in the early stages. SUFK's business model is that of a service provider, charging corporate clients according to the scope of space and facilities offered to them. Capitalising on an established network built over the previous decade of supporting German firms in mainland China, SUFK was able to minimise marketing expenses by targeting companies with a recognised need that SUFK knew it could address. As well as minimising outflows, this approach brought early clientele to gain very important, stable, and positive cash flows. Furthermore, establishing manufacturing infrastructure in a foreign country attracts long-term investors who take years to build up and stabilise. Where service companies may have low capital costs, factories cannot fold up and move on a whim, meaning that each client gained by SUFK offered a meaningful and long-term relationship.

Through demonstrated stability in the business model, SUFK gained increasing favour in the German '*mittelstand*' – Germany's successful and stable network of small and medium enterprises. This was, in hindsight, only natural, as small and medium sized firms were not usually capable of setting up independent infrastructure to make an entry into a relatively unfamiliar market space. Unlike larger companies which could afford the overhead of market exploration on their own, the *mittelstand* companies were on the lookout for a shared service provider who could offer them affordable market entry information services.

Ongoing need for reinvention

During the early years of SUFK, most customers were from the automotive sector. Since companies shared factory and office space, there were some initial doubts about conflict of interest. However, only a small number of entities were unable to establish in SUFK for these reasons. Reitmeier, however, was concerned about the risk of over-reliance towards a single industry sector. Should the automotive sector experience a downturn, SUFK would likely be adversely impacted. Reitmeier proposed two new ideas to future proof SUFK.

Idea A - Smart Factory Kunshan: Established in 2017, Smart Factory Kunshan is a sector-agnostic laboratory of sorts, exposing customers to the benefits of a smart factory. Founded on Industry 4.0 principles, SUFK offers a programme to educate stakeholders on current and future trends in manufacturing. Industry 4.0 refers to vertically and horizontally integrating manufacturing systems through technology enabled connectivity with the aim of systems being able to control their own manufacturing processes (Lasi *et al*, 2014; Dalenogare *et al*, 2018). Germany's Federal Ministry of Education and Research was quick to support the movement, with the German speaking world being noticeably progressive in adoption mindset (Lasi *et al*, 2014). As a platform for demonstrating, integrating, developing, and marketing Industry 4.0 technologies (smartfactorykunshan.com, 2022), the Smart Factory Kunshan plays on Germany's competitive reputation as a national leader in Industry 4.0, with China's reputation as being the manufacturing centre for the world. Although not a significant money maker as at spring 2022, the Smart

Factory Kunshan positions it firmly at the forefront of advanced concepts and technologies in industrial engineering, and crucially helps in diversifying its customer base, with software development, robotics and other sectors coming to represent more of its clients.

Idea B – Equity stake: In the interest of a long-term involvement into the companies and facilities SUFK was helping create and develop in China, Reitmeier started an incubation programme that involves SUFK acquiring a minority stake in companies taking the programme.

These ideas helped make the business model more robust, investing SUFK into a deeper, more strategic, and more engaged role with its customers founded not simply on the idea of service provision, but with a stake in the future development of the client base.

Consolidating the governance structure

As Reitmeier was making strides in his innovative venture, he was not one to underestimate the importance of having a strong team to make those strides longer and more impactful, on the solid grounds of Kunshan. As it gained local credibility and fame, he was well aware that his partners needed to be as committed and hard-driving as he was. As at spring 2022, SUFK operated via a seven-member management and partner team, each person with a different expertise when it comes to the arcane and specialised skills of setting up and operating complex industrial systems. As an old China hand, Reitmeier also realised that professional skills are only part of the success equation. In Asia, as they often say, "it's not just about what you know, it's about who you know, and how well you know them". So, he picked a team very much like him, professionally competent, but also personally able to form and maintain personal relationships that often form the most important part of business success in the Chinese environment.

Opportunities exist for SUFK to expand into the United States. Compared to mainland China, the United States is quite a different ballgame, perhaps a different ballpark, or even a different sport, when it comes down to it. The involvement of governments in encouraging businesses to establish in various territories is there, but far less than either in China or even Germany, for that matter. Industrial policy in the USA is driven by a different set of factors, with a different set of incentives and a different measure of what constitutes a horizon. On an overall level too, governments in the USA tend to involve themselves less into local industrial policy, have a decided preference for large businesses than for typical German-style *mittelstand* organisations, and are currently more enamoured of the high-tech, service economy type of business, rather than the bread-and-butter, bricks-and-mortar, blood-and-sweat enterprise that forms the backbone of manufacturing in Germany or China. Reitmeier is far from intimidated, though. With a strong partner in place, SUFK might be forced to change its initials soon, unless it sets up in Kansas, for example. The future of manufacturing, after all, is common to countries, related to the sharing of knowledge, people, facilities and business processes.

Conclusion

The Start-up Factory Kunshan exemplifies how a rejected idea has potential to grow into an icon amidst an industry that is seeking to redefine itself – through the adoption of 'Industry 4.0' in this instance. The case has narrated key milestones in the development of SUFK by following the individual experiences of its founder, Mr. Bernd Reitmeier. Whereas entrepreneurial theory may correctly assert the need for intentional and planned behaviour for a new venture to succeed over time, the story of SUFK highlights that entrepreneurial intention is itself not necessarily immediate. Failure and / or rejection to adopt an idea within an existing eco-system may be an igniting facture behind the inspiration of 'going for it alone'.

As highlighted by Blank (2000), start-ups may be characterised by their speed and responsiveness towards change. Yet, they may equally be characterised by their fluid approach towards planning. We see this in SUFK's emergent strategy towards allying itself with Germany's *mittelstand* companies – arguably an obvious move in hindsight. Equally, as the entity has grown and matured, so too has its need for consolidating a governance structure that involves competent people with expertise covering all core aspects of the business – not only technically, but also with regards to astuteness towards the intricacies of doing business in China. The case of Start-up Factory in Kunshan therefore offers valuable insights and learning for those interested in entrepreneurial activity, whether in China or overseas.

References

Ambler, T., Witzel, M., & Xi, C., (2016). *Doing business in China*. Routledge. Chapter 4.

Ajzen, I., (1991). The theory of planned behaviour. *Organisational behaviour and human decision processes*. Vol 50 (2), pp.179-211.

Atherton, A., & Smallbone, D., (2013). Promoting private sector development in China: the challenge of building institutional capacity at the local level. *Environment and Planning C: Government and Policy*, *31*(1), 5-23.

Blank, S., (2000). Why the lean start-up changes everything, *Harvard Business Review*. May Issue. Available from: https://app.glueup.com/resources/protected/organization/699/event/1153/0b2fc8f8-f57c-4250-8833-408e353137ba.pdf (Accessed 28th April 2022)

Carter, N., Gartner, W, & Reynolds, P., (1996). Exploring Start-Up Event Sequences. *Journal of Business Venturing*. Vol 11, pp.151-166. http://dx.doi.org/10.1016/0883-9026(95)00129-8

China.ahk.de., (2022) *AHK Greater China*. Available from: https://china.ahk.de/ (Accessed 28th April 2022)

Cohen, S., Fehder, D., Hochberg, Y., & Murray, F., (2019). The design of startup accelerators, *Research Policy*. Vol 48 (7), pp.1781-1797.

Dalenogare, L., Benitez, G., Ayala, N., & Frank, A., (2018). The expected contribution of Industry 4.0 technologies for industrial performance, *International Journal of Production Economics*. Vol 204, pp.383-394.

Ho, O., (2004) Determinants of foreign direct investment in China: A sectoral analysis. Available from: https://www.digital.uwa.edu.au/__data/assets/pdf_file/0019/102556/04_18_Ho.pdf

Krueger, N., Reilly, M., & Carsrud, A., (2000). Competing models of entrepreneurial intentions, *Journal of Business Venturing*. Vol 15 (5-6), pp.411-432.

Lasi, H., Fettke, P., Kemper, H., Feld, T., & Hoffman, M., (2014). Industry 4.0, *Business Information Systems Engineering*. Vol 6, pp.239-242.

Lin, J., (2011). China and the global economy, *China Economic Journal*. Vol 4 (1), pp.1-14. Smartfactorykunshan.com., (2022). *Sharing ideas*. Available from: https://www.smartfactorykunshan.com/

Startupfactory-china.de., (2022). *Our vision*. Available from: https://www.startupfactory-china.de/en/about-us/our-vision/

Tianshu, P., (2011) Place attachment, communal memory, and the moral underpinnings of gentrification in postreform Shanghai. In: Kleinman A., Yan, Y., Jun, J., Lee, S., Zhang, E., Tianshu, P. Fei, W., & Guo, J (2011) *Deep China: The Moral Life of the Person*. University of California Press: London

Yueh, L., (2010). *The Economy of China*. Edward Elgar Publishing, Inc: Cheltenham, UK.

Discussion questions

1. What are the primary motivators for an entrepreneur to launch a new entity?

2. This case highlighted how relationships with local government may favourably impact the future performance of a start-up. Within the context of your current location, what support mechanisms does the local and/or regional government have available to support start-ups?

3. This case highlights the constant change and evolving strategy that is commonly deemed inherent within a start-up. How does this relate to conventional thinking about writing a business plan? What are the strengths and limitations of business plans?

Transformation Journey of a Global Chemical Company in China

Annette Metz
Co-founder: CONBEN Deutschland GmbH

Abstract

This case study describes the transformation journey of a global chemical company in China which fought its own under-representation in the growing Chinese market with a transformation journey. By creating cross-unit initiatives, the organisation overcame the rather fragmented set-up of separately led Business Units. Finally, those cross-unit initiatives became the foundation for the strategic orientation of the company to grow its business. Dialogic Organisation Development interventions as well as agile project management approaches guided the process.

Introduction

Headquartered in Switzerland, Company X, of which the parent company was created through a spin off and IPO in the 1990s, is one of the globally leading Chemical companies in its field. With 15,000 employees across more than 50 countries, Company X realises a global turnover exceeding four billion Euros. The company offers a variety of benefits to a diverse group of customers via three global business units (BUs): it offers customer solutions from consumer care to industrial applications; it adds value to clients in the petrochemical field by making their use of finite raw materials more efficient; and it supports clients in the additives market in achieving a lower carbon footprint by enabling circularity.

The growing sustainability focus as well as the enhanced wish from business customers for safe and healthy solutions offer new growth potential for Company X. China represents forty percent of the global chemical market and sixty percent of the global growth in the chemical market between 2016 and 2021 was realised in China (Yuan et al. 2021; Chen and Reniers 2020; Fernandez 2022). Therefore, the China chemicals market itself provides a tremendous growth opportunity. However, benefiting from this favourable market situation is challenging for Company X as it faces fierce competition not only from existing multinational corporations (MNCs) but also from new aggressive Chinese players. The China ecosystem in the chemical business shows structural differences compared to other regions due to reasons such as the influence of the Chinese government supporting state owned enterprises (SOEs), easy access to capital for private entrepreneurs and strong willingness to accept risks (Yuan et al. 2021; Chen and Reniers 2020).

The set-up of Company X in China includes ten production sites and three R&D centres serving the three business units. The China entity has approximately 1,500 employees and realises ten percent of global turnover.

Problem statement

Although the overall China market represented forty percent of the global chemical market, Company X only realised ten percent of its business in that market. Consequently, Company X needed to bundle China resources to gain market shares. However, the China business comprised three BUs which were strongly led by global BU leaders. The BUs co-existed in China and did not actively search for synergies. Although the matrix structure foresaw a combination of BU and regional approach, the reality portrayed a clear BU-focus: the China BUs had disciplinary reporting lines to the Global BUs and dotted reporting lines to the China President. The BUs were supported by several Supporting Units (SUs) like procurement, logistics, finance, HR, legal etc. As the SUs followed the BUs' demands, they also did not use the opportunity of uniting the China business. This rather fragmented set-up contradicted the need of an aligned China strategy of Company X.

Given the worldwide economic tensions caused by the pandemic, the Global Headquarters was eager to address the mentioned challenge. The Headquarters' major target was to close the 10-40-Percent-gap as China represented the primary growth engine of the whole organisation.

Therefore, the company's Board decided to put China in the centre of its global strategy by developing local capabilities in China to reach ambitious growth targets. Given the diverse situations in the different market segments withing the BUs, Company X wanted to achieve these growth targets partly by organic growth and partly by taking advantage of suitable merger and acquisitions (M&A) opportunities. Capability development embraced expanding production capacities (constructing new manufacturing plants and explore the mentioned merger and acquisition opportunities), enhancing the local innovation capabilities (new regional R&D centre), and empowering China (changes in governance model).

Given this tailwind from the global Headquarters, the China President of Company X wanted to use the momentum to strengthen the buy-in and excitement within his China leadership team and the whole China organisation for the China-focus-strategy. The China President of Company X was a non-Chinese who had been serving the organisation in different regions and positions for over two decades, including a position in China in his earlier career and who was newly appointed into his role as President. Given this unique career development, he had built both a trusted network in the global Headquarters as well as in China. Given the China-focus-strategy from global Headquarters, BUs and SUs needed to align their forces to address the needs and opportunities in the Chinese market. In addition, it was crucial to unite the fragmented voices towards the Headquarters in a one-China-voice without losing the unique strengths of the different BUs. To address those challenges within the China organisation, the China President decided to launch a transformation journey in 2020. Its major purpose was to enhance the cross-unit collaboration as basis for the mentioned growth.

Theory

Organisation Development (OD) is defined as all planned interventions to increase organisation effectiveness and health (Beckhard 1969). Given the corporate volatile, uncertain, complex, and ambiguous (VUCA) environment, OD can be described as an organisation's ongoing journey of improvement. Already most of the OD founding fathers from the 1940s and 1950s played a double role as academics and as consultants (Cheung-Judge and Holbeche 2015). Due to this dual emphasis of theory and practice, OD is assessed as a suitable perspective for the given transformation journey of Company X.

Meanwhile, the literature distinguishes between Diagnostic OD and Dialogic OD. While Diagnostic OD views change as a planned process with unfreezing, movement, refreezing phases, Dialogic OD emphasises discourse and emergence to foster change (Bushe and Marshak 2014, 2015a). Some of the principal beliefs that Bushe and Marshak (2014) describe as basis for Dialogic OD are the following:

- Change is part of a continuous process of self-organising
- New organisational behaviours emerge rather than being prescribed
- Adoption of new ways of thinking and behaviours may be accelerated by fostering supportive conditions
- Organisational reality is a social construct that emerges through dialogic processes
- Narratives are coherent stories that help organisation members to make sense of the past, current as well as future situations

While diagnostic OD relies mainly on upfront diagnosis and often quantitative data-feedback, dialogic OD emphasises emergence and generativity during the process. "Generativity creates change by offering people new images that allow them to see old things in new ways, and to make new actions available that couldn't be conceived before" (Bushe and Marshak 2014: 2). Consequently, a possible disadvantage of dialogic OD is to get buy-in of people who are especially comfortable in using analytical, left-brain-oriented methodologies.

When working with larger groups, a diagnostic OD consultant normally plays the role of a facilitator, while the dialogic OD consultant "is described by some as a choreographer or stage manager who helps to create a 'container' and designs and fosters conversations among the participants" (Bushe and Marshak 2014: 2). In the dialogic OD field, this role is often described as convening instead of facilitating, as the latter is mainly focusing on the process of making something easier (Neal et al. 2011). This convening role can be taken either by an internal or an external consultant. Experience shows that external consultants often create the mentioned container more easily than internal consultants, as they are not part of the internal power structure and are viewed more neutrally. In summary, in dialogic process consulting, the consultant engages in multiple ongoing convening interactions with the target to make the system more effective (Bushe and Marshak 2015a). Following this line of thought, dialogic OD is representing the theoretical foundation of the described transformation journey of Company X.

Actions taken

Company X hired an external OD consultant, who had been involved in the company's talent related development for ten years, to support the transformation journey. The advantages of this long-term cooperation were that the consultant had gained trust within the China organisation on different hierarchical levels and was familiar with the business. Furthermore, the external consultant had the advantage – in comparison to internal consultants - of being perceived as neutral and of standing outside of internal power dynamics. As will be described below, the transformation was handled as an organically evolving process. Looking back, the journey of 1.5 years embraced the major elements as shown in figure 1.

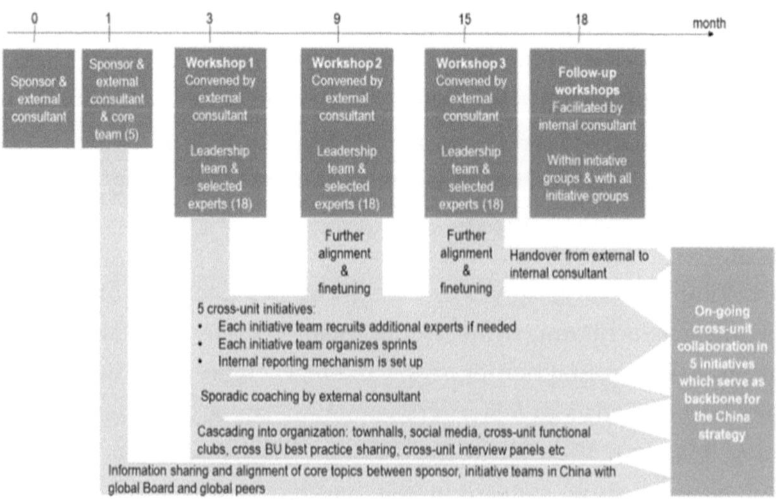

Figure 1: *Overview of Transformation Journey*

In a first step, the President of Company X in China articulated the future direction with the help of the consultant. In the next step, a core team of five colleagues (leadership team members from BUs and SUs) agreed that cross-BU-initiatives would be a suitable way to use the synergies between the BUs as basis for further China growth. At this point in time, it was clear that cross-unit-initiatives seemed to be a promising way to go. However, in that moment neither the buy-in of the leadership team nor the content of the initiatives existed. The core team and the consultant discussed an iterative approach, in which one step would be designed, tested, evaluated before the next step is designed according to the results. As the content in each iterative cycle was not yet defined, the amount and lengths of iterations were open.

In the following step, key stakeholders in the China organisation were identified. It was a group of 18 individuals which included the leadership team members as well as selected experts. The experts were defined by the leadership team as being especially relevant for cross-unit cooperation (e.g., cross-unit processes), which was the major purpose of this transformation journey as the way to reach the targeted growth. Out of a first workshop with the 18 individuals, convened by the consultant, five topics emerged as relevant cross-BU-initiatives. The topics were linked with customer experience, innovation drive, footprint enlargement, optimised processes and with engaged people. Voluntary groups – who take the ownership for the initiatives – were built. Those initiative groups involved other colleagues from the organisation who possessed needed expertise. In line with agile project management approaches, each initiative group worked out its next sprints. In an agile project, a sprint is a time-boxed period in which the team works to complete a given task (Sutherland 2015). In addition, the team agreed upon an internal mechanism for following-up on the sprints.

The President acted as sponsor as well as participant in one of the initiatives. Although this double role of a top leader can create confusion in a hierarchical organisation, the developed buy-in of the whole team into the concept of collective leadership, in alignment with the dialogic OD values of collaboration and participation on eye-level, made this double role work well. Furthermore, the President led the communication with the global

Board. In addition, all initiative groups identified ways of informing and involving the relevant global peers. Finally, the China organisation was onboarded through townhall meetings, social media information, cross-units functional clubs, cross-BU best practice sharing, cross-unit interview panels etc. During the first 1.5 years of the transformation journey, the consultant sporadically coached the sponsor and stakeholders, when the need arose. This coaching particularly covered questions regarding the shaping of a collaborative company culture which were the basis in all five initiatives.

The core team agreed to arrange every six months a workshop with the external consultant. During those workshops, the next steps regarding the five initiatives, the interconnections between them as well as the overall cross-unit and local-global cooperation emerged; those represented then the next iteration in the transformation process. After fifteen months, an internal facilitator/consultant started to support the initiative leaders to build routines with quarterly updates by focusing on external factors with cross-BU impact (achievements, challenges, risks, opportunities etc.) and by bridging the conversations between the initiatives. At this moment, the external OD consultant stepped back.

Evaluation

When evaluating the transformation journey, particularly two success factors emerge: first, the buy-in of the extended leadership team to the overall direction – which is also consistent with literature on successful change management (Kotter 1995) - and, second, the generative nature (as presented in the theory section) of the process.

Regarding the overall direction, dialogic OD interventions helped to paint an image of how Company X looks like when cross-BU-SU collaboration is reality. Visualisation and story-telling elements were applied to develop a narrative with a common direction. Dialogic OD interventions also helped to develop the generative nature of the process which is challenged in the beginning as the described BU-focused set-up creates a certain degree of power struggle. Dialogic OD interventions in this transformation journey do not only equalise speaking-time among participants but also slow down, make participants listen deeply and wholeheartedly, avoid quick judgements, and hold space for difference. The participants regularly express their surprise towards the consultant that it is possible to create this kind of joyful, seemingly informal, and still very productive setting which is in literature often described as container. A container is about creating the physical and energetic field within which the participants meet; a container gives security as well as safety and it builds an alive atmosphere based on connection which helps meaningful conversations to emerge (Neal et al. 2011).

Still, the process was not always comfortable. In the generative conversation phase, frictions emerged. Some team members got impatient, and the consultant needed to find the fine line of letting conversation go and getting back into guiding mode. This fine balancing - which cannot be pre-planned - required for a consultant with solid group dynamic experiences. Agile project management approaches supplemented the experimental nature of the dialogic OD interventions. While agile methodologies emphasise responsiveness to changing business needs (Martin 2017), dialogic OD interventions highlight the long-term health of an organisation (Cheung-Judge and Holbeche 2015); this means both approaches are complementary, as they offer two complementary perspectives on continuous improvement of the organisation.

Furthermore, the President's role was crucial. His firm conviction that cross-unit cooperation will lead to growth created trust in the team, especially as he – as non-Chinese – genuinely exuberated a long-term interest for the China entity. Literature shows that the willingness to put organisational matters over self-interests leads to integrity as a major component in trust-building (Mayer et al. 1995). His supportive and helpful nature exampled a mindset that is in literature referred to as the basis for collective leadership: he believes that leadership is collectively produced in the community, not the individual (Bateson and Brubeck 2016). In addition, the President took the role of sharing information with the global Board and of aligning selected questions with global peers. This global-local bridging was also highly important.

Overall, the organic development of the process - first forming the cross-unit initiative teams, then agreeing on an initiative leader and at a later stage involving an internal consultant - enhanced the ownership of all parties, as all those steps happened naturally and in a participative manner. It allowed sufficient time to test and experiment which cooperation and communication models were suitable to enhance the cross-unit collaboration. One-and-a-half years into the transformation process, the five cross-units initiatives became the backbone of the China strategy of Company X. This was a great achievement of cross-unit collaboration, as previously the China strategy consisted of individual BU strategies listed next to each other. The five strategic cross-units initiatives were fully owned and continuously shaped by the China team and recognised as well as appreciated by the global headquarters.

Conclusion

In conclusion, creating conditions for collective thinking that allow new insights to emerge are crucial for reaching people's buy-in for transformation. The combination of Dialogic OD interventions, mainly driven by the external consultant, and agile project management practices, applied by the initiative teams, worked well as both approaches are characterised by an iterative and experimental nature.

In this transformation journey, the trustful link between the external consultant, the sponsor and the leadership team was core. In addition, the sponsor's mindset and behavior that mirror the OD democratic, humanistic, and collaborative values (Bushe and Marshak 2015b) helped to build credibility in the team. Those values let the sponsor appear rather as inclusive host than as lonesome hero.

Finally, it was important to realise that the underlying tension in this transformation journey represents a polarity, not a problem. The tension can be termed as 'global-local' or as 'centralisation-decentralisation'. If it would be a problem, there would be a way to solve it. However, a polarity cannot be solved. Instead, a polarity needs to be continuously managed. Therefore, although the fragmented collaboration between BUs in China might look like a pure China challenge at the first glance, the involvement of the global organisation into this transformation journey was equally important for the success.

References

Bateson, Nora; Brubeck, Sahra Bateson (2016): Small arcs of larger circles. Framing through other patterns. Axminster, England: Triarchy Press.

Beckhard, Richard (1969): Organization development: Strategies and models. Reading, MA: Addison-Wesley.

Bushe, Gervase R.; Marshak, Robert (2014): Dialogic organization development. In B. B. Jones, M. Brazzel (Eds.): The NTL handbook of organization development and change. 2nd. Wiley-Pfeiffer. San Francisco, CA, pp. 193–212.

Bushe, Gervase R.; Marshak, Robert (2015a): Introduction to the Dialogic Organization Development Mindset. In Gervase R. Bushe, Robert J. Marshak (Eds.): Dialogic organization development. The theory and practice of transformational change. First Edition. Oakland: Berrett-Koehler Publishers, Chapter 1.

Bushe, Gervase R.; Marshak, Robert J. (Eds.) (2015b): Dialogic organization development. The theory and practice of transformational change. First Edition. Oakland: Berrett-Koehler Publishers.

Chen, Chao; Reniers, Genserik (2020): Chemical industry in China: The current status, safety problems, and pathways for future sustainable development. In *Safety Science* 128, p. 104741. DOI: 10.1016/j.ssci.2020.104741.

Cheung-Judge, Mee-Yan; Holbeche, Linda (2015): Organization development. A practitioner's guide for OD and HR. Second edition. London: Kogan Page.

Fernandez, Lucia (2022): Chemical sales market share in China 2010-2020. Edited by Statista. online. Available online at https://www.statista.com/statistics/1247221/market-share-of-global-chemical-sales-value-china/, checked on 4/3/2022.

Kotter, John P. (1995): Leading change: why transformation efforts fail. In *Harvard Business Review* (March-April), pp. 59–67.

Martin, Jane (2017): Agile Organizational Change. Leveraging learnings from software development. In *OD Practicioner* 49 no. 3, pp. 39–41.

Mayer, Roger C.; Davis, James H.; Schoorman F. David (1995): An integrative model of organizational trust. In *Academy of Management Review* 20 (No 3), pp. 709–734.

Neal, Craig; Neal, Patricia; Wold, Cynthia (2011): The art of convening. Authentic engagement in meetings, gatherings and conversations. 1st ed. San Francisco, CA: Berrett-Koehler; London.

Sutherland, Jeff (2015): Scrum. The art of doing twice the work in half the time. London: rh Business Books.

Yuan, Yufeng; Pan, Weiguang; Di Sha (2021): Analysis on Export Competitiveness of Chinese Chemical Products. In *JSS* 09 (12), pp. 139–156. DOI: 10.4236/jss.2021.912011.

Discussion questions

1. For entities undergoing a strategic and/or transformational change, the role of the leader involves showing clear direction whilst leaving room for the collective wisdom of the team to emerge. Although a rather easy statement to agree with, acting out the balance must require something beyond the ordinary, or otherwise more leaders would be able to achieve it. Discuss.

2. How may continued growth in the China region of a multi-national corporation result in increased need actively to manage global-local tensions? What sort of tensions may arise and what recommendations would you offer to the leadership responsible for navigating these tensions?

3. Many organisations opt to work with an external consultant to facilitate the change process. Close alignment between sponsor, core team and external consultant is crucial. What factors should external consultants be aware of when introducing tools such as agile project management to drive internal change within a VUCA industry environment such as the China market?

Utilising A Design Thinking Approach to Improve Employee Retention

Xiaolei Yang
Talent Director, APAC: Sensata Technologies

John Storm
Senior Lecturer: The University of Aberdeen, United Kingdom

Abstract

Employee turnover of 30-50% is common within the automobile sector in mainland China. Although performing well against peers, this project utilises the Design Thinking model to engage with core stakeholders associated with Sensata (China), to improve understanding around root issues behind high turnover in the sector, and propose creative solutions that guide operational managers on how to meaningfully 'Care and Connect' with their respective people groups. The project output is a systematic action plan to roll-out a customised coaching leadership approach that aligns every day organisational culture with recently revised value statements.

Company introduction and macro-environment

Sensata Technologies Holding plc (herein referred to as Sensata) is a US headquartered organisation that focuses on sensor-based solutions. With operations in 13 countries and a workforce of 19,000 employees, Sensata targets annual revenues of around $3.5 billion – 70% of which is generated from the automotive sector (Sensata.com, 2022). Sensata (China) maintains two principal manufacturing sites in Changzhou and Baoying, as well as an Asia head office in Shanghai. Together, these facilities account for 21% of Sensata's revenues (Sensata, 2021, p.11). The strategic importance of China in Sensata's global strategy correlates with the rapid growth in China's car sales, growing from 12 million in 2012 to 28 million in 2017, before subsequently pulling back to 23.4 million in 2020 (Ministry of Public Security, 2020). Equally, this growth has occurred during a period that included (i) increased political tensions between the US and China, raising questions about the need to shift some manufacturing outside of China (Sensata, 2021, p.17); (ii) Covid-19, creating significant disruption to operations that contributed towards an 11.8% drop in Sensata's 2020 global revenues (Sensata, 2021, p.26), and moreover, (iii) China's car industry entering a period of adjustment in 2017 following Government initiatives to stimulate growth in new energy vehicles that now account for 10.9% of car sales in China (CHYXX.com, 2021; Zhiyan Consulting, 2021).

The combination of these factors induces significant external pressure onto Sensata. China-US tensions encourage local automotive companies to consider substitutes. New energy trends have resulted in a wave of new technologies and competitors entering markets (Javaid *et al*, 2021). Chip shortages arising from Covid-19 clash with China Government's growth policies for new energy solutions, resulting in increased aggression during procurement negotiations (Ting-Fang and Li, 2021). The impact on labour markets is increased competition as new innovative companies poach talent during a period where the appeal of working for a large American brand begins to wane. This is a particular challenge for HR executives as Covid-19 prompts increased life reflection from employees around the world regarding their own health and well-being, thus creating another stimulant to drive high employee turnover as many opt for change (Kurbetti and Maheshkar, 2021; Hagos, 2021). Although the global war for talent is not a new phenomenon (Beechler and Woodward, 2009), the urgency for change has grown to new heights as millennials and their demands for more authentic leadership now account for over 50% of labour workforces (Gallup, 2019). Creative responses to talent solutions are increasingly necessary as the benefits of company branding and compensation schemes are replaced by the need for increased managerial openness, learning agility, integrated and adaptive HR systems, as well as an innovative and responsive organisational culture (Beechler and Woodward, 2009; Gallup, 2016). Ultimately, Sensata (China) operates in an industry environment where annual labour turnover of 30-50% is not uncommon. Whilst Sensata (China)'s voluntary turnover of 15-20% is competitive against sector peers, the business challenges and implications remain considerable. May improvement opportunities exist for a company who pro-actively responds to employee needs within this environment?

Project identification

Sensata has internally placed "Care and Connect with our People" as a core business priority since 2020. Clear direction is significant in spearheading positive change (Isern and Pung, 2007). Equally, change takes time and there is regularly disconnect between visionary statements, strategy implementation and methods for evaluating performance (Allison, 2019). The way in which 'Care and Connect' is to be exhibited through observable behaviour needs to be clearly communicated in order to be coherently recognised and inspired throughout the workforce (Bardi and Schwartz, 2003). The inference towards leadership is in itself insufficient, as leadership theory is proliferated by a plethora of frameworks, making the term itself messy and often impractical, not only as each manager may approach the concept with different perspectives but as they themselves get discouraged by the significant time investment into their subordinates who frequently leave due to the accepted industry environment of high staff turnover. A project was devised with the following objectives:

- Explore leadership impact on employee retention and employee engagement,
- Generate data and feedback from core stakeholders regarding areas perceived to impact turnover,
- Gain alignment and define core areas requiring change,
- Recommend an effective leadership approach to guide operational managers on how to implement 'Care and Connect' with their respective people groups.

Critical overview of actions taken

Design Thinking may be used as a managerial framework to approach complex projects within an ambiguous and changing environment. Comprising five stages, Empathy, Define, Ideate, Prototype and Test, Design Thinking orientates around a component critical to the nature of this project i.e., whereas most frameworks orientate around an analytically-based management approach towards problem solving, Design Thinking emphasises entrepreneurial creativity and value creation via deeply integrating the diverse perspectives and viewpoints of core stakeholders (Brenner, Uebernickel & Abrell, 2016; Storm, 2021a).

Stage 1 – Stakeholder engagement (Empathy)

Essential starting questions were (i) Empathise with whom (ii) How do we empathise? (Storm, 2021b). For the purposes of this case study, , the answer to the first question was simplified into a core stakeholder map comprising:

Stakeholder group 1 - Sensata (China) executive team: Included on the assumptions of Executives being motivated towards maintaining or improving organisational performance, being in a position to gain from reduced staff turnover (in terms of both traditional performance metrics as well as emotional mindset) and being in a position of general understanding towards the issue as a whole given their role.

Stakeholder group 2 - Previous employees: Included on the assumptions that previous employees left for a reason(s) and that learning more about the reason(s) may help in determining core areas needing improvement and/or initiate creative response. Due to the volume of turnover, contacted previous employees were limited towards those who left no more than 24 months prior and whose contact details were readily accessible – potentially skewing bias of findings towards a sample pool more favourable towards positive communication.

Stakeholder group 3 - Colleagues within the China HR department responsible for exit interviews: Included on the assumption that HR colleagues involved in exit interviews would be most informed with regards to turnover trends, review policies and issues arising within the themes of employee experience, engagement, and retention.

The first round of dialogue with each stakeholder group was initiated by survey via the Wenjuanxing App and distributed by WeChat to optimise convenience for those engaged. Although specific responses are sensitive and not suitable for public disclosure, response rates resulted in the representation of 70% of the China Executive Team, <10% of previous employees leaving during the prior 24 months, and 100% of HR colleagues involved in exit interviews. As raised above, the use of convenience sampling (i.e., connecting with formal colleagues with whom contact details were readily accessible) not only limited the size of the sampling pool, but may also reduce reliability of findings (Patton, 1990). To move closer towards authentic dialogue and gain a deeper understanding of insights raised (Kohlrieser 2007), follow-up interviews were conducted.

Findings supported trends that may be attained by analysing the up-to-date literature of reputable consultants and executive search advisory services – such as market data provided by the 2020 Mercer China Talent Attraction and Retention Practice Survey Summary Report (Mercer, 2020). This included findings around the rate of turnover, average period of tenure pre-turnover, primary reasons for turnover, primary reasons for retention, and core initiatives of companies to improve retention, employee expectations of management and employers, etc. Ultimately, primary reasons for turnover were career development, industry prospects, compensation, company culture, and work-life balance. Although Sensata remains competitive when benchmarked with industry peers, this should not provide an excuse to limit ongoing improvement.

Acknowledging China's new energy vehicles market to be dominated by domestic manufactures with over 80% of the market share and arguably increasing that position through responsive innovation and growth policies that poach talent (KPMG, 2021), an unexpected point raised was the need for leadership more greatly to emphasise the importance of social capital within organisational settings in general as frequent changing of jobs often means restarting the relationship building process within a new workplace and culture (Christian, 2021).

An important finding from dialogue with HR colleagues involved in the exit interviews was that discussion often orientates around the reason why employees choose to leave, rather than the reason why employees decided to explore outside opportunities – defined by Belete (2018) as turnover intentions. The latter may support the development of pro-active initiatives to reduce turnover, although equally requires a level of emotional intelligence that cannot be universally assumed (Bradberry and Greaves, 2009).

A further finding was that the expectations of millennials in respect of management and employers placed increased levels of demand towards demonstrable leadership approaches and certain characteristics of the corporate culture – with millennials particularly likely to consider referrals from their extended networks when considering job opportunities. Although not unique towards Sensata, this adjusted emphasis towards leadership approach gains importance when cross-referenced against internal records that group Sensata's 18,925 employees by generation and hierarchical level, revealing an executive team that currently does not include representation from anyone born after 1980.

Stage 2 – Define

Upon analysis of stakeholder findings within the context of both a wider literature review and the context of Sensata (e.g., a technology organisation that understandably emphasises technological ability when considering promotional opportunities), a final clarifying question was posited: "How can we better retain critical talents?" Following which, the need to recommend an effective leadership approach that may guide operational managers on how to implement 'Care and Connect' with their respective people groups was rearticulated as a core focal point for the project.

Stages 3 to 5 – The design cycle

The chosen design cycle comprised several stages as outlined in Figure 1. Observers may criticise the constant presence of the researcher throughout the process as increasing the risk of perspective bias. Equally, the context of raising the project for academic study rather than purely work-based purposes - initiating the project outside of the traditional corporate structure - combined with cultural factors where a more relational and personable approach to sensitive topics is preferred within mainland

China, the provided approach was taken with acknowledgement towards its limitations.

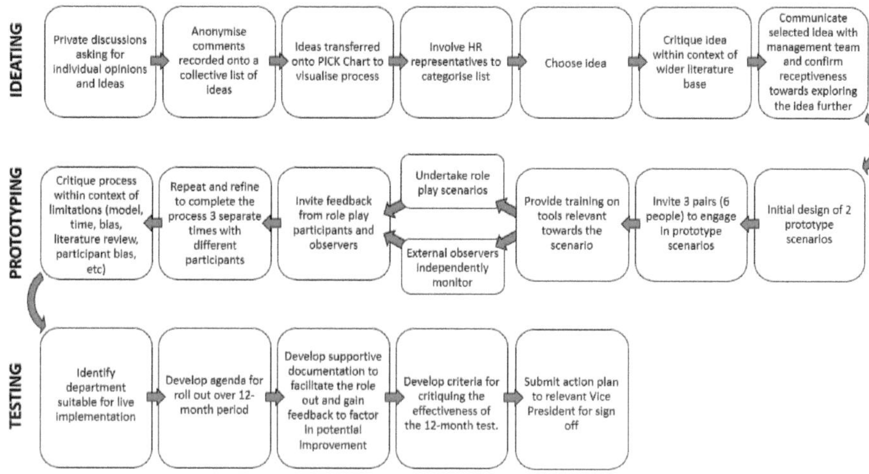

Figure 1: *Design cycle process*

To combat intrinsic limitations of researcher bias, time limitation and limited authority within the hierarchy, references towards the wider up-to-date literature base from reputable practitioners and consulting agencies (such as DDI reports, Korn Ferry Reports, etc) was made and viewpoints from several stakeholders were integrated at different parts of the process to help generate consensus when considered most necessary. It was finally considered important to integrate the project into wider corporate systems in order to facilitate buy-in. This point is clearly established within McKinsey & Company's (2015) "Influence Model" that comprises the fundamental components of role modelling, fostering understanding, developing skills, and reinforcing within formal mechanisms. For example, Sensata has an existing development programme entitled 'Sensata Global Tech Ladder'. Integration within existing systems helps to reduce perception of the test being a one-off project, improves buy-in, and facilitates knowledge-building across the company. Within the context of improving staff retention, this integration into a more structured and mid-to long-term system is of particular importance in combatting the short termism underlying much of the workforce turnover.

Evaluation

The proposed solution involved embedding a tailored coaching leadership approach within Sensata management practice in an effort to influence positive cultural change that may manifest the declared business priority of "Care and Connect with Our People". Although the internally proposed model utilises well known tools such as GROW (Grow, Reality, Options, Will) and ADKAR (Awareness, Desire, Knowledge, Ability, Reinforcement), literature highlights the need for leadership style to adjust according to situational context, otherwise misuse may cause frustration for both employees and managers (Hersey and Blanchard, 1997). There are further instances where coaching strategies are not advisable (Goldsmith, 2007). Equally, research is increasingly highlighting that coaching leadership styles are preferred by the millennial generation, particularly important as they are gaining increasing importance within the labour force (LaCore, 2015) and that engaged employees are up to 43% more productive and 87% less likely to leave (Kruse, 2012).

In a practical setting, the need for balancing a perfect solution with the everchanging constraints of a VUCA (Volatile, Uncertain, Complex, Ambiguous) world compels an informed – though most probably imperfect – decision. Through prototyping and testing, this project was able to demonstrate that the proposed approach for coaching leadership positively promotes and encourages behaviours that will support management within their operational roles. With a coaching mindset that involves employees in decision making, invests in employee development, stimulates 2-way feedback, and embraces failure as a learning opportunity, coaching leadership may truly reflect Sensata's values and legacy of "Integrity, Excellence, One Sensata, Passion, and Flexibility".

Whilst the project undertaken received consent from the relevant Vice-President in Head Office, the project was materially affected by being confined to a very limiting timeframe and only informal backing from formal hierarchy. The Design Thinking model pushes project leads to engage with a broader range of stakeholders than may perhaps otherwise be taken. Equally, truly caring and listening to stakeholders is highly time-consuming and makes it highly probable that the project will encounter delay. It also should not be taken for granted that information will be freely provided, as authentic dialogue requires relationship development. Herein the decision to wrap up the project by feeding the project learning and action plan back into wider systems has been of particular importance.

Conclusion

Within a sector environment where 30-50% employee turnover is common, a Design Thinking approach was utilised in an effort to reduce the rate of turnover by improving understanding around root issues behind high turnover and proposing creative solutions that guide operational managers on how to implement a key company initiative i.e., 'Care and Connect'. Acknowledging constraints within the project methodology, the project output is a systematic action plan to roll-out a customised coaching leadership approach that aligns every day organisational culture with recently revised value statements. In true Design Thinking fashion, the output is not final, but merely the first step of an ongoing and iterative process.

References

Allison, J., (2019) Mission Statements and Vision Statements: Examining the Relationship Toward Performance Outcomes, *Global Journal of Management and Marketing*. Vol 3 (1), pp.1-21. Available at: https://www.igbr.org/wp-content/uploads/articles/GJMM_Vol_3_No_1_2019-pgs-1-21.pdf.

Bardi, A., & Schwartz, S., (2003) Values and Behavior: Strength and Structure of Relations, *Personality and Social Psychology Bulletin*. Vol 29 (10), pp.1207-1220.

Beechler, S., & Woodward, I., (2009) The Global "War for Talent", *Journal of International Management*. Vol 15(3), pp.273-285. doi.org/10.1016/j.intman.2009.01.002

Belete, A., (2018) Turnover Intention Influencing Factors of Employees: An Empirical Work Review, *International Journal of Research in Business Studies and Management*. Vol 5 (7), pp.23-31. Available from: https://pdfs.semanticscholar.org/c3a2/6253e522d8b3a4cfc15b24c86f841d4e837c.pdf.

Bradberry, T., & Greaves, J., (2009) *Emotional Intelligence 2.0*. San Diego, CA. TalentSmart.

Brenner, W., Uebernickel, F., & Abrell, T., (2016) Design Thinking as Mindset, Process and Toolbox. **In:** Brenner W., & Uebernickel, F., (Eds) *Design Thinking for Innovation*. Springer, Cham. Available at: https://doi.org/10.1007/978-3-319-26100-3_1.

CHYXX.com., (2021) 2020 年中国汽车销量连续十二年全球第一（附乘用车、商用车、新能源汽车产销量，汽车区域产销量，以及市场集中度. Available from: https://www.chyxx.com/industry/202103/935251.html

Christian, A., (2021) *'Great Flirtation': Should Workers Constantly Job Hunt?"* https://www.bbc.com/worklife/article/20211022-is-hr-ever-really-your-friend.

Gallup., (2016) *How Millennials Want to Work and Live*. Gallup Inc. p.3.

Gallup., (2019) *Millennials Workplace Management Report*. Gallup Inc. p.1.

Goldsmith, M., (2007) *What Got You Here Won't Get You There*. Hachette: New York, pp.55-57.

Hagos, A., (2021) *The Impact of Covid-19 on Employees' Wellbeing and the Role of Human Resource Management.* Available from: https://www.researchgate.net/profile/Aron-Hagos/publication/350087940_The_Impact_of_Covid-19_on_Employees_Wellbeing_and_the_Role_of_Human_Resource_Management/links/6050210d299bf17367465315/The-Impact-of-Covid-19-on-Employees-Wellbeing-and-the-Role-of-Human-Resource-Management.pdf

Hersey, P., & Blanchard, K., (1997) *Situational Leadership*. **In:** Dean's Forum. Vol 12 (2), p.5.

Isern, J., & Pung, C., (2007) Driving Radical Change. *McKinsey Quarterly*, Vol 4 (24).

Javaid, M., Haleem, A., Rab, S., Singh, R., & Suman, R., (2021) Sensors for Daily Life: A Review. *Sensors International*. Vol 2. doi.org/10.1016/j.sintl.2021.100121

Kohlrieser, G., (2007) The Power of Authentic Dialogue, *Annals of Spiry Haret University: Sociology and Psychology Series*. 2, pp.125-130.

KPMG., (2021) *China's Automotive Industry Intensifies Electrification*. Available from: https://home.kpmg/cn/en/home/news-media/press-releases/2021/01/2020-china-leading-autotech-50.html

Kruse, K., (2012) *Why Employee Engagement? These 28 Studies Prove the Benefits*. Available at: https://www.forbes.com/sites/kevinkruse/2012/09/04/why-employee-engagement/

Kurbetti, S., & Maheshkar, S., (2021) A Study of Hr Issues and Challenges of Global Auto Component Industries, *Vidyabharati International Interdisciplinary Research Journal*. Vol 12(1), pp.416-419.

LaCore, E. (2015) Supporting millennials in the workplace. Strategic HR Review.

McKinsey & Company., (2015) *The Science of Organizational Transformations*. pp.59-71. Available from: https://www.mckinsey.com/business-functions/people-andorganizational-performance/our-insights/the-science-of-organizational-transformations

Mercer., (2020) *2020 Mercer China Talent Attraction and Retention Practice Survey Summary Report*. Mercer China.

Ministry of Public Security., (2020) *National Car Parc 2020*. Sourced from the National Bureau of Statistics. Available from: https://www.mps.gov.cn/n7944517/n7944597/n7945888/c7478950/content.html

Patton, M., (1990) *Qualitative Evaluation and Research Methods*. **In:** Designing Qualitative Studies, pp.169-186. Beverly Hills, CA: Sage.

Sensata., (2021) *Annual Report for the Year Ended December 31, 2020*. Available from: https://s22.q4cdn.com/327799861/files/doc_financials/2020/2020-IFRS-Annual-Report-final.pdf *Page.26*

Sensata.com., (2021) *About Us*. Available from: https://www.sensata.com/about

Storm, J., (2021a) A Design Thinking Workshop to Kickstart Sustainability Initiatives: For Entrepreneurs and SME Leaders. **In:** *EdMedia+ Innovate Learning*. Online. Proceedings pp.407-412.

Storm, J., (2021b) Developing A Design Thinking Mind-set to Stimulate Sustainable Development in Chinese SMEs. **In:** *Proceedings of the IIBG Academic-Industry Exchange 2021 Conference on Business as Usual: How do we Turn the New Normal into Normal*. Hong Kong. Proceedings pp.43-67.

Ting-Fang, C., & Li, L., (2021) *How the Chip Shortage Got So Bad – and Why It's So Hard to Fix: Surging Demand and Political Tension Play Havoc with Global Supply Chains*. Nikkei Asia. Available from: https://asia.nikkei.com/Business/Business-Spotlight/How-the-chip-shortage-got-so-bad-and-why-it-s-so-hard-to-fix

Zhiyan Consulting., (2021) 2021-2027 年中国汽车行业竞争格局分析及投资前景规划报告. 智研咨询.

Discussion questions

1. The Design Thinking model is characterised by its simultaneously broad and deep engagement with stakeholders. Whereas the formal hierarchy may facilitate access to a wider range of stakeholders, hierarchical position may equally create a distance between a project lead and the stakeholder base. How should project leads balance the needs of a project with the opportunities and challenges of working within formal hierarchical structures?

2. Executive appointments typically take into consideration the extent of an individual's related career and ability to bring transferable experiences into oversight and decision making. Recognising that generational differences do occur, should executive teams be expected to be more representative of their wider workforce demographic?

3. Employee turnover of 30-50% is common within the automobile sector in mainland China. What trends do you think feed into this reality, and how does this compare with employee turnover in your own business context? Consider from both a sector as well as geographic perspective.

Warm House Daycare Center: A Case Study in Organisational Culture and the Application of the Cultural Web

Yinan Jiang
Co-founder / Operational Deputy Director: Warm House Daycare Centre

Abstract

This case study considers organisational culture and provides an example of the application of a particular model, the cultural web, to a specific organisation in the childcare sector in Mainland China.

Introduction

This case considers the issue of organisational culture and, in doing so, applies a particular model, that of the cultural web (Johnson, 1992; Johnson & Scholes, 1997; see also Hoyas, 2022), to an organisation, Warm House Daycare Centre ('Warm House'), which operates in a key sector, childcare, in Mainland China. The case highlights how the cultural web model can be used to underpin, communicate, develop and, where necessary, correct aspects of culture in the interests of employees and the customers they serve.

National context

Over the past twenty years in Mainland China, kindergarten enrolment has mainly focused on children who are over 3 years old, with a limited number of private centres approved to enrol children over 2 years old. Although there are some early education training institutions for children below the age of 3 years, they primarily focus on short courses for parents e.g., sixty minutes' duration once or twice a week and intended to help parents to enhance the quality of interaction with their children. However, with few realistic child care options available, many Chinese couples have to rely on their own parents to look after their children or hire expensive nannies (Qi & Melhuish, 2016).

At the national level, and not dissimilar to many other countries, including developed economies, childcare has become a major issue for Chinese parents, and particularly so after the country removed the one child policy, established in 1979, and enacted a two-child policy in 2016 i.e., couples were allowed to have two children. This was further increased to three children in 2021. However, the lack of care services for extremely young children in particular is seen as a key reason young people are not having more children. According to a survey conducted by the Women and Children's Committee of The State Council (2017), 35.8% of parents of children under the age of 3 need childcare, and 69.7% of them hope to send their children to professional childcare institutions.

To meet growing public demand, the Chinese Government released guidelines to encourage more services for infants under three years of age. On 9th May 2019, the State Council issued the guidelines on *Improving Care Services for Infants and Children Under Three Years Old.* This is the first time that the Government has introduced a policy on childcare services for infants under 3 years of age, leading to 2019 being known as "the first year of a childcare services era" in Mainland China. After 2019, the Government introduced more policies to promote the development of the sector. Under the country's 14th Five-Year Plan (2021-2025), the availability of child care services will increase by 150% so that there will be 4.5 day care spots for every 1,000 people, or 6.3 million spots nationwide.

At present, the Government has given strong support to the development of childcare as a supporting measure of China's population policy. In the Government's Work Report, presented at the 13th National People's Congress in Beijing on 5th March 2022, one of the main targets for 2022 is for China to improve support measures for its three-child policy, easing the financial burden on families by adding care expenses for children under three years old into the special deductions list for Individual Income Tax. The need for such incentives was illustrated in data from the National

Health Commission (NHC), July 2021, showing that China has about 42 million children under the age of three and that parents of one-third of them have strong demand for childcare services (Xinhuanet, 2021). However, the country's nursery enrolment rate of children under three is only 5.5%, according to statistics revealed by a survey. More than 4,000 childcare institutions had been registered with the NHC by the end of June 2021 and some 10,000 more are in the pipeline for application (this data is derived from an on-site report by Yang Wenzhuang, an official of the NHC, on July 21, 2021). These figures show clearly the market demand for childcare services but there is a gap between demand and affordable supply, representing both a clear social need and an opportunity for providers of high-quality childcare services. Such high-quality is more likely to be demonstrated if the organisational culture is one which promotes and facilitates it.

Warm House Daycare Centre

Warm House belongs to DTS Education Company ('DTS') which was established in 2014, a private enterprise operating in Chengdu, Sichuan Province, China. In 2017, DTS obtained approval to establish Warm House to offer childcare services. It is the first daycare centre on the Chinese Mainland allowed to accept the 0–1-year-old babies. It also supplies curriculum-related products and management technologies to other institutions. Warm House is one of three separate divisions within DTS, each managing an independent brand, see Table 1, and, as at March 2022, has 785 employees. Its three divisions and split of employees is shown in Table 2.

Brands of DTS Education	**DTS International kindergarten**	**Warm House Daycare Centre**	**Guang He Hui Daycare Education Resources Forum**
Division	Kindergarten Business	Childcare Business	Industry Development Business
Service for	2-6 years old child	Baby to 3 years old child	Other institutions of education for 0-6 years-old children
Numbers	7 campuses in Sichuan Province, China	20 centres on Mainland China	No physical tre
Situation	All campuses are for-profit kindergartens. However, as the penetration rate of national public kindergartens increases and the Government advocates inclusive kindergartens, the private for-profit kindergarten market is shrinking.	The service for 0-3 years old children is an industry strongly supported by Central Government and is also a key development project of the company as at March 2022.	"Asset-light" strategy - supplies curriculum-related products and management technologies to other institutions for children 0-6 years old.

Table 1: *The three brands of DTS Education Company*

Division	**Employees**
Kindergarten Business	330
Childcare Business	410
Industry Development Business	10
Head Office (management / finance / admin / HR)	35
Total	**785**

Table 2: *Warm House structure and employees*

The Kindergarten Business Division launched seven DTS international kindergartens for children aged 2-6. The Childcare Business Division launched twenty Warm House Daycare Centres on Mainland China for babies and children up to 3 years old. Of the 785 employees, 470 (60%) are child teachers and 315 (40%) work in the administration and logistics departments. Each kindergarten campus and each daycare centre have administrative and logistics staff. The author is a co-founder of DTS and, in 2015, took charge of the establishment and operation of the first kindergarten.

At the end of 2015, when Warm House was planning to expand its business, it also considered becoming an early education agency for children under the age of 3 years. However, there were many famous brands on the market at that time and the market was already mature. At the beginning of 2016, during a staff development and exchange visit to Singapore and Japan, we saw that babies aged several months were in childcare centres, but this mode of provision was not available in the 0-3 years old market in China. With the development of China's economy and the increased awareness of women as to the possibility of living independently, this demand also existed in Mainland families. As a result, we began to prepare this project after we returned to Chengdu.

With the development and strategic planning of the company the business was expanded in 2016 to cover children under 3 years old and the first daycare centre was founded in 2017, in Chengdu, providing high-quality childcare services for 0-3 years old children. This also is the first day care centre in Mainland China with approval to care for infants under 1 year old.

Beginning with the start-up team, we believe that the staff of educational institutions is the key to ensuring the quality of education. We value staff in promoting happiness and positivity. Daycare is a relatively new service on the mainland and a key challenge is how to attract more people to join and stay in our centres. In meeting this challenge, the organisational culture and its brand are regarded as being of particular importance. The brand's name, Warm House, is intended to reflect its core culture. We provide sincere and warm care for children aged 0-3 years, as well as a loving and growth-oriented working environment for teachers and support staff. This culture drives us to improve our services, makes our teachers willing to work in the environment, give of their best, and makes our brands popular with customers. In 2019, the brand began to expand from Chengdu to the whole country. At present, it has centres in Chongqing, Tianjin, Wuhan,

Changsha and Guiyan. In total, as at March 2022, it has twenty daycare centres across Mainland China. The author now is the Deputy Director of Operations of the all the daycare centres, in charge of the teaching research training department and the quality control management department. The annual turnover of DTS education was RMB 114m in 2021 and Warm House is RMB 60.5m. Warm House is also an important project in DTS development strategy and plans to open an additional fifty physical centres nationwide by 2025.

One of the challenges facing organisations is how to motivate and inspire employees, and Warm House is no different. The behaviour of employees will greatly influence the quality of teaching and care in the kindergarten.

Organisational culture

Organisational culture refers to the shared characteristics among people within the same organisation. It includes the values, norms of behavior, routines, traditions, perspectives, and beliefs of individuals. Culture matters for numerous reasons, not least because it offers a way for employees to understand their organisation, to voice their views and to develop connections and common purpose. It is also important for organisations continually to assess their culture as an organisation's purpose and values will affect the standard and quality of many aspects of its operations, including its customer service, and influence the engagement and retention of its people. 'It defines what is important and unimportant in the company and, consequently, directs everyone in the organisation toward the "right way" of doing things. You might think of organisational culture as company's DNA – invisible to the naked eye, yet a powerful template that shapes what happens in the workplace' (McShane & Glinow, 2018, p338). This definition is useful but it overlooks the fact that aspects of culture may actually be visible. Schein (1990), for instance, identifies three levels of culture, see Table 3.

Level	Description
Artifacts	On entering an organisation, it is possible to observe and sense its culture through its artifacts. This may include physical layout, the dress code, the manner in which people address each other, the smell and feel of the place, its emotional intensity and other phenomena. These may be observed along with more permanent archival evidence of culture such as company records, its products, statements of values etc.
Espoused Values	Through various survey methods, a culture's espoused (and sometimes documented) values and norms can be evaluated.
Underlying Assumptions	Through more intensive observation, it is possible to identify and understand the taken-for-granted, underlying and usually unconscious assumptions that determine behaviour, attitudes, statements, perceptions, feelings and so on. Once these assumptions are understood, such phenomena become easier to understand.

Table 3: *Levels of culture*

Based on the theory of these three levels, it can be seen that organisational culture is a complex form, in part tangible and visible, shown, for example, by documents, the environment viz. physical layout and decor, dress codes, office rituals etc., and in part intangible and invisible, including processes, tacit assumptions, widely-held beliefs e.g., 'us against them' or 'we're all in this together' may be contrasting views on management held on a shopfloor. On the first day when someone enters an organisation (and perhaps, through prior engagement, even before entering), the way of communication, interpersonal relationships and interactions will characterise and reflect the organisation's culture. There are numerous models for evaluating organisational culture, and one is that of the cultural web. The nature of organisational culture and its evaluation by use of the cultural web can be illustrated by the case of Warm House.

The cultural web

Developed in 1992 by Gerry Johnson and Kevan Scholes (see Johnson & Scholes, 1997), the cultural web model helps define the 'paradigm,' or the lived reality, of working within an organisation. It comprises six inter-related components, shown in Figure 1, which collectively constitute a 'paradigm'. Moreover, it is a method of exploring the different elements of a company and how these elements can shape the experiences of those that work for an organisation and, also, for its customers. In addition, it is a way to explore:

- The power structures that exist within an organisation
- The collective 'history' of an organisation
- How behaviours or 'rituals' within an organisation are formed and continued.

A disadvantage of the model is that the process can be time-consuming and requires a systematic approach, analysis and, where necessary, actions to correct or change the culture or policies relating to it. In turn, this requires collecting and interpreting data and finding solutions if required. Such work also needs a team, one that really understands the history of the organisation even if not all members have necessarily experienced it. Despite these potential disadvantages, the cultural web model is a way to understand an organisation's present culture and the elements that can help shape its future.

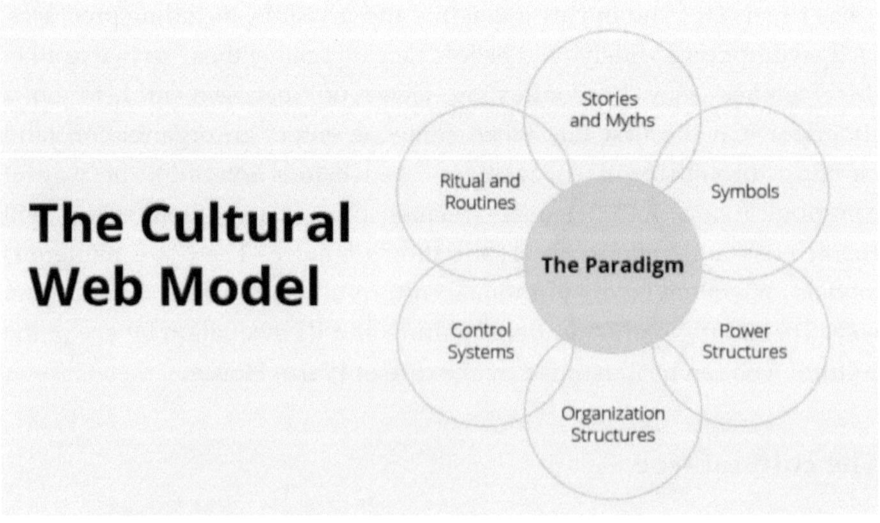

Figure 1: *The cultural web model*

The model provides a useful way by which an organisation's culture might be created and developed, and this can be illustrated by Warm House.

Warm House Culture and the cultural web

Stories and myths

This component can be considered the collective 'memory' of an organisation. For this element, it is helpful to think about the 'stories that organisations tell', the narrative or the words that are used to describe the company, its history, and its future.

Figure 2: *Warm House story*

In our new employee training, the first lesson that is shared with everyone is the "warm house story". The intention is to ensure everyone knows how the brand was built and where the organisation wants to go. The story of Warm House, see Figure 2, illuminates its core values, indicating warmth and caring, the behaviours they determine, and which are worthy of exemplifying. Stories encourage employees to follow certain paths and enable them actually to become part of the history.

Thirty-seven degrees approximates to the most suitable temperature for the human body and makes people feel comfortable. We also adhere to the core values of sincerity, care and protection, and hope that the thirty-seven degrees of love in Warm House can remain constant. See Figure 3.

Figure 3: *Warm House core values*

Ritual and routines

These are the various behaviours and actions that are acceptable in a company, and which help reinforce and perpetuate its culture. Routines can also be understood as expectations, which could include what an employee can expect coming into work every day, the behaviour of the organisation they may experience once they leave work at the end of the day (e.g., whether they might receive or be expected to respond to emails outside normal working time), and what typical activities throughout the day look like.

At Warm House, babies and children up to 3 years old are of course very young and need an adult's care. What do the children's parents, Warm House's customers, expect when they choose us? How do we uphold our standards and high-quality services? To this end we have established the SOP (standard operating process) system, covering aspects of provision including care, logistics, sales, and administration. The SOP allows employees to understand the organisation's processes and what they are intended to achieve. Warm House was the first childcare services institute in China to achieve ISO9001, the international standard that specifies requirements for a quality management system. See Figure 4 (Note:

Chengdu Nuanfangzi Education Consulting is the official name of the company registered in the Government Department of Industry and Commerce; Warm House Daycare Center is the brand name).

ZTC
中泰认证

QUALITY MANAGEMENT SYSTEM CERTIFICATION

Registration NO : 29019Q01076-12R0S

Chengdu Nuanfangzi Education Consulting Co., Ltd.

Unified social credit code:91510108MA6CL5NG42

Registered Address:No. 16 Attached to No. 62 2/F, No. 63 2/F, No. 66 3/F, Shuangcheng Three Road, Chenghua District, Chengdu City, Sichuan Province

Office Address:No. 16, Shuangcheng Three Road, Chenghua District, Chengdu City, Sichuan Province

Business Address:No. 16, Shuangcheng Three Road, Chenghua District, Chengdu City, Sichuan Province

Established Quality Management System Accord With
GB/T 19001-2016 idt ISO9001:2015 standard

Through the certification scope is as follows

Childcare Services

The release date for the first time : 27-12-2019
Exchange certificate date : 27-11-2020
Will be valid until : 26-12-2022

Approval of the second | Approval of the third surveillance audit

Issuer :

ZhongTai Union Certification Co., LTD.
Tel : +86 028-62521000 www.ztccc.org

0018537

Figure 4: *ISO9001 Certification*

Being awarded ISO9001 reflected the efforts made by Warm House in producing an operations handbook, with full details relating to all frontline education services and all support services including logistics, human resources (HR), administration, marketing, and project preparation. By means of such documentation, all the employees in different departments can learn how they are expected to behave and what constitutes 'normal' behavior, it is what has become normalised as part of the company culture. The processes also underpin a safe environment, a place for children aged 0-3 can develop, grow, where a 'warm house' is created, a second home for children. At our facility, when clients walk in for a consultation, they are given carefully selected glass cups from which to drink, replicating behaviour at home in China where guests would be treated with great respect and be given the best utensils a household has to offer rather than disposable items. In terms of employee behavior, we encourage teachers to be active, helpful, and warm-hearted. Book clubs, art salons and youth club activities are all part of this environment.

Warm House also attaches great importance to parents' feedback and seeks to optimise care services, in part reflected by and based on an annual family questionnaire. Table 4 shows some questions from the family survey in 2021 of those parents whose children are currently at Warm House. A total of 670 responses were received, representing a 76% response rate. The responses indicate parents' recognition of the Warm House culture and their trust in the quality of childcare.

2021 Warm House Parents Feedback Questionnaire		
Would you recommend Warm House to a friend?	Rate	
	Yes	99%
	No	1%
	Total	100.00%
So far, how satisfied do you believe your child is at Warm House?	Rate	
	Very Satisfied	59%
	Satisfied	38%
	Neither satisfied nor dissatisfied	3%
	Total	100%
Please make an overall evaluation of the center your baby attends?	Rate	
	Excellent	59%
	Very Good	39%
	Average	2%
	Poor	0%
	Total	100%

Table 4: *Annual parents feedback survey extract*

Symbols

Symbols play their role in the cultural web model as part of employer branding, or organisational branding more generally. This includes all things visual: logos; branding; the way the office looks; dress codes at work; advertisements, and more. Both internal and external, it is the visual communication of a company that influences perception of the brand. See Figure 5.

暖房子
warm house

Figure 5: *Warm House brand*

The above is Warm House's logo, illustrating a house and including symbols of the organisation's values:

- Transparent: This transparent house icon represents the open attitude of Warm House. We will openly communicate with our children and their parents/guardians about their life and all activities in the centre to establish a crucial sense of trust. For example, parents often feel anxious when their young children enter the daycare centre. We will not only provide a detailed list of baby items to prepare but also give to parents a baby separation anxiety parents manual. We also carefully record any changes in the baby's behaviour in the first month and make an electronic photo album to share with parents.

- Diligently： This glowing heart shape represents a warm house, one that is focused on the child and demonstrates an empathetic attitude and a process of nurturing and caring for life. All possible care is taken of the child and, in doing so, we need to observe and interpret children's behaviour attentively, to give them scientific and effective support for their growth.
- Hug: This part of the graph looks like two hands embracing, representing the love and patience given to babies and children aged 0-3.

For each interviewee who comes to Warm House, we will give them a gift reflecting the corporate culture, such as a Warm House postcard on which is written the concepts underpinning our approach to education.

These values are also intended to be represented in the uniform. See Figure 6, illustrating the Warm House work uniform. In terms of design, it not only conforms to the colour of the brand but also has many functional designs that are convenient for teachers to use at work. The colour of the teacher's standard uniform is grey, a kind of cool colour to reflect strict but caring standards of childcare, and the smile of each staff member represents our patience and love when interacting with children, raising warm children in a warm environment.

Figure 6: *Warm House uniform*

When a new staff member joins the team, a professional photography agency takes a photo of each employee. Using this photo reminds them of their key role as a professional childcare teacher. All the teachers' working photos and their profiles are displayed on an image wall. This is a source of pride for our teachers and also lets our customers – the children's parents - learn about the professional background and behaviour of the teachers, the individuals in whom they are placing so much trust as they place their child in their care. In the event an employee leaves Warm House, they are presented with a framed copy of the photo as a gift, to remind them of their working time accompanying and facilitating the growth of children in Warm House. This can be captured in the photo and the warm memories it might evoke.

DTS and Warm House also try to help its employees in relation to their own childcare. When running the kindergarten, parents sometimes would ask if they could enrol their children under 2 years old, a request often made when parents did not have help available from their own parents or family and friends and they could not afford a babysitter. In this situation, one of the parents will often need to resign from their jobs and devote their time to looking after their child. DTS itself experienced such an example and lost an excellent staff member who left after having a baby because no family member or friend was available to help her, and she was unable to afford the cost of a nanny. DTS, and Warm House, does have an employee discount scheme in place, with varying rates of discount depending on years of service. This is not only of practical benefit to employees but is also, of course, a good advertisement for the company in that if employees wish to send their own child to Warm House it demonstrates employees' recognition of the warm and educational culture. However, even with a discount, not all employees are able to pay the fees and unfortunately the loss of an excellent staff member has been experienced.

Control Systems

This component is based on how control is exerted in an organisation. We may also think about this in terms of performance management, how employees are graded on how they work and how they succeed in their various roles. This includes financial systems, quality control, fringe benefits and bonuses. These are the ways in which good performance is encouraged and poor performance managed and addressed.

Warm House uses evaluations of effectiveness or ineffectiveness of the organisation's culture, including Monthly Performance Appraisal and Annual Employee Satisfaction Survey. Summary results of the 2021 survey of the 410 employees of the Childcare Business Division (see Table 2) is given in Table 5. The survey is conducted anonymously and completed using mobile phones. Employees are requested to complete the survey within two days of it going live but it remains open until a minimum response rate of 75% has been achieved. In 2021, the number of responses received within two days was 343 i.e., 84% response rate.

The survey results indicate a high level of agreement with the statements to which employees were asked to respond. There are issues for management to consider, e.g., over one in five respondents (22%) stated that centre management is the main cause of stress being experienced, but this needs to be seen in the context of other responses indicating a high level of trust and support.

Table 5 Warm House Annual Employee Satisfaction Survey 2021 – Extract

Statement	**Response**	%
I feel a strong sense of belonging to the centre	Strongly Agree	48
	Agree	43
	Neither Agree nor Disagree	8
	Disagree	1
	Strongly Disagree	-
	Total	100
I am satisfied with working relationships in the centre	Strongly Agree	47
	Agree	45
	Neither Agree nor Disagree	6
	Disagree	2
	Strongly Disagree	-
	Total	100

Table 5 Warm House Annual Employee Satisfaction Survey 2021 – Extract

Statement	Response	%
My supervisor trusts employees equally	Strongly Agree	51
	Neither Agree nor Disagree	6
	Disagree	1
	Strongly Disagree	1
	Total	100
I am satisfied with the welfare benefits of the centre (staff birthday, team building, holiday benefits)	Strongly Agree	44
	Agree	50
	Neither Agree nor Disagree	4
	Disagree	1
	Strongly Disagree	1
	Total	100
I have a great sense of accomplishment in my current position	Strongly Agree	48
	Agree	41
	Neither Agree nor Disagree	7
	Disagree	3
	Strongly Disagree	1
	Total	100
I feel my abilities are being fully utilised at work	Strongly Agree	51
	Agree	36
	Neither Agree nor Disagree	12
	Disagree	1
	Strongly Disagree	-
	Total	100

Table 5 Warm House Annual Employee Satisfaction Survey 2021 – Extract		
Statement	**Response**	**%**
What is the main source of any current stress you may be experiencing?	Childcare development	38
	Centre management	22
	Public opinion	31
	Other branches of government	9
	Total	100
What is your main motivation at work?	Children development	45
	Self-development	53
	Industry competition	1
	Company development	1
	Total	100
I feel I can always get help from management	Strongly Agree	50
	Agree	45
	Neither Agree nor Disagree	4
	Disagree	1
	Strongly Disagree	-
	Total	100
I am satisfied with the study options at the centre	Strongly Agree	51
	Agree	41
	Neither Agree nor Disagree	5
	Disagree	2
	Strongly Disagree	1
	Total	100
I feel there is equality in terms of workloads and study opportunities at the centre	Strongly Agree	39
	Agree	47
	Neither Agree nor Disagree	10
	Disagree	3
	Strongly Disagree	1
	Total	100

Table 5: *Annual employee satisfaction survey extract*

Organisation structures

An organisational chart of Warm House shows a very clear organisational structure i.e., who works where, who reports to whom and who ultimately has final decision-making power. The structure is quite flat, reflecting a more collegial approach to management within Warm House, and departmental. It is also explained to staff on induction, and this allows employees to be very clear about their responsibilities and reporting lines. The organisational structure has significance in terms of culture as an employee's department and supervisor are also the direct transmitters of organisational culture. In order to ensure that each department maintains the same cultural values, Warm House evaluates employees' understanding of the values. For example, there will be different types of employee surveys every year to understand employees' opinions and obtain their feedback on organisational management. To this end, annual questionnaires and quarterly sampling interviews are undertaken, enabling Warm House to understand employees' perception of their department culture and its alignment with Warm House culture. It also provides an opportunity for employees to give feedback and suggestions.

Power structures

The final component of the cultural web is that of power structures, what some call 'real power' within an organisation. It is essentially the centre of power, and it can take many different forms. It could be one person, a handful of executives, an entire group or a department that has influence over the entire company. The key here is knowing which people have the greatest say, how an organisation runs and how their opinions dictate strategic direction.

The power structure in Warm House includes the Board of Directors ('the Board') at the top of the hierarchy and is responsible for strategic planning and setting strategic goals. Reporting to the Board is the Operation and Management Committee (OMC) and is composed of the General Manager, Deputy General Manager, Chief Financial Officer, HR Director and two Business Division Directors. The OMC discusses and decides on the operational decisions and any problems within the Centre. In this way, the core values and culture of the company can permeate each business segment. At the same time, employees should also be an important part of the power of the company, and employees' understanding and recognition of corporate culture play a vital role in ensuring the quality of work. Each department head will organise staff communication regularly to understand the work trend. As stated above under 'control systems', the HR Department conducts an annual Employee Satisfaction Survey to obtain employees' feedback on various issues relating to the management of the company. It provides important intelligence relating to organisational culture and its effectiveness. For example, in the 2021 Employee Satisfaction Survey particular questions were asked, including ones relating to employees' satisfaction with corporate culture, working environment and support from line managers, and which demonstrated very positive feedback. See Table 5. This approach is similar to employee surveys conducted in organisations around the world in that it is somewhat top-down but is consistent, perhaps, in general with Chinese organisational culture where employees expect and welcome leadership and direction. It is, however, supplemented by monthly performance appraisal discussions and informal one-to-one and group discussions where feedback can be obtained.

Conclusion

Culture is an abstract concept, usually hard to describe, but important nonetheless. The cultural web is a useful tool in understanding and providing a comprehensive assessment of an organisation's culture and, in doing so, it offers a visual way by which it might be perceived and evaluated. It can help provide a holistic vision and road map, based on key areas, to bring about real change in an organisation, where such change is needed. At Warm House, it has been of great benefit in capturing and understanding the culture and helped in the identification of strengths and weaknesses. As a company, especially as an education company, it is very important to retain and enhance the positive aspects of service provision and its operations as a business. The components of the cultural web can help employees, particularly new employees, easily understand where Warm House has come from, how it does things and where it is going. As the company expands, new centres will be opened in different cities and, in ensuring the Warm House culture is successfully created in each new centre, the cultural web is an excellent means by which this can be achieved. However, it is also important to realise that culture is dynamic and not static, reflecting a process of continuous evolution. To this end, all employees should, for example, see themselves as not simply accepting the story of Warm House but, rather, as being able to add to it, to contribute to Warm House's development. This is particularly relevant to an educational establishment, one which should be open to new ways of thinking, to evaluating and applying as appropriate the latest pedagogic research relating to young children. In summary, the cultural web is extremely useful as an analytical tool, but it should also facilitate critical consideration of the future and not simply the past and the present.

The adjective 'warm' is a powerful one, and perhaps it is one that is more likely to be used in describing an individual's personality or a family home rather than a workplace. This is precisely the reason why it was chosen by DTS Education Company, to reflect and also drive the creation and development of a culture reminiscent of one's home, a safe environment for children, for the parents whose children are in the kindergarten and for employees. Warm House will continue to enrich its warm culture, transfer its influence to more people and ensure that the company lives up to its name.

References

Hoyas, J. (2022). 'Cultural Web Model: What Is It & How Can To Use It? (sic) 9th February https://factorialhr.co.uk/blog/cultural-web/

Johnson, G. (1992) 'Managing strategic change: strategy, culture and action' *Long Range Planning* 25, 1, 28-36

Johnson, G. and Scholes, K. (1997) *Exploring Corporate Strategy*. London: Prentice-Hall https://www.personio.com/hr-lexicon/cultural-web-model/

McShane, S.L. & Glinow, M. A. V. (2018). *Organizational Behaviour* (7th Edition). Beijing: McGraw Hill Education and China Machine Press

Qi, X. & Melhuish, E. C. (2016). 'Early childhood education and care in China: history, current trends and challenges' *Early Years* 37, 3, 268-284 http://dx.doi.org/10.1080/09575146.2016.1236780

Schein, E. H. (1990). Organizational Culture 'American Psychologist, 45, 109-119 http://ciow.org/docsB/Schein%281990%29OrganizationalCulture.pdf

State Council (2017). 'A survey on the needs of childcare services for children under 3 years old' 29th November http://www.nwccw.gov.cn/2017-11/29/content_186813.htm

Xinhuanet (2021) 'Childcare services in strong demand for Chinese toddlers: health official' 21st July http://www.xinhuanet.com/english/2021-07/21/c_1310075752.htm

Discussion questions

1. Does your organisation explicitly define and display its values? If so, how were they agreed and how prominently are they displayed? Does your organisation live up to them? If values are not formally defined, what would you say are the dominant cultural values within your own organisation, and why?

2. Are there any aspects of your organisation's culture that you regard as being particularly positive or negative? Organisational culture is not necessarily homogeneous, there may be sub-cultures, e.g., across or within different countries or cities if the organisation has a presence in more than one country or city. Does your organisation have sub-cultures? If so, how would you describe them? What is their significance?

3. Does your organisation make any efforts to measure aspects of its culture? If so, how? Consider how useful the cultural web model may be when applied to your own organisation.

4. Does your organisation's culture, however you might define it, act as a source of competitive advantage in the sector in which it operates and, if so, how?

www.ingramcontent.com/pod-product-compliance
Ingram Content Group UK Ltd.
Pitfield, Milton Keynes, MK11 3LW, UK
UKHW041643031026
15587UKWH00001B/471

9 781804 410004